PIDGIN MAGAZINE

ISSUE NUMBER NINE

PRINCETON UNIVERSITY SCHOOL OF ARCHITECTURE

CONTENTS

**PIDGIN
NUMBER
NINE**
Fall 2010

G-ALYP ENRIQUE RAMIREZ	5
NAUGHTY FLUFF JOSHUA LONGO	17
INTERVIEW THOMAS HIRSCHHORN WITH GARRETT RICCIARDI + JULIAN ROSE	27
STATUES IN GARDENS ROBERTO BURLE MARX TRANSLATED, WITH NOTES AND ILLUSTRATIONS, BY CATHERINE SEAVITT NORDENSON	39
ARCHITECTURE IS ALL IN THE HEAD JORGE OROZCO GONZALEZ	59
DRAWING [ON] THE SUBLIME MARCUS CARTER	81
FULL DISCLOSURE FIVE FELLOWS	99
SCENES FROM A LATE 20TH CENTURY AUTOGEDDON PATRICK CICCONE	115
CHANDIGARH AT 50 PHOTOS BY RAGUNETH VASUDEVAN	127
"IM ANFANG WAR DIE BEKLEIDUNG" LISA LEE	139
FOAM ADVOCATES BRANDON CLIFFORD + WES MCGEE	149
THE FORM OF DISORDER UMBERTO ECO TRANSLATED, WITH NOTES AND INTRODUCTION, BY BRITT EVERSOLE	161
UNTITLED BRYONY ROBERTS	181
RE-CREATING THE PRIMEVAL WILDERNESS JOSEPH CLAGHORN	187
OBSTRUCTION JIMENEZ LAI	199
NEW MONUMENTALITY OSNAT TADMOR	211
INTERVIEW ANNE TYNG WITH SAM STEWART-HALEVY	223
PERFORMING ON TWO STAGES JOHN COOPER	231
GHOSTS OF THESES PAST NICHOLAS DE MONCHAUX INTERVIEWED BY PIDGIN	241
DC ON WHEELS INSERT BY JESSE LECAVALIER	

Inaugural flight of BOAC Comet G-ALYP, 2 May 1952

G-ALYP

ENRIQUE RAMIREZ

On the morning of January 10, 1954, British Overseas Air Corporation (BOAC) Flight 781 took off from Rome's Ciampino Airport en route to London's Heathrow Airport. The equipment used for Flight 781 was a De Havilland DH-106 Comet (registration G-ALYP), the world's most advanced aircraft at the time. With a sleek, stressed metal fuselage, state-of-the-art "Ghost" turbojet engines, and pressurized passenger compartments, the Comet inaugurated the world's first passenger jet service. Twenty-six minutes after take off, at 10:31am, Flight 781 exploded in mid-air.[1] All 6 crew and 29 passengers died. The pieces of the jet fell to the Mediterranean Sea off the coast of the island of Elba. This was not the first incident involving a Comet, nor would it be the last. Investigators found that a series of fatal accidents in 1952 were attributable to pilot error.[2] And it was not until April 1954, when a BOAC Comet leaving Rome for Cairo crashed near Naples, that Britain's Ministry of Transport decided to ground all Comet operations until further notice.

Although local fishermen already retrieved victims' bodies as well as some pieces of the wreckage of Flight 781, the Royal Navy began salvage operations on January 25, 1954, the date that a new organization, the Aircraft Accidents Investigations Branch (AAIB), assumed control of the operation. The vessels H.M.S. *Barhill* and H.M.S. *Sea Salvor* sailed into the waters of the Elba coast and scoured the accident area with heavy salvage and dredging equipment and underwater television cameras. By March 1954, over 80 percent of the Comet's wreckage had been recovered and sent back to England for closer examination. The pieces were reassembled at the Royal Aircraft Establishment (RAE) a collection of buildings and laboratories near Farnborough airfield in Hampshire.

In 1954, AAIB reassembled the pieces of Flight 781 at the RAE's Material and Structures Laboratory. The arrival of the wreckage was a momentous occasion. The Comet was built, tested, and revealed to the public at the RAE, a place that has become a nexus of Cold War British "Hot Science." The immediate postwar years were particularly fruitful ones for the RAE. Not only were scientists designing and testing advanced jet and supersonic aircraft at Farnborough, but they were also outsourced to other aeronautical establishments such as NASA. The Comet was the crown jewel of England's scientific and technical industries. Rolls Royce and De Havilland, frequent users of RAE facilities and equipment, were also the undisputed world leaders in turbojet technology. Finding the cause for the Comet's demise was a national priority.

Shortly after the accident, Sir Winston Churchill authorized an investigation to discover what had happened to the Comet and why. Churchill appointed the aerospace engineer Sir Arnold Hall to head the investigation. Under Hall's supervision, the team ruled out dif-

Figure 1: Testing Structure, Comet G-ALYU, RAE Farnborough, England

ferent causes for the disaster. They concluded that the only reasonable cause was a massive, explosive decompression inside Flight 781's cabin.[3] The presence of human body parts and interior upholstering plastered to various parts of the airframe suggested as much. Engineers reasoned that the most plausible cause for such an explosion was metal fatigue. Their charge was to find a structural weakness in the aircraft that would cause it to pop like a balloon in mid-air. A remarkable piece of detective work ensued, one that would rely on the construction of a testing facility next to the Materials and Structures Laboratory.

RAE engineers built a portable laboratory used to recreate atmospheric flight, a temporary steel-framed structure covering the fuselage of a grounded Comet (registration G-ALYU). [fig. 1] It was a building

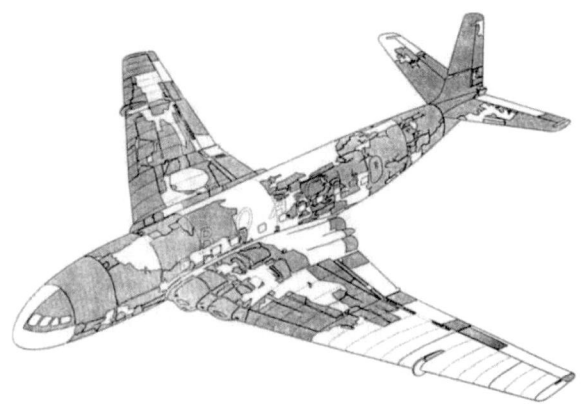

Figure 2: Diagram showing amount of wreckage recovered, Flight 781 (1954)

designed with a very specific and important function: to determine precisely the Comet's structural weak points. The interiors of both the Comet fuselage and the testing structure were filled with water. However, the fuselage was filled with still more water, enabling engineers to simulate the difference between internal cabin pressure and outside atmospheric pressure during flight operations.[4]

Repeated testing provided the answer that Hall and AAIB engineers were looking for: a crack just underneath the port navigator's window.[5] At high altitudes, enough pressure would escape through the crack with such force that would cause the Comet to explode in mid-air. The AAIB confirmed their hypothesis once salvage crews recovered part of Flight 781's roof section. Using this piece of the fuselage, RAE metallurgists were able to trace a network of very small cracks originating in the Comet's top observation windows.[6] They found that the particular type of riveting used on the Comet created miniscule cracks in the airframe's thin aluminum skin.7 Repeated pressurization and depressurization—a common occurrence in the operational life of an airliner—allowed the cracks to lengthen and enlarge, eventually contributing to the Comet's structural failure. Flight 781's demise was the result of a design flaw.

The discovery of this flaw marked a poignant moment in the history of British aviation. BOAC was forced to substitute its jet fleet with less-advanced propeller aircraft. It eventually reintroduced a newer, faster, and safer version of the Comet in 1958. Four years after the crash of Flight 781, two American aircraft, the Boeing 707 and Douglas DC-8, began passenger service, only to become the first commercially successful jet aircraft. De Havilland could not recover from the Comet mishap. Aerospace engineers and Airline operators learned much from the tests at the RAE, lessons that enabled designers to build safer commercial jets.

Even before the Flight 781 disaster, the Comet captured the imaginations of many Britons. Branded as "the most beautiful aircraft ever built", the Comet's design was the frequent subject of many publications. The first stage of lectures at the Institute of Contemporary Art (ICA), from 1952 to 1954, even featured several talks by the Comet's lead designer, Ronald Bishop. This must be taken as a bellwether for the level of interest the Comet garnered in design communities. Yet it is the relationship between architecture and the Comet that merits attention.

Whether on the floor of the Mediterranean Sea or in pieces inside a hangar at Farnborough, the Comet was a dissociated object—a collection of mangled scraps of metal, wire, and plastic. A series of images produced by AAIB photographers are the best indications of how the Comet is a disassociated object. One drawing showed how the pieces recovered from the wreckage of Flight 781 fit on the aircraft.[8] [FIG. 2] Here, the artist depicted the Comet's fuselage, wings, forward cabin and tail assemblies in light colors. The pieces of wreckage, however, were a darker color. The difference in shading thus suggested two different readings of the airplane. In the first, the Comet was an intact object. In the second, the Comet was dissociated, suggesting how a series of panels and pieces make up a whole aircraft.

Another image showed one of these panels, the exact location of the Comet's metal fatigue on the top of the forward fuselage.[9] [FIG. 3] The "B" of BOAC's white and blue livery was visible underneath a large crack. Another series of cracks propagated from the two aerial observation windows. One of them continued down towards two port observation windows. One of the windows was completely destroyed. The other still held fragments of broken glass. The serrated edges of the forward fuselage paneling gave a sense of the force of the explosive decompression. A caption label stating "Portion of Blue Band Which Made Impact on Wing" also suggested the force of the explosion.

These two images hint at the De Havilland Comet's systemic nature. On the one hand, like the process of manufacturing, an aircraft accident brings the interconnectivity of an aircraft to bear. In 1954, as crews from the *Sea Salvor* and *Barnhill* scoured the seafloor for fragments of Flight 781's wreckage, the fruit of this search was the recovery of literal bits and pieces. Wire, glass, aluminum, plastic, rubber, cloth—when combined, these became the components of an aircraft. On the other hand, the incident of metal fatigue, with the structural failures that followed after the initial crack in the fuselage's aluminum skin, also pointed to the systemic nature of this aircraft. In other words, determining the cause of the acci-

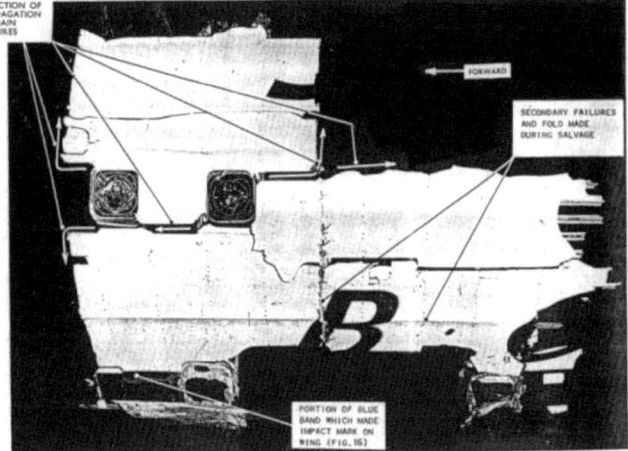

FIGURE 3: Recovered fuselage showing metal fatigue, RF aerial port, Flight 781 (Comet G-ALYP) (1954)

dent required that the accident investigator think of the aircraft as a system. The investigator located the evidence (or if possible, the cause of the accident) and mapped out its effects over time, in effect reading and interpreting the accident. And yet the creation of this narrative anticipated the same idea of a "holistic phenomenon" that Christopher Alexander announced in "Systems Generating Systems," published in a 1968 issue of AD: a "*holistic phenomenon which can only be understood as a product of interaction among parts*."[10] In the case of the De Havilland Comet, the metal fatigue was the literal line of continuity that joined the result of an accident to its cause. It was a line that also cut across separate pieces of the aircraft as well.

Architecture played an unusual role in that it presented an obstacle to the very notions of systemic thought underlying the accident investigation. By "obstacle", I am not referring to a conceptual or methodological impasse. The obstacles I reference here are quite

Figure 4: (Above) Front nose assembly of Comet G-ALYP, RAE Farnborough (1954)

Figure 5: (Below) Recovered tail section, Flight 781 (Comet G-ALYP), RAE Farnborough (1954) literal. The above-mentioned testing rig was thus one example of a physical barrier. Inside the rig, the Comet G-ALYU appeared unnaturally static and incapable of flight. It also defied any holistic conceptions of flight by literally separating the aircraft into two objects: wing and fuselage. Whereas technicians and RAE staff subjected the Comet's fuselage to extreme changes in pressurization, the wings were left alone. Within the testing rig, it then became impossible to conceive of the aircraft as a flying system, or more specifically, a complex grouping of objects assembled as a larger object that once flew in the air.

The investigation relied on architecture to make sense of the accident's cause in other ways. Images by AAIB investigators depicted how RAE technicians attempted to reassemble the pieces of Flight 781. In one image, the crumpled front nose assembly showed the physical damage that the Comet sustained during the accident. [FIG. 4] In another, the tail assembly was severed completely from the rear fuselage.[11] [FIG. 5] Lastly, another photograph showed the remaining aircraft pieces assembled on the floor of a hangar.[12] [FIG. 6] This last image was remarkable for two reasons. First, it showed how technicians placed the pieces of wreckage in places approximating their actual location on the aircraft. Nosepieces were reassembled in the approximate location of the forward fuselage assembly. Wing fragments lied alongside the fuselage, as if the fuselage were really there.

Second, this image suggested that the absence of a main fuselage is significant for what was there in its place. The photograph showed wood frame scaffolding holding the Comet's remains together.[13] On the one hand, this image could suggest how that most basic of architectural apparatuses—wood framing—could be used to make sense of the accident. The building of the pressurization test rig would be another example of this as well. But like the rig, the wood scaffolding only inhibited a systemic reading of the aircraft. The scaffolding in the main fuselage section, for example, never read as a suggestion of a fuselage. No bits of wreckage were appended to it. Nothing hanged there as evidence of a structure that was there previously. In this image, therefore, the front and rear sections of the Comet were conjoined by a gaping absence. Although it may be easy to read an individual piece of an aircraft as something that use to belong to and be part of another system, assembling some of those pieces together complicated the reading of a system.

What, then "is the concept of history embedded in the accident investigation that begins while crushed aluminum is still smoldering?"[14] In other words, why are we interested in the demise of Flight 781? We are interested because of the role that architecture played in the lifespan of this aircraft. The De Havilland Comet was born in a wind tunnel. It died in Sir Arnold Hall's testing structure, the very place where the jet's design flaws came to light. This birth and death shares a condition, and that condition is architecture.

Yet architecture here provides a corrective to the epistemologies of accident investigation. Indeed, the rigs and scaffolding helped RAE technicians make sense of the Comet's form. As for the cause of the accident, however, architecture provided very little of a guide. The investigators assembled many of the recovered pieces onto the wood scaffolding. The absence of parts from the middle fuselage sections, however, did help in understanding the power and magnitude of the explosive decompression. However, none of this would make sense without recovering the piece that contained the original source of metal fatigue. And without this piece, RAE engineers and architects would have never conceived of the testing rig to corroborate metal fatigue as the cause of the Comet's demise.

NOTES

1. Much of the literature concerning the crash of Flight 781 is of two different types. The first is a "technology buff" literature that does not consider the De Havilland Comet in historical terms and looks at the airplane solely in terms of design. The second is heavily engineering-oriented in nature and considers the accident investigation from a purely technical standpoint. However, this analysis draws from the government documents regarding the Comet's design and subsequent accident: *Material Specification, Aluminum-Coated High Tensile Aluminum Alloy for Sheet and Coils, DTD 546B*, Ministry of Supply (London: HMSO, 1946); Baron L. Cohen, W.S. Walmer Farren, W.J. Duncan and A.H. Wheeler, *Report of the Court of Inquiry into the Accidents to Comet G-ALYP on 10 January, 1954 and Comet G-ALYY on 8 April, 1954* (London: HMSO, 1955); and Atkinson, R.J., W.J. Winkworth and G.M. Norris, *Behaviour of Skin Fatigue Cracks at the Corners of Windows in a Comet I Fuselage* (9th edn. ed.) R&M 3248 (London: HMSO, 1962).

2. Baron L. Cohen, W.S. Walmer Farren, W.J. Duncan and A.H. Wheeler. *Report of the Court of Inquiry into the Accidents to Comet G-ALYP on 10 January, 1954 and Comet G-ALYY on 8 April, 1954* (London: HMSO, 1955), accessed at <http://www.geocities.com/CapeCanaveral/Lab/8803/fcogalyp.htm>.

3. *Ibid.*

4. Geoffrey De Havilland, *Sky Fever: The Autobiography of Sir Geoffrey De Havilland* (London: H. Hamilton, 1961), pp. 182-183.

5. Atkinson, R.J., W.J. Winkworth and G.M. Norris, *Behaviour of Skin Fatigue Cracks at the Corners of Windows in a Comet I Fuselage.* (9th edition), R&M 3248 (London: HMSO,1962), n.p.; *Report of the Court of Inquiry into the Accidents to Comet G-ALYP on 10 January, 1954 and Comet G-ALYY on 8 April, 1954*, n.p.

6. *Ibid.*

7. P.A. Withey, "Fatigue Failure of the De Havilland Comet I," *Engineering Failure Analysis*, Vol. 4, No. 2 (Sep., 1996), p. 148.

8. *Report of the Court of Inquiry into the Accidents to Comet G-ALYP on 10 January, 1954 and Comet G-ALYY on 8 April, 1954*, n.p.

9. *Ibid.*

10. Christopher Alexander, "Systems Generating Systems" *Architectural Design*, No. 38 (Dec., 1968), p. 606.

11. Robert J. Serling, Richard K. Smith, and R.E.G. Davies, *The Jet Age (The Epic of Flight)* (Alexandria, Virginia: Time-Life Books, 1982), p. 48.

12. *Ibid.*

13. *Ibid.*

14. Peter Galison, "An Accident of History" in Peter Galison and Alex Roland, eds. *Atmospheric Flight in the Twentieth Century* (Dordecht, Boston, London: Kluwer Academic, 2000), p. 3.

FIGURE 6: (background) Assembly of Flight 781 (Comet G-ALYP), RAE Farnborough, (1954)

NAUGHTY FLUFF
A TALE FROM LONGOLAND

JOSHUA LONGO

Seven-thirty. The alarm chimes its modern apple song. The Moose thinks it's time. He needs to pee. His bladder is the size of an apricot. I guide him under the covers. He nuzzles into my right armpit head first. Eight o' clock. Repeat. Eight thirty. Repeat. Nine o' clock. Moose won't get under the covers again. His tiny fuzz covered belly is about to explode. I check my e-mail on my phone as if my eyes are even focused to handle such a task, but I am slave to that tiny rectangle. I put a small bed at the foot of my own so this seven pound butter sausage can jump down without hurting his tiny chicken wings and pork chops. He dances ass first as I attempt to put his harness around his neck and chest. As I get closer he tries to help the process by lowering his head to ground. It doesn't help, but I don't discourage his enthusiasm. I want him to think he's doing a good job. **THE WALK GOES AS FOLLOWS.......SNIFF, SNIFF, SNIFF, WAIT.....SNIFF, SNIFF, OH OH MAYBE, NO, SNIFF...... SNIFF, PEEEEEEEEEEEE, "YOU'RE SO MACHO, WHO'S SO MACHO, YOU ARE, YOU ARE"............WALK, WALK, HURRY,**

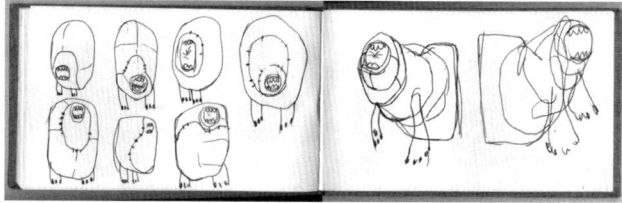

HURRY, HURRY,........WHAT'S THAT!!!!???.....HE RETREATS HURRIEDLY FROM A PLASTIC BAG CAUGHT IN A SMALL WIND.....SNIFF.......SNIFF........HE PROCEEDS TO WALK IN A CIRCLE AND...... RELEASE........ We get back to the door. He begins to dance. His ass is the bull and his body is the cowboy fighting to stay on. It's breakfast time. I don't leave food out for the Moose. He has no self control. None. If I did we'd be seeing him on a reality tv show velcro-ed to mobility scooter with a bag of cheese balls and diet root beer. I schmoosh the food down into the bowl to prevent him from inhaling it. A half a minute goes by. lick, lick, lick, lick, lick. I pick him up. He tries to kiss me. **"PLEASE DON'T KISS ME RIGHT**

18/19

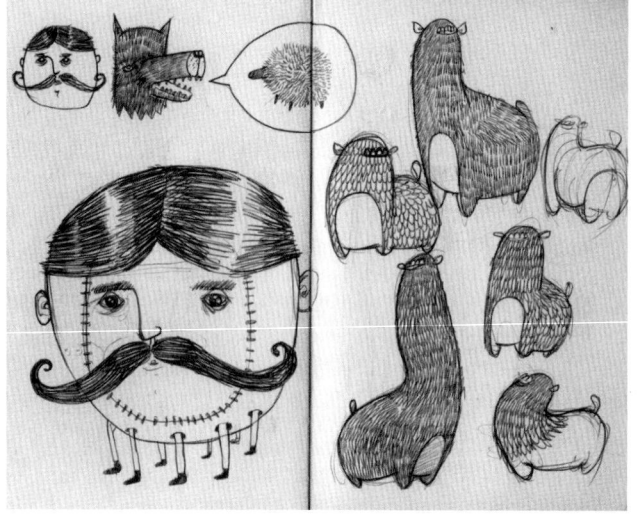

NOW……COME ON CHIMICHANGA". I put him back on the bed. He lays down like a gentleman and proceeds to lick his paws. He stares at me. He stares as if he is about to confess his secrets. He stares right into my eyes, waiting…..waiting patiently for his words to softly kiss the air. I touch his tiny nose and pat his fuzzy butt. (He bought the nose at the "Small & Tiny" store along with his eyebrows) Maybe he will kill his duck this morning, tear him limb from limb, but he had a rough morning. A tyrannical plastic bag, with all of its fury almost erased him from this very earth. It's ten o' clock. Somehow the moose has gone from the bed to my lap. He sleeps. My day can start. I will spend the remainder of the day trying not to distract myself with pretty faces, random doodles, and the NY times. My day will be filled with changing modern, traditional, geo, ethnic, floral prints just ten percent. Just enough that "they" don't get sued. When I reach a point of floral suffocation, I exhale, I exhale, I take a deep breath and enter a place of monsters and shadows. Plump, fuzzy, dancing meatballs.

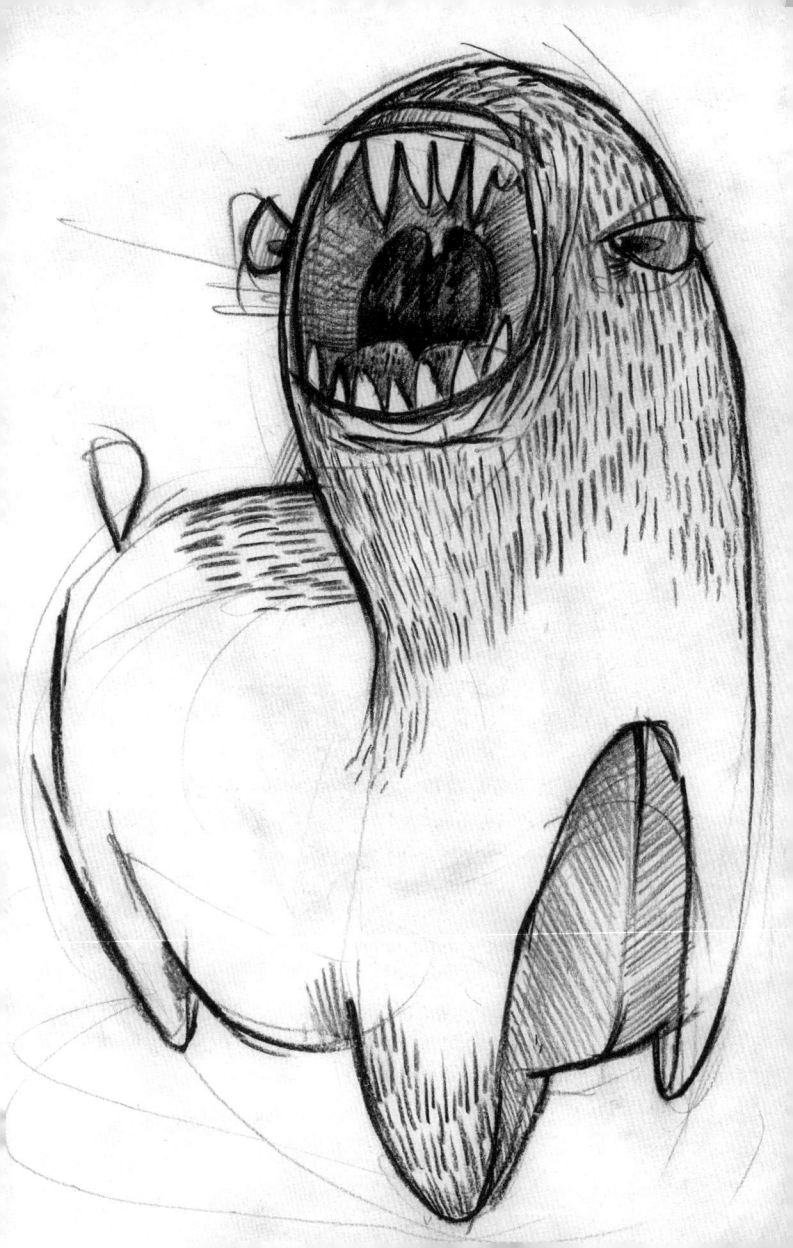

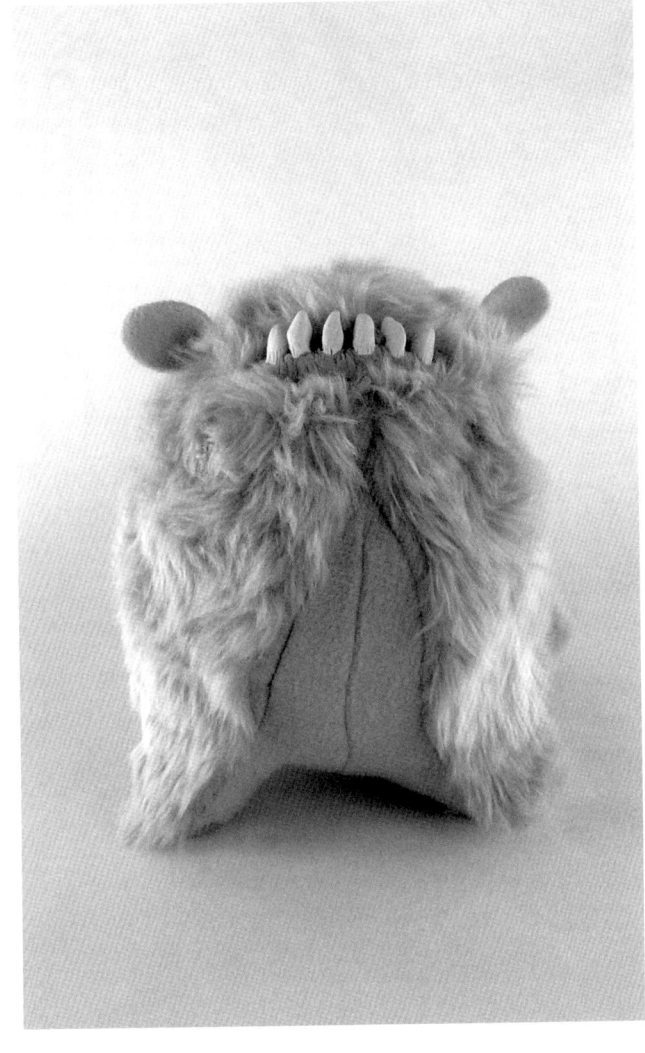

24/25

27

INTERVIEW

THOMAS HIRSCHHORN
WITH GARRETT RICCIARDI + JULIAN ROSE

Background: Thomas Hirschhorn, *Théâtre Précaire 2*, 2010 (*Les Ateliers de Rennes*-Biennale d'Art Contemporain, Rennes)

HIERARCHY

Garrett Ricciardi + Julian Rose: You have stated your desire to make work that is non-hierarchical, and this resistance to hierarchies seems to be at the root of your social and political project. In his "Critical Dictionary", Bataille's fundamental critique of architecture is that as a representation of social order it is inevitably hierarchical. In your work, you create spaces that hold the potential for inhabitation and use (libraries, places for speaking, meeting, etc.). One might even refer to these spaces as "programmed," to borrow an architectural term, but they do not seem to submit to the hierarchies architecture is normally entangled in. How and where do you see these hierarchies most clearly dissolving in your work?

Thomas Hirschhorn: To do a non-hierarchical work is neither a social nor a political project, it is an art-project, it is my artproject. In my work I dissolve hierarchies by creating sculptures in which everything is important, in which everything can be important and in which nothing is unimportant. Every element in my work has the same importance and could be important for somebody. Nothing is unimportant or less important. I can't accept that someone else decides for me what is or should be of importance and I don't decide what is important for the other. That is precisely what I want to give form to. To establish hierarchies or to establish what should be considered "quality" are procedures of exclusion which—in art—do not make sense. Art goes beyond hierarchy, art touches beyond all hierarchy, I am convinced of this. In my work I want to fight hierarchy-thinking and quality-thinking by deliberatly using non-intimidating forms. I only use inclusive forms. All single forms I use in my work are inclusive, which means they must have the power to include—at one to one—the spectator. And all materials I use in my work must be incusive and non-intimidating. A non-intimidating material is a material with no plus-value, this is the only kind of material I use. In my work, guidelines such as "Less is Less, More is More" contribute to avoid absurd quality-evaluation and demagogic hierarchy-thinking. Hierarchy is avoidable, but the artist must pay

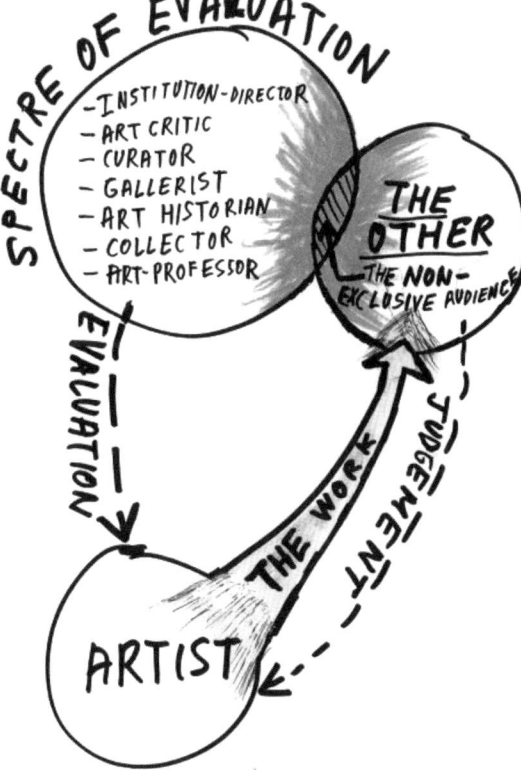

Thomas Hirschhorn, *Spectre of Evaluation*, 2008

for it. That is why I have the will to do too much in order that things don't lie anymore.

I always want my work to address the "Non-exclusive Audience" or 'the Other' (see previous page). By doing this I can avoid establishing hierarchies because the "Non-exclusive Audience" is my neigboor, it is the unexpected, 'the Other'. The "Non-exclusive Audience" is what I oppose to the "Spectre of Evaluation" which wants to etablish hierarchies or wants to keep the old hierarchies. I do not want to establish a new hierarchy—I want to refuse all hierarchy. This desire of non-hierarchy is the desire of the *real* against the acceptance of reality. To do a non-hierarchical work is to have the ambition of universality. To do a non-hierarchical work is resistance toward exclusivity, luxury, inaccessibility and toward aristocracy—all of which are forms of exclusion and injustice existing not exclusively in art, but also in art.

COLLAGE

YOU HAVE SPOKEN OF COLLAGE, AN IMPORTANT TECHNIQUE IN YOUR WORK, AS A WAY OF PUTTING THINGS TOGETHER THAT CANNOT BE PUT TOGETHER. BUT AT THE SAME TIME THAT COLLAGE HOLDS THE PROMISE OF ENGAGING THIS KIND OF OTHERNESS, IN THE WORK OF SOME ARTISTS IT GIVES A GLOSS OF OVERALL STYLISTIC UNITY, TO THE POINT THAT CRITICS OR HISTORIANS OCCASIONALLY USE THE TERM "COLLAGE AESTHETIC" TO DESCRIBE WORKS PRODUCED BY COLLAGE. HOW DO YOU RETAIN TRUE HETEROGENEITY IN YOUR COLLAGE, AND WHAT IS VALUABLE TO YOU ABOUT THE EXISTENCE OF SUCH RADICAL OTHERNESS IN YOUR WORK? DOES PUSHING COLLAGE FROM TWO TO THREE DIMENSIONS HELP YOU ACHIEVE THIS?

When I do a collage, I really do a collage, that means I literally glue things together, with glue! Pushing collages from the second dimension into the third (into the space) and into the fourth dimension (into the head of the spectator) is the technique that I have been using for years: to glue together, to really glue! This is how to be truthful to collage and this my invention. I think that the "overall stylistic" comes from the fact that instead of a collage pieces are often montage or photo-montage. But a montage is something different then a collage. A collage is made with the fact that the two parts are kept as two different parts but glued together by decision of the artist. In a montage the "gloss" can come from the temptation to unify, to *uniformize*, to make it cleaner or make it fit more closely to "reality". This is what I avoid and never do. On the contrary, I am interested in using the differences of sizes, of printing, of material of both parts of a collage, and it's an absolute necessity to keep these as such in order to create something *real* and not "reality".

In order to keep the heterogeneity of a collage and the heterogeneity of doing collages I need to keep it simple, very simple. The obvious feature of a collage consists of creating a new world —a new *real*— from only two elements of the existing world. Therefore I want to connect two images to one another, to bring them together. I want to glue them together into a new worldview only with glue. What connects the two elements before I have glued them together is that they are both images of the existing world surrounding me. They are elements, images of our undivided world—our only world. They are elements of the world I live in: complex, chaotic, cruel, beautiful and wonderful. To do a collage means to act headlessly and to take the risk of being accused of stupidity and even making a ridiculous work, because it is ridiculous to have the ambition to create a new truth. But this is exactly what a collage allows! When doing a collage you don't have to be smart, it is no longer a collage if you want to be smart in doing it!

Yes, it is fun to make a collage and at the same time it arouses suspicion: it is too easy, too fast. For many it is not respectable enough and many label it as immature. So collages are mostly done at youth (young people make collages, not montages by the way). A collage is resistant. It is resistant and as such it escapes control—even the control of the one who made it. That is its resistant character. To make a collage always has something to do with headlessness. That is precisely what interests me, because there is no means of expression with such great explosive and heterogeneous power. There is no technique more common throughout the world than the collage. Almost everybody in this world has done a collage at some point in their life. That is the associative element of a collage, almost everyone, has tried to make an image of this world. In doing collage and in insisting with it, I want to constitute a "critical corpus" with my work.

THE PRECARIOUS

You have used the term "precarious" in relation to your work. While the word could describe the fragile, unbalanced quality of many of your materials and structures, you seem to understand "precarious" in a more extended way to describe a quality of space or even experience. It is almost as if certain material qualities implicate the viewer, soliciting a certain type of attention and therefore producing a corresponding psychological response to the environment you have created. What is the connection between these two levels of precarity, and more generally, how do you understand the connection between the material and experiential dimensions of your work?

First of all, I do not make a linguistic distinction between 'precarity' and 'precarious'. With both words—to me—it's about the same term, the same notion. There is only one level in 'precarious' and it is not a psychological one. To me precariousness is only physical. Precariousness is only the working-out, the visual, the form. There is nothing precarious in the idea, the experience, the consequences, the confrontation, or the enrichment. This is why I make a distinction between precarious and ephemeral. Ephemeral is what comes from nature, precariousness is human. Precariousness is not negative. Precariousness is the photography of an endless movement.

Precariousness is not the end and not the beginning, it is an instant, a moment. It is the unique moment. In order to reach this moment I have to be present and I have to be awake, I have to keep my eyes open all the time! I have to stand up, I have to face and I have to risk myself. This is why the work—as an artist—has to be deconstructed every day, every hour, every moment in my own brain. The endless re-building and constant reconstruction of my work gives it—I am sure—its power to touch eternity. Nothing is more boring than something definite, something sure, something safe, because it just isn't the truth. The truth can only be touched in Art with hazardous, headless, contradictory and hidden encounters.

I want to re-establish the word 'precarious'. Precariousness can be a tool to work out contemporary problems involving economic, social, religious, political and cultural issues. The logic of the precarious is, to me, the logic of precocity. The precocity of doing encounters and creating an event through the precarious, thanks to the precarious or instead of the precarious. As an artist, to do a work which claims to be precarious is to risk exposing myself to an incredible challenge without foreseeing or measuring the difficulties. It is the difficult to create something today. My love for the precarious comes from my understanding of each human activity as precarious, from the belief in doing things instead of considering the incommensurable precarity they will unavoidably own. My love comes from the strength and the courage that is necessary to create something instead of the precarity of things, the precarity of all things and the precarity of life.

The logic of the precarious is one of necessity and emergency and it is contrary to ephemeral logic, which is the logic of death. My adherence to precarity comes from my life, from my experience, from what I love—from the precarious forms I love—and from what I understand of it.

I am really pleased to know that Judith Butler, Emmanuel Levinas, Hal Foster and also Manuel Joseph (a French writer and friend) among many others, have developed serious thoughts about 'precariousness,' but I learned about the term 'precarious' myself. My tendency is, I admit, to avoid to go "deeper" into the term because I need, yes I need, my own strange, wrong, headless, misunderstood, bad, stupid—but my fucking own—relation to preserve and to develop the 'precarious'. This is not an opposition to theory or a refusal of theory—absolutely not—it has to do with being open to what comes from myself, to what comes only from myself. It makes me happy to know that I am not alone with my interest in "precarity" because I do have the ambition in doing my work to intervene—through the notion of 'precarity' or the 'precarious'—in the field of art.

ADDITION/SUBTRACTION

Many of your works are constantly in flux and so fundamentally dynamic. Not only are some of them assembled through a kind of logic of aggregation, but often elements can be added to or subtracted from them even after they are "complete." In contrast, architectural form is traditionally understood as static. The renaissance architect and theorist Leon Battista Alberti, for example, used the term "concinnitas" to describe the idea that buildings achieve beauty by taking a form to which nothing can be added and from which nothing can be taken away. What motivates the dynamic nature of your work? Is your emphasis on change part of an effort to avoid making form, and what would you describe yourself as making, if not form?

I cannot accept any architectonic or formalist self-satisfaction, but I am not fighting against architects or architecture. I am an artist doing art. I want to define, through my work, new terms for art. As an artist I need to ignore architecture and work with it, not for it and not against it, but with it in order to go beyond any easy and self-calming prescripts. I think that today in this complex, cruel, incomprehensible, but also graceful, beautiful and hopeful world, to be static, to "keep the level," to be for security, tradition, and identity leads to a certain death. I am for change, the change of the world. I am for movement, intensity, and exaggeration. I am for headlessness, insistence, and the offensive, for the dream, for the decision and for production—the production of a generous, energetic statement. I want to make a statement about form with each one of my works.

Making a statement through form is obviously the most important problem for the artist. I see this as most important, not the form as such, but the decision and the act of "giving form". The crucial point for me is to distinguish between "making form," and "giving form". "Giving form," is a form which comes from me, from me only, which can only come from me because I see the form that way. I understand it that way and because I am the only one to know that form. To give form—rather than to make form—means to be "one" with it. I must stand alone with this form. It means raising the form, asserting this form and defending it against everything and against everyone. It means to ask the question of form for myself and try to answer through giving form. I want to try to confront the great artistic challenge: How can I give a form which takes a position? How can I give a form that resists facts? I want to understand the question of form as the most important question for an artist. I understand the difference between "making form" and "giving form" as essential. "Giving form" means giving from me, giving everything from myself, giving only from me. How can I give away something so close to me, so personal, so intimate without going into the private? Something, so individual, that it can have the power to be universal? The key— and this is the departure from "making"—comes through "giving". Giving form does not implicate a target, a use, a demand, a result or a contract. Giving form means giving what only I own, what only I know, what only I see like this, and what only I, personally, can take responsibility for. "Giving form" means to fight the dictatorship of information, documents, facts, and journalism. "Giving form" means to stand up, to say "yes!" to the absoluteness of art. It is a movement beyond justification, discussion and explication. "Giving form" is an engagement that does not step back. "Giving form" and not "making form" is the only way I can reach a kind of equality. In my work I always ask myself, "Does this form really come from me?" and "Can this form create a truth beyond cultural, political, aesthetic habits?"

POINTS AND LINES VS. VOLUMES AND FORMS

Many of your spaces have a raw, unfinished feeling, perhaps rooted in the logics of addition and subtraction noted above. This feeling implies a kind of unplanned space, built through immediate accumulation of materials rather than resulting from a preconceived process of formalization. At the same time, you have said that you prefer to think not in terms of volumes or spaces, but in maps, plans, or networks of points and lines. How would you describe your process of creating space? Do you use materials to shape space directly, or is there a preparatory stage or some other kind of mediation between your conception of a work and its material existence?

I am not interested in doing something "unfinished," I want to finish my work as every artist does. I want to take responsibility for the entire, finished work, but I refuse to do what one can call overworked, overpolished, or overdone work. I think that technically overfinished artworks often hide a lack sense. I want to do my work in "Low control". This could be misunderstood as lack of rigor, but acting in "Low control" —as a technique—means refusing to be "in control". It means putting myself at a level of "Low control", like someone on the ground, at the bottom, overwhelmed, completely submerged but still unresigned, unreconciled and uncynical.

I like trash and I like trash-art. I like artists who do exaggerated work. I myself want to do a work which is completly exaggerated but also completely precise. I want to work in a rush of precipitation. I am not interested in the "tidy" or the "untidy," I am interested in doing a powerful and biting work—that is what I want! My guideline for working in "Low control" is 'panic is the solution!'. I do not fight against the space nor work for the space. I want to work with the space available. I do no planning and I don't prepare or model the lay-out of the elements in space. What I do is a mental preparation of all the elements needed for my work, because there is a reason, a logic to why I need those elements. When the elements are made—either in my mind or in my studio—I have to put or to glue them together, like in a collage, in the given space. I can do this only in a rush, in precipitation and with a certain blindness. This is why 'panic is the solution!' helps me to give form. Of course I am interested neither in 'panic' nor in 'solution' but both words describe the mental catastrophe in which I am—as the artist—working out my project in the exhibition space. I am a "mentally-catastrophé"—yes!

Interview conducted via email by the authors in April 2010.

Tanks on *Avenida Presidente Vargas* in front of the former *Ministério do Exército*, the Ministry of the Army, in Rio de Janeiro, circa 1964. Beyond is the clock tower of *Central do Brasil*, the city's main rail station. The coup of March 31, 1964 ushered in 21 years of a repressive military dictatorship in Brazil.

*Burle Marx, Roberto. "Estátuas em Jardins." *Cultura: Conselho Federal de Cultura*. Ministério da Educação e Cultura. Ano 2 – No. 14. Rio de Janeiro, Agôsto 1968.

STATUES IN GARDENS*
ESTÁTUAS EM JARDINS

ROBERTO BURLE MARX
TRANSLATED, WITH NOTES AND ILLUSTRATIONS, BY CATHERINE SEAVITT-NORDENSON

The Brazilian Conselho Federal de Cultura (Federal Council of Culture) was created by decree in November 1966, two years after the 1964 coup that began a 21-year right wing military dictatorship. The first Conselho Federal de Cultura consisted of 24 members, appointed directly by the President of the Republic, Humberto de Alencar Castello Branco. The Council was comprised of four divisions: Arts, Letters, Social Sciences, and National Historic and Artistic Patrimony. The landscape architect Roberto Burle Marx (1909-1994) was appointed as a member of the Câmera de Artes. Some of the Conselho Federal de Cultura's other well-known members, all of whom shared an interest in the national projection of Brazilian culture, were sociologist Gilberto Freire, novelist Rachel de Queiroz, and literary critic Adonias Filho. Meanwhile, many other significant Brazilian cultural figures spent this period in political exile. This conflux of culture and politics, and specifically a nationalist cultural policy as implemented by a military dictatorship, is particularly unique. The Council was active for more than twenty years; after the end of the dictatorship in 1985, the Ministério da Cultura was created by the federal government, and in 1990 the Conselho Federal de Cultura was formally dissolved.

FIGURE 1: *Praça Paris*, Glória, Rio de Janeiro, photographed at its opening in 1929. The park was designed by Alfred Agache and modelled on the Parisian *belle époque* gardens.

The landscape work produced by Roberto Burle Marx during the period of the military dictatorship, 1964-1985, is quite different from his work during the preceding years. The majority of Burle Marx's projects from 1934-1964 are public parks. These range in scale from the small town squares of Recife of his early career, to the landscaped plazas of important public buildings such as the Ministério de Educação e Cultura and the Rio de Janeiro airport terminal, to the large parks executed in Pampulha, Araxá, Rio de Janeiro, and Caracas. After the military coup of 1964, Burle Marx's projects are smaller in scale and often privately commissioned. Perhaps Burle Marx saw his position as a Counselor as providing a forum in which to develop and promote his ideas of the Brazilian landscape in relation to the public realm, and as a way to deliver his cultural position to the federal government. He often read his statements directly to the President of the Republic. As illustrated here in the vehement (yet humorous) opinion delivered in 1968 to both the President and his fellow members of the Council, Burle Marx felt passionately about the quality of commemorative sculptures placed in public spaces. His position clearly equates public sculpture (and by extension, public art) with a reflection of a society's culture. And, embedded in the critique of statues, there also are a few subtle critiques of the military dictatorship. [FIG. 0]

MR PRESIDENT AND FELLOW COUNSELORS:

I would like to deliver a statement regarding the use of statues in our cities, and, above all, to the role they play in public plazas, parks and gardens.

A great majority of our statues do not attain the level of artistic quality that they should. However, they continue to proliferate and multiply. Today, Rio de Janeiro is a city that has been "bust-ified." The Directors of the Department of Parks and Gardens, seduced by clever sculptors, have inappropriately satiated public spaces with sculptures lacking both aesthetic standards and direction. A sculpted *herma* had significance in ancient Greece; however, today's parodies of heads on pedestals seem ridiculous. They embody a lack of taste; it is impossible to justify their placement in our public parks. Is it not a sufficient commemoration to perpetuate the names of great heroes with the names of streets, plazas, and even cities? Must we accept these horrifying stone heads, just because their actual owners were indeed meritorious? When Michelangelo created the Medici tomb, he was not preoccupied with resemblance, but rather with the quality of his sculpture.

Here in Rio, just examine the original design made by the urban planner Alfred Agache[1] for the *Praça Paris* with the situation today. [FIG. 1] Here, sprouting up around the four original *herms* representing the four seasons, are a huge number of busts, such that the garden has completely lost its original feeling of an economical use of sculptural elements. And add to this the mutilation of the flowerbeds and the lawn, which were intended to act in contrast to the volumes of the trees and planted shrubs. You can clearly perceive the interference of poorly trained gardeners, lacking both sufficient knowledge and concern for the park.

FIGURE 2A: *Monumento ao Marechal Floriano Peixoto*, erected in 1910, with the *Theatro Municipal* and *Avenida Central* (now *Avenida Rio Branco*) seen beyond. Photograph circa 1919.

Statues do not complement gardens—that is, when they are used in a purely sentimental manner. This problem occurs in *Botafogo*, in *Praça Marechal Floriano*, and in the *Passeio Público*; in fact, it is a problem in the majority of plazas in this city.

Of course there exist exceptional spaces that merit large and important statues, but unfortunately they often result in truly carnivalesque compositions. I do not object to the allegorical floats that are made specifically for Carnival, for these are created for the ephemeral duration of just a single night, filled with noise, colors, and lights. By contrast, in the case of this type of statuary, we are obliged to endure them for an entire lifetime.

A sculptural ensemble at *Cinelândia*,[2] [FIG. 2A] erected as a pompous allegory and, frankly, of poor quality and in bad taste, is topped off by **PIDGINS**.* [FIG. 2B] This has transformed the intentions for a serious and reverent commemorative sculpture into a ridiculous note at the very center of our city.

Figure 2B: Detail of the *Monumento ao Marechal Floriano Peixoto*, with PIDGINS*.

Figure 3A: Itinerant *lambe-lambe* photographer taking portrait photographs in the *Campo de Santana*, a public park in downtown Rio de Janeiro, 1969.

Figure 3B: Another *lambe-lambe* photographing at the *Jardim do Méier*, Rio de Janeiro, 1969.

* On the occasion of this publication of Pidgin Number Nine *pombos* has been translated as PIDGINS.

FIGURE 4A: Equestrian statue of the *Duque de Caxias*, in its intended location along an allée of palm trees at the *Largo do Machado*, Catete, Rio de Janeiro.

These sculptures might be compared with the *"lambe-lambe"* photographers[3] who frequent our public parks and plazas. These photographers transform the plazas into charming backdrops for portraits, but their work does not attain the level of photography as a visual art, as it certainly should today. [FIG. 3A+3B]

It is curious that here in Rio, statues go walking. They roam around neighborhoods, often abandoning the locations for which they were compositionally intended and specifically constructed. This is the case of a notable work by Rodolfo Bernadelli,[4] originally found in the *Largo do Machado*. [FIG. 4A] It was perfectly proportioned to the plaza and its surrounding residential buildings, beautifully scaled to the observer, to the passersby, who could contemplate its bas-reliefs and the details of its equestrian figure. But in 1949 this statue was transferred without any reason, and certainly with no landscape-based criteria, to the plaza in front of a gigantic edifice, where it is now completely out of proportion. [FIG. 4B]

FIGURE 4B: In 1949, the statue of the *Duque de Caxias* was transferred, along with the Duke's remains, to a pantheon plinth in front of the Ministry of the Army on *Avenida Presidente Vargas*.

FIGURE 5: Statue of São Sebastião, erected in 1965 in Glória's *Largo do Russel*, Rio de Janeiro.

FIGURE 6: Memorial to the soldiers killed in the 1935 *Intentona Comunista*, now at *Praia Vermelho* in Urca, Rio de Janeiro.

Figure 4c: Roberto Burle Marx (1909-1994). Garden Design. Duque de Caxias Square, Rio de Janeiro, Brazil. Plan. Drawing date: 1948. Gouache on paper, 33 ¾" x 56". Gift of Philip L. Goodwin (SC44.1948). The Museum of Modern Art, New York, NY, USA. The gray rectangle at the center of the plaza was the location of the Bernadelli equestrian sculpture. Designed by Burle Marx in 1948, the plan was never executed.

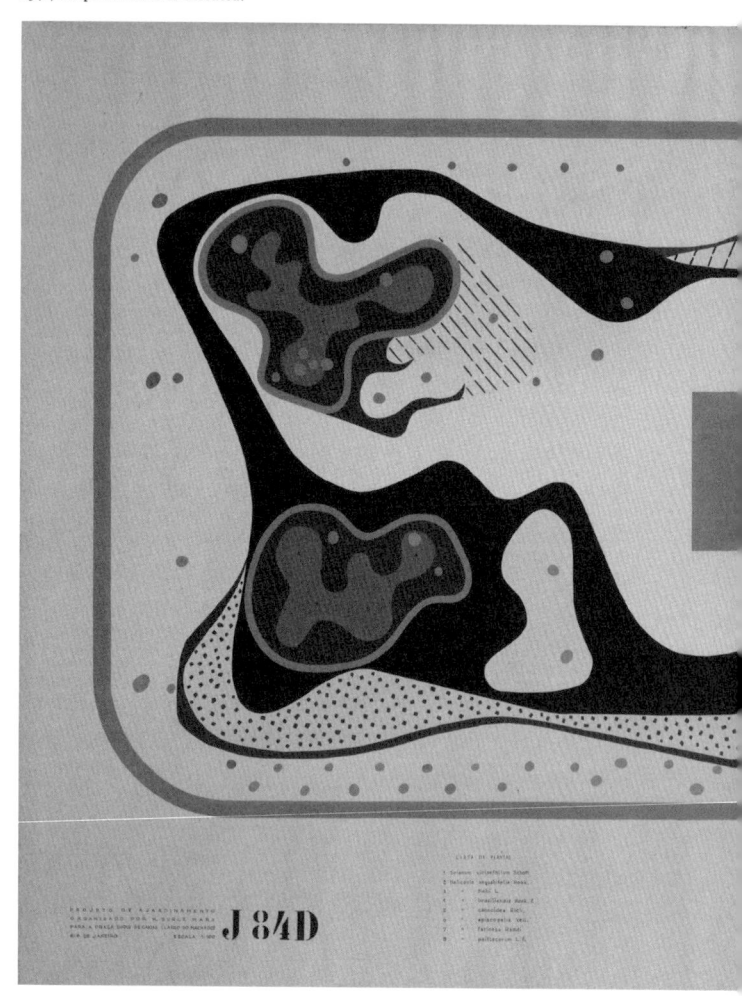

46
47

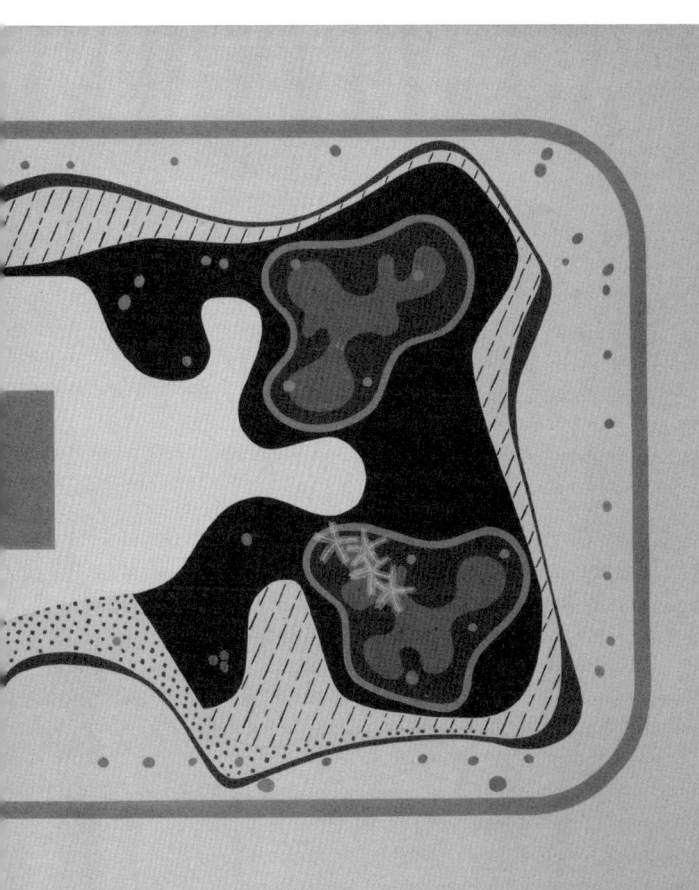

FIGURE 7: Entrance to the *Passeio Público*, the oldest public park in Rio de Janeiro, circa 1920.

In the *Passeio Público*, [FIG. 7] there is a bronze of a female journalist that appears to have been put through a grinding mill.[5] These particular examples, where the intentions were to create a respectful homage, have instead resulted in complete caricature.

The sculpture of Saint Sebastian, in *Praça Baden Powell*, has today been transformed in effect into an altar for practitioners of macumba.[6] [FIG. 5] There also exist examples in which statues are removed from cemeteries and then used in public parks. This is the case with the memorial statuary for the victims of the *Intentona* of 1935,[7] [FIG. 6] which was moved from the Cemetery of Saint John the Baptist to the *Praia Vermelha* at the base of Sugar Loaf Mountain. Often of poor or questionable artistic merit, these are monuments that would certainly be better off in the places for which they were intended. Since there seems to be such a need to exalt and visualize so many heroes and prominent public figures, and since there are certainly so many more to come, perhaps it would be wise to create a public park in the manner of a necropolis, containing tree-lined lanes of busts and statues of lesser artistic interest. I believe that the descendents, admirers, and pious souls would thus be able to envelope themselves with the sentimentality associated with the grouping of such sculptures, and in this association the sculptures would acquire a greater value than when isolated.

Cities such as Brasília, Rio, and others have restrictions and laws governing building construction. Yet the preoccupation of their mayors is to erect statues. Recently, the *Praça de Atibaia* was renovated while the façade of its adjacent church was being restored and re-stuccoed. Right in front, a luminous fountain was constructed, like a checkerboard, covered with glazed tiles and with a tailor's dummy in stone offered as sculpture.

During the period in which I was director of Parks and Gardens in Recife, I had the impulse to assess, demolish, and remove sculptures from the gardens that did not rise to a level of greatness corresponding with the real heroes. This was the case with the monument to the heroes of *Casa Forte* and Admiral Cochrane.[8] The latter had the unusual situation of having a *kepi*, the military field cap, screwed into the statue after the fact, by official decree. [FIG. 8] I return today to this same issue, to propose judicious and sensible regulations that might restrain somewhat abuses of this sort.

Sculptures in gardens and parks should be well-proportioned to the spaces for which they are created, with an aim to attain an elegant relationship between dimension, scale, and proportion. Many sculptures are of white marble; this brightness contrasts with the green masses of the trees, and potentially creates rhythmic patterns. When well-composed, the use of sculpture to creating order and sequence helps emphasize certain focal points, such as reflecting pools. Sculp-

FIGURE 8: *Praça de Casa Forte*, Recife, shown in April 1938 shortly after its 1935 renovation by Roberto Burle Marx. This was one of his earliest public park designs, conceived as an aquatic garden incorporating native species from the Amazon and Atlantic rainforests. The *Colégio Sagrada Família* and the *Matriz de Casa Forte* are seen beyond the pool of *Victoria regia* water lilies.

50/51

FIGURE 9: Re-structuring of the eroded slopes of Cantagalo hill, seen from the *Lagoa Rodrigo de Freitas*, Rio de Janeiro. This work was planned and executed by the engineer Raymundo de Paula Soares after the devastating landslides caused by rainstorms in 1966 and 1967.

ture might be used dramatize important places, where the volumes and masses of plants, water, and sculpture together shape a totality in such an idealized manner that if one were to extract one element, the whole composition would be destroyed. Such sculptures may be seen in isolation, yet the most important factor is the conception of the entire composition.

Unfortunately, it seems that a concern for public parks and for the natural landscape itself is lacking in our country. Even those with a limited capacity of observation would perceive, without too much effort, the offenses committed on our natural landscapes. The worst case must be at the Sugar Loaf Mountain. A company has erected a large illuminated advertising panel. Another offense is an enormous panel announcing the time of day. To crown this all off with a shining halo of poor taste, governmental authorities have painted white all of the public erosion control works [FIG. 9] that they have initiated in the entire city, leaving an impression of gigantic adhesive tape, accentuating the wounds provoked by heavy rains and deforestation.9 The value of this commendable government work should not be highlighted in such a manner. This just implicates our culture's lack of understanding of the problems involving our landscapes, and speeds our arrival to this inversion of aesthetic values.

The examples are interminable. The statue of Quintino Bocaiúva at the *Lagoa*, besides lacking artistic value, has an even worse spatial placement. The statue of Mahatma Gandhi, [FIG. 10] one of the great figures of humanity, appears to be more like a caricature of a comic.

It is troubling that there exists not just a glorification of so many *"post mortem"* heroes, but also of those individuals still living, particularly in the case of Presidents of the Republic. There are sculptors who function as veritable factories. In their studios they are warehousing hindquarters and heads of horses, legs and shoulders of soldiers, to be used in the creation of future equestrian statues. These are modified in accordance with specifics; protuberances and lines are expanded or retracted in accordance with the hero's rank.

At times, the motivation behind these statuary tributes compromises the better judgement of our society. There exists, in *Praça Saens Peña*, a statue of the *"Rádio-Ginasta"* (Radio Gymnast), [FIG. 11] honoring the work of the radio-broadcast exercise and work-out pioneer.[10] On *Avenida Vieira Souto* one finds a monument to a King who visited us, once.[11] And there are innumerable statues imposed on us by foreign consulates, seemingly sympathetic to this impulse to deform our city.

The charity of the rich is also credited in statuary. At the beginning of this century, a generous lady gave, at her expense, a bronze statue erected in honor of "the poor of Botafogo," in the words of the tourist guide *Guia Rex*.

Inside the *Theatro Municipal*,[12] busts appear in inappropriate places, with no relationship to the architecture. I do not negate the merit of these homages. But we must cite the impropriety of statuary that is lacking a compatible artistic quality. An homage is perpetuated by statuary that communicates this tribute with a high level of artistic quality. One does not consecrate a name by deforming it into a poorly sited, banal sculpture.

In France, the placement of inappropriate busts in the gardens of Versailles or the Tuileries would never be permitted. We have an obligation to establish limits based on the idea that sculptures must have certain intrinsic qualities, and not be valorized by cheap sentimentality. As these sculptures are intended for public spaces, they must serve and benefit everyone. We must end once and for all these double standards, where a manifestation of bad taste is elevated and confused with a work of art. It is important to keep in mind that a culture measures itself by its artistic creation—not by works that perpetuate sentimentality. [FIG. 12]

Based on these concerns, current observations, and my professional experience as a landscape architect, I have taken the initiative to bring to this honorable Council the suggestion of organizing stronger and more restrictive legislation, and establishing procedures for the approval of the design and construction of monuments and statuary. In addition, I would propose a regulation and approvals process for their placement, particularly when they are proposed for public parks, streets, and the grounds of public buildings.

FIGURE 10: Statue of Mahatma Gandhi, erected in 1949 near *Cinelândia*, Rio de Janeiro.

FIGURE 11: Inauguration of the commemorative *Rádio-Ginasta* monument erected in 1957 at the *Praça Saens Peña*, Tijuca, Rio de Janeiro.

FIGURE 12: *Passeata dos cem mil* (March of 100,000), Rio de Janeiro, June 22, 1968. The most important manifestation against the military dictatorship since its onset, the march occurred just two months before Roberto Burle Marx wrote *Estátuas em Jardins*.

NOTES

1. French architect and urbanist Donat-Alfred Agache (1875-1959) published a Beaux-Arts master plan for Rio de Janeiro in 1930, a 300-page document that drew upon sociological ideas to provide the Brazilians with a plan for urban and national development along with socioeconomic and moral reform. The *Praça Paris*, a formal garden, was constructed near the center of downtown Rio along the Bay of Guanabara in the open space that was produced by the flattening of the *Morro do Castello*, an "insalubrious" hill in the center of town. The hill had been the site of informal housing erected by the poor.

2. Burle Marx is referring to the monument to Marechal Floriano Peixoto (1839-1895), the second president of Brazil, in the center of *Praça Floriano*. The work of the sculptor Eduardo Sá, it was cast in Paris and erected in 1910. In the 1920s the plaza became known as *Cinelândia*, named after the many movie theaters incorporated into the ground floors of the new office buildings framing the western edge of the plaza.

3. These are the traditional itinerant photographers who took portrait photographs in the parks and plazas of Brazil, using the park as a backdrop. Occasionally they would provide their own painted canvas backdrops, often of a picturesque natural scene.

4. Rodolfo Bernadelli (1852-1931) is one of Brazil's most significant sculptors. He trained at Rio's Imperial Academy of Fine Arts, and later became the Academy's director in the Republican period, when it was renamed the National Academy of Fine Arts. The sculpture referenced by Burle Marx is Bernadelli's 1899 equestrian sculpture of the Duque de Caxias (Luís Alves de Lima e Silva, 1803-1880), who, because of the critical role he played in Brazil's struggle for independence, is considered the father of the Brazilian Army. Intended for Rio's *Largo do Machado* (also known as the *Praça Duque de Caxias*) the

statue was transferred in 1949 to the *Praça da República*, in front of the former Ministry of the Army building on *Avenida Presidente Vargas*. Burle Marx must have been particularly unhappy about this move, as he had designed a transformation of the *Praça Duque de Caxias* in 1948, the year before the statue was transferred. His plan, focussing on the equestrian statue, was not executed.

5   The *Passeio Público* is oldest public park in Brazil. It was designed by the sculptor Mestre Valentim da Fonseca e Silva (c.1745-1813) in the 1780's and renovated by the French landscape architect Auguste François Marie Glaziou (1828-1906) in the 1860's. In the early 20th century, the *Passeio* was ornamented with many busts of famed Brazilians; by 1912 the park was referred to as the *parque de hermas*. The bust cited by Burle Marx is that of the writer Júlia Lopes de Almeida (1862-1934). It was executed by her daughter, Margarida Lopes de Almeida in 1935 (who was also the model for the hands of the famous statue of Christ on Corcovado). Ironically the bust was stolen by thieves in 2004; they presumably saw value in melting down the bronze.

6   Saint Sebastian is the patron of the city of Rio de Janeiro; the official name of the city is *São Sebastião do Rio de Janeiro*. In the polytheistic religions of *macumba* and *condomblé*, widely practiced in Brazil, Catholic saints were syncreticized with specific African deities, called *orixás*. Saint Sebastian is associated with Oxossi, the god of the forest and hunting, and offerings to Oxossi are often left at the statue.

7   This monument commemorates thirty soldiers of the Third Infantry Regiment Military School of Praia Vermelha, killed during the *Intentona Comunista* of November 1935. This was an attempted coup by the Brazilian Communist Party against the government of Getúlio Vargas.

8   Burle Marx, at the age of 25, was appointed the Director of Parks and Gardens in the northeastern city of Recife, where he worked from 1934-36. The renovation of the *Praça de Casa Forte* in 1935 was one of his first public park designs; conceived as an aquatic garden, it was planted with representative native species from both the Atlantic rainforest and the Amazon region. The plaza is the historic site of the *Casa Forte* uprising, a 1645 conflict between the residents of the state of Pernambuco and the Dutch army known as the *Insurreição Pernambucana*.

9   Burle Marx is referring to the stabilization and reinforcement of the city's granite hills, subject to erosion and rockslides. Much of this "patching and stitching" work was begun in 1966 by the engineer Raymundo de Paula Soares (1926-1992), the chief public works engineer in the State of Guanabara. Paula Soares also insisted upon a vast reforestation project in order to prevent further erosion of the hills.

10 This statue is an homage to Professor Oswaldo Diniz Magalhães (1904-1998), who broadcast a morning radio gymnastics program, *Hora da Ginástica*, for 51 years.

11 Albert I, King of Belgium (1875-1934), indeed visited Brazil, once. His bust was erected in Ipanema, Rio de Janeiro.

12 The *Theatro Municipal do Rio de Janeiro* is located in the center of the city's downtown at *Praça Floriano*, also known as *Cinelândia*.. The mayor (and engineer) Francisco Pereirra Passos (1836-1913) included the building as part of his "hygienic" reconstruction of the city's downtown in the early 20th Century, and the theater was inaugurated in 1909. Inspired by Charles Garnier's Paris Opera, it is one of the most important theaters in South America.

Stan Allen (2009) ink on watercolor paper 8.5" x 10.5" [*detail*]

Architecture is all in the Head -- Le Corbusier is the title of the artwork.

ARCHITECTURE IS ALL IN THE HEAD*

JORGE OROZCO GONZALEZ

1. The portraits will be of:
   a. Architects whose work seems to come up a lot in relation to my work during a review or desk crit.
   b. Architects whose work seems to be mentioned or discussed a lot at the school.
   c. Architects who have directly played an important role in my education as an architect.
2. Almost all of the work will be made over the course of three summers. As such it began in the beginning of the summer of 2009 and will end at the end of summer 2011.
3. All of the portraits will be drawings.
4. All of the images used as a reference for the drawing will be found through a Google image search.
5. All of the drawings will be rendered through stippling.
6. They will all be ink on paper.
7. They will all be roughly around letter size.

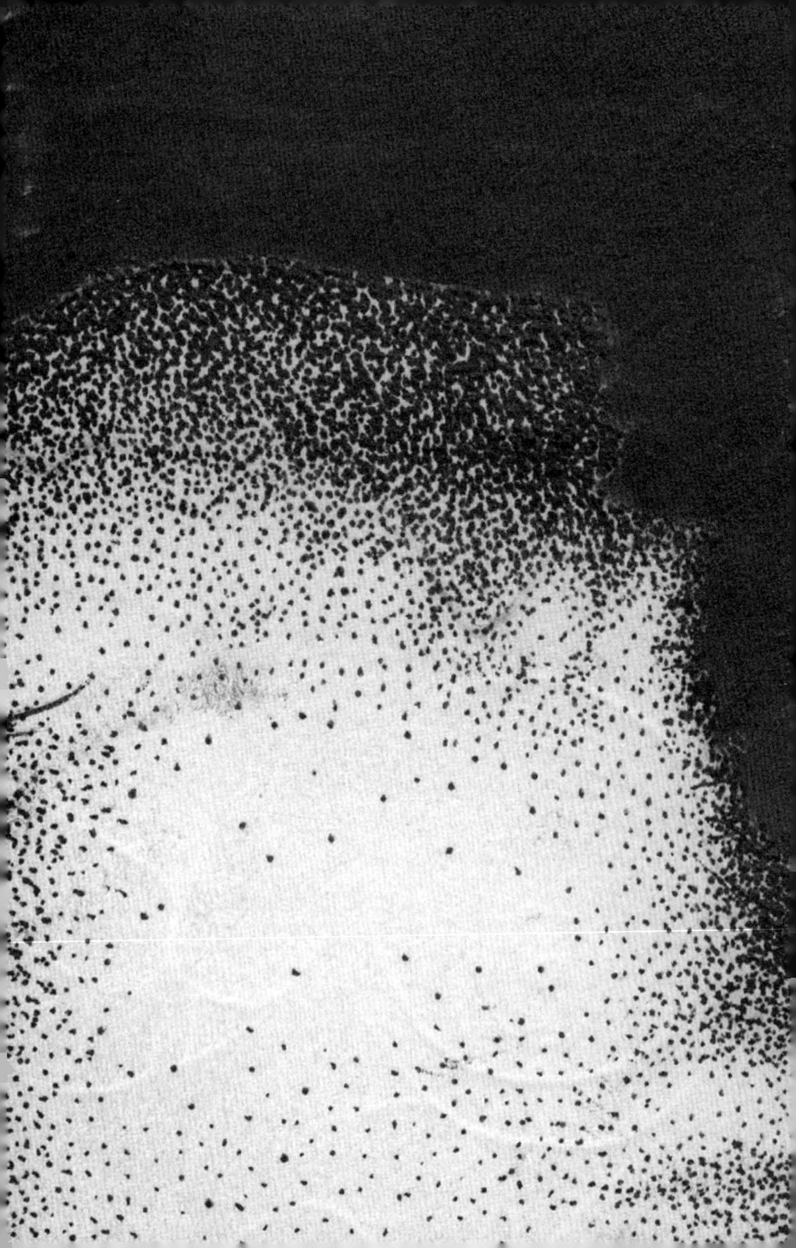

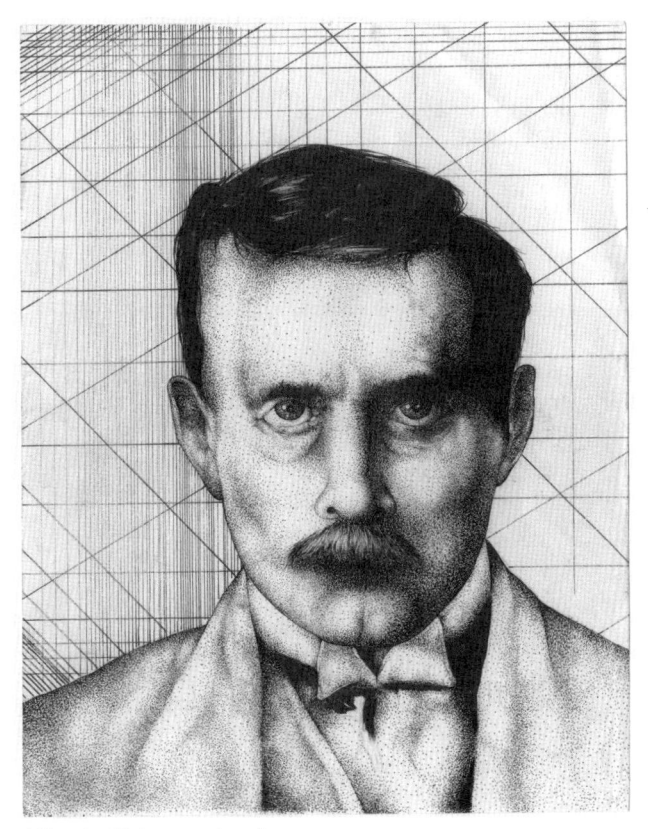

Adolf Loos (2008) ink on paper 9" x 11.5"

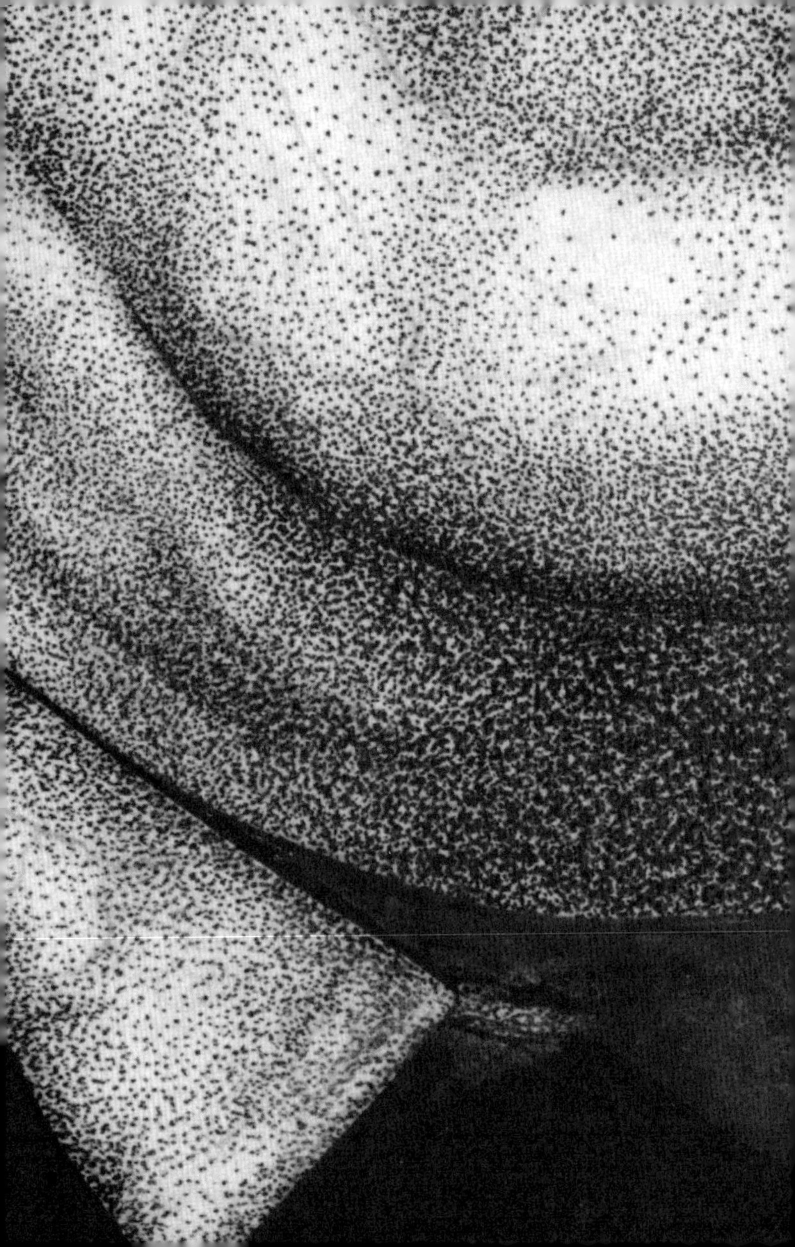

James Stirling (2008) ink on bristol board 7" x 9"

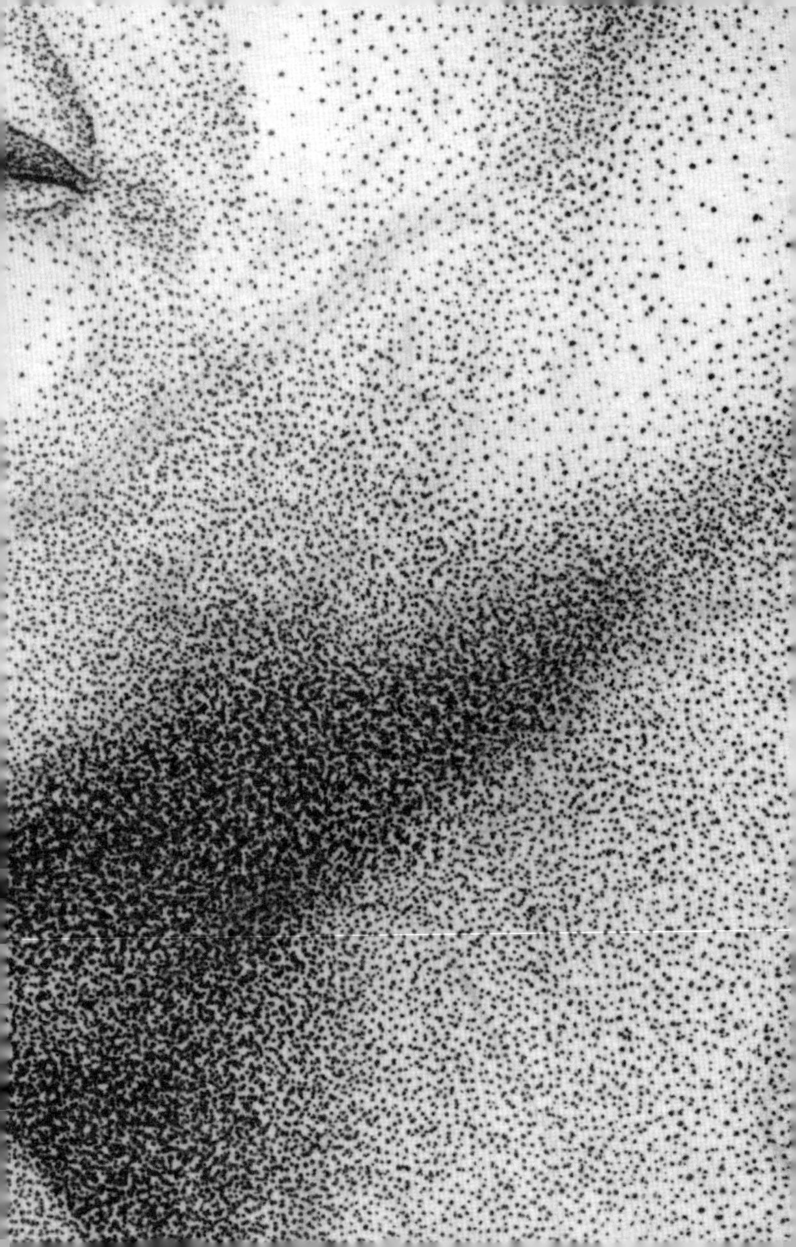

Le Corbusier (2008) ink on bristol board 9" x 12"

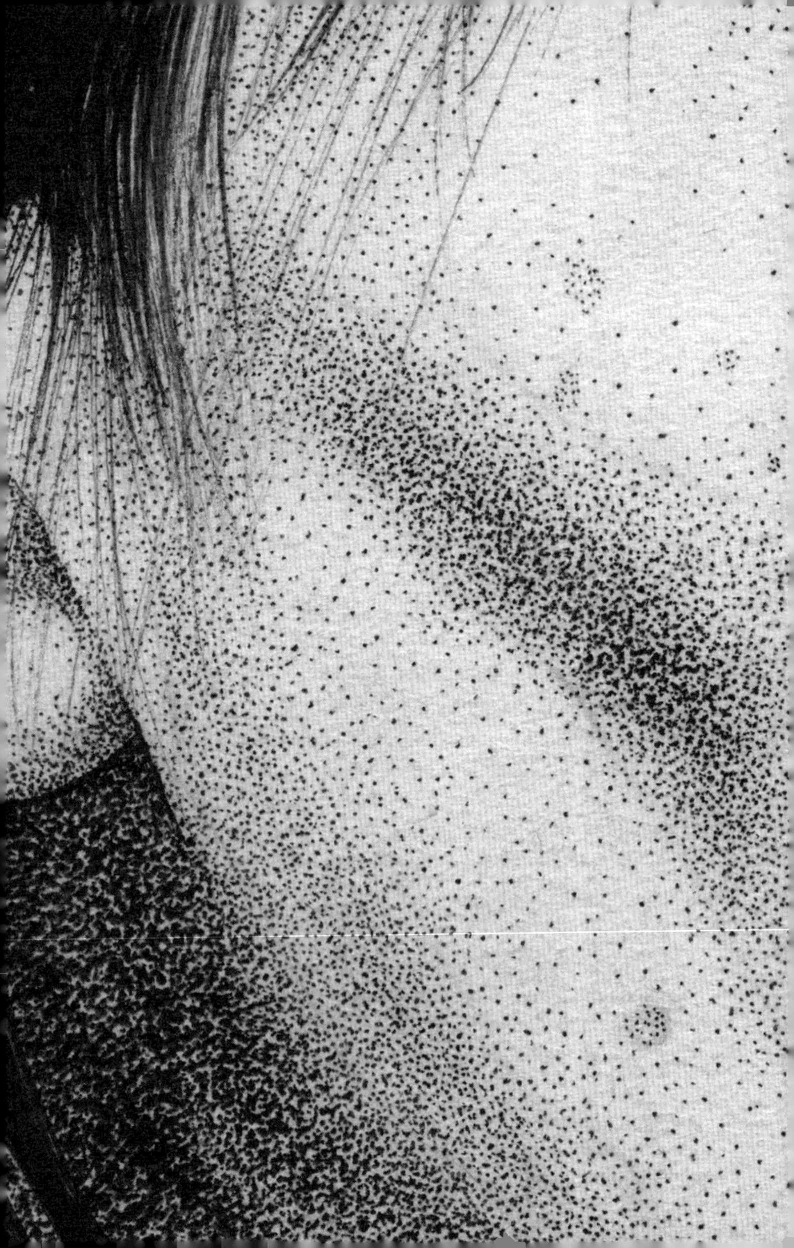

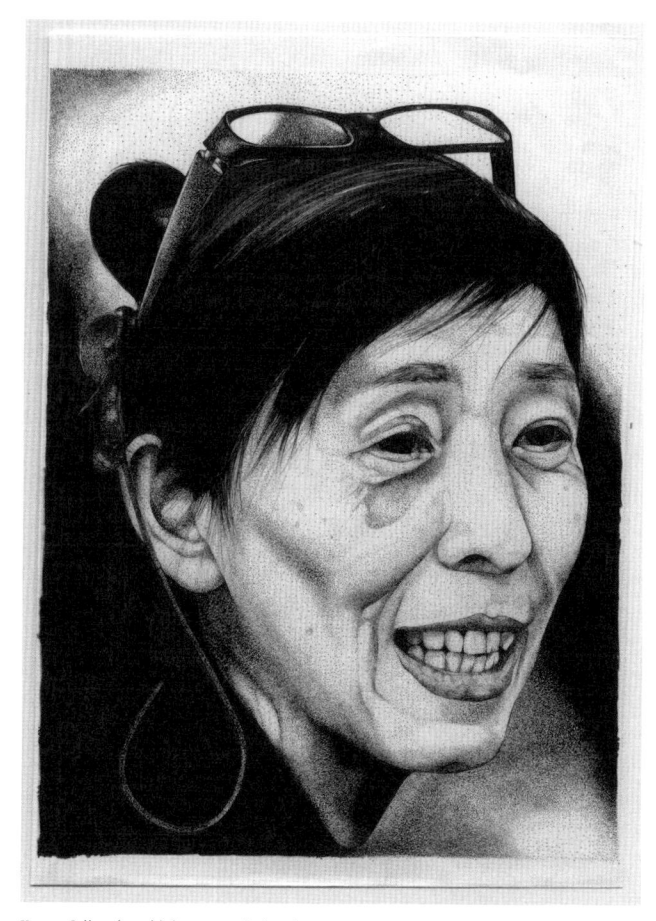

Kazuyo Sejima (2009) ink on paper 8.5" x 11"

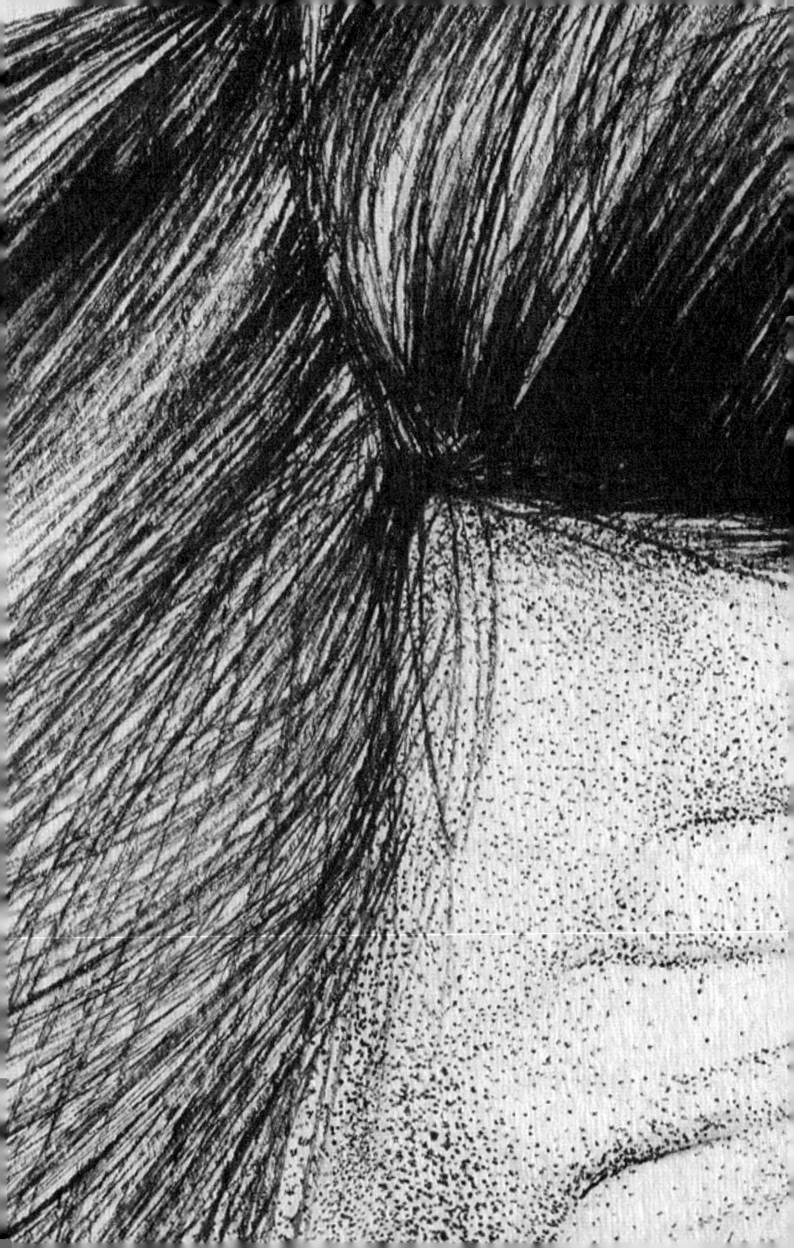

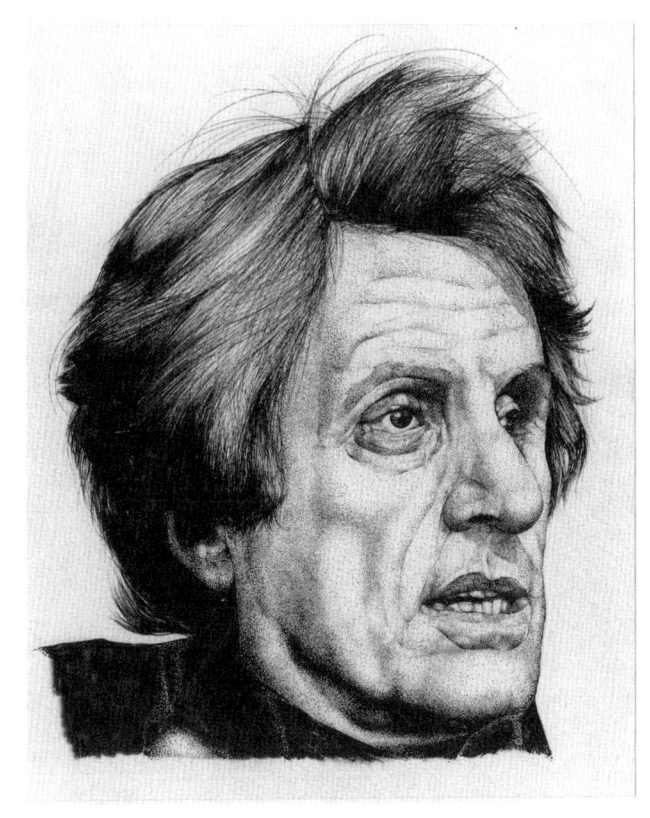

Iannis Xenakis (2009) ink on watercolor paper 8.5" x 10" -

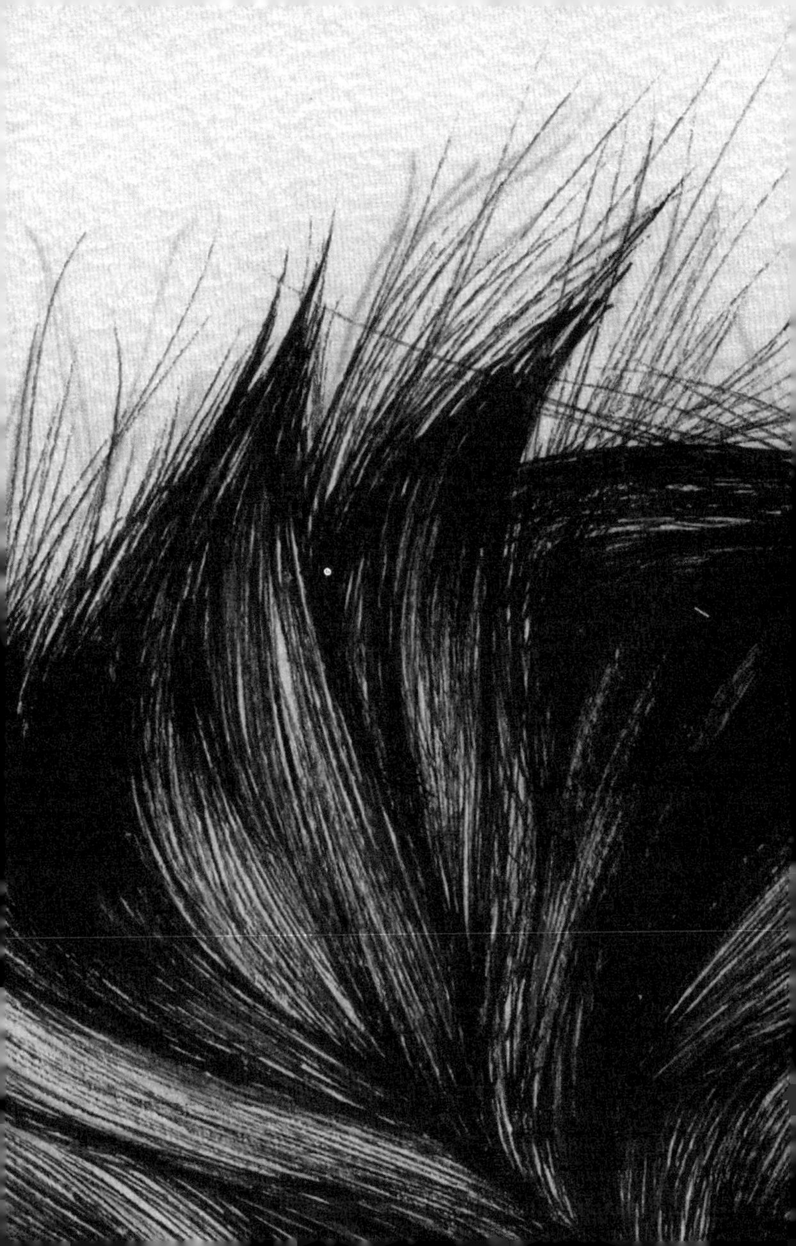

Bjarke Ingels (2009) ink on watercolor paper 9.5" x 12"

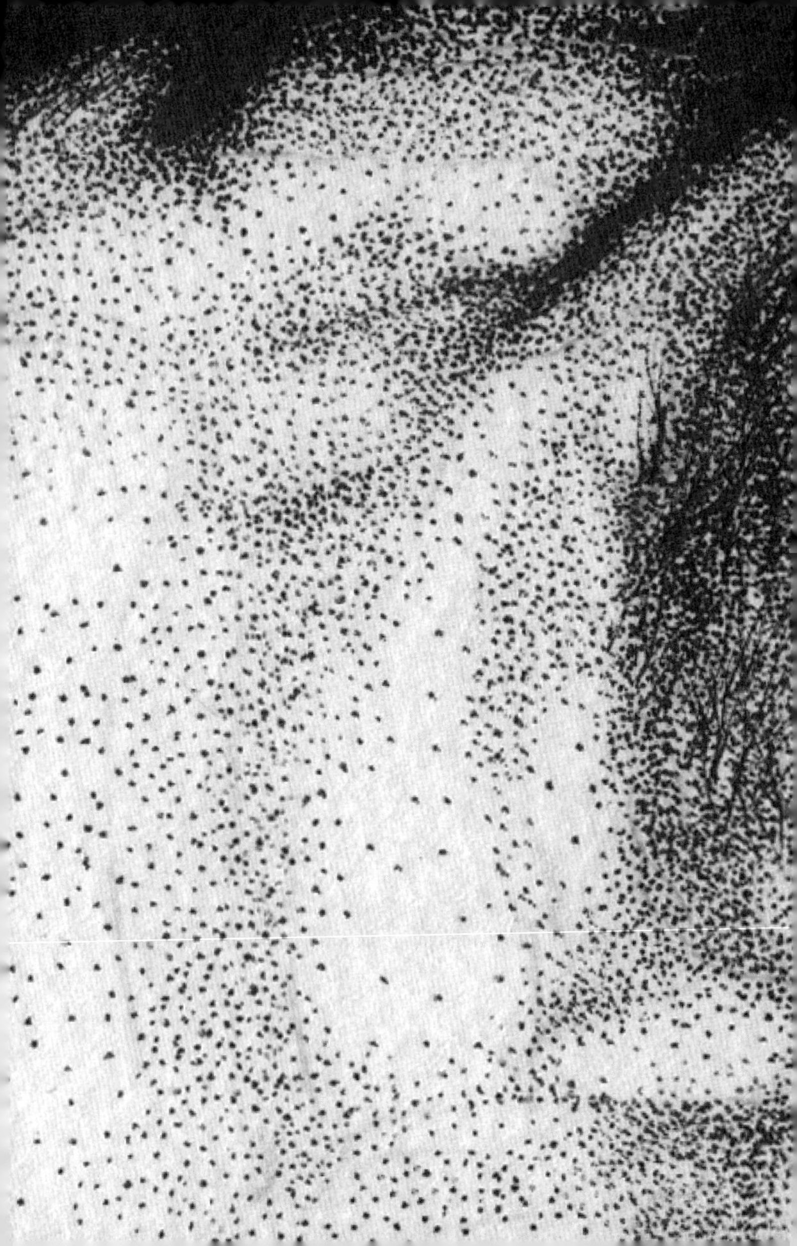

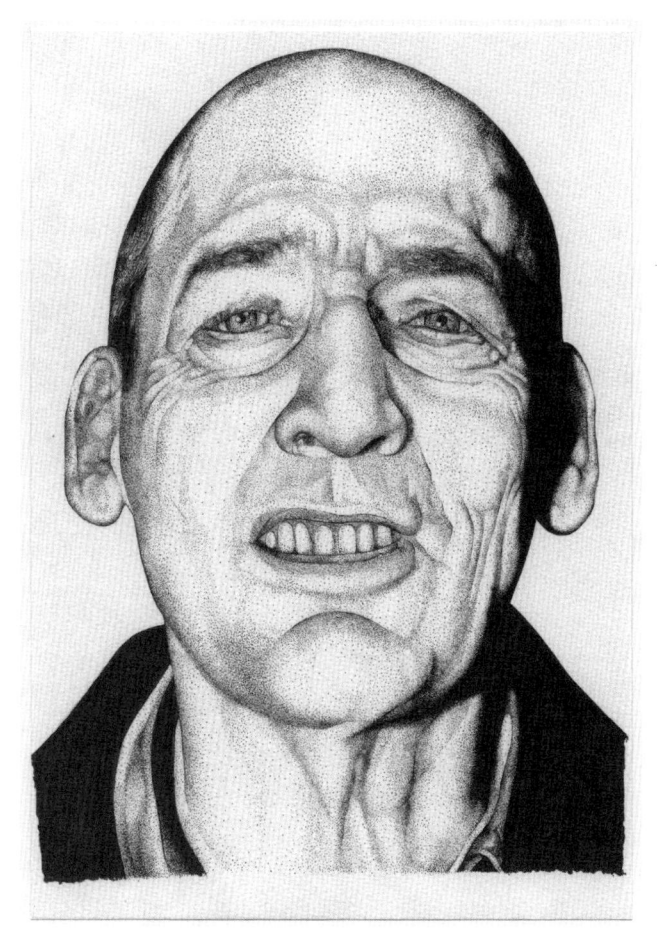

Rem Koolhaas (2009) ink on watercolor paper 8" x 11"

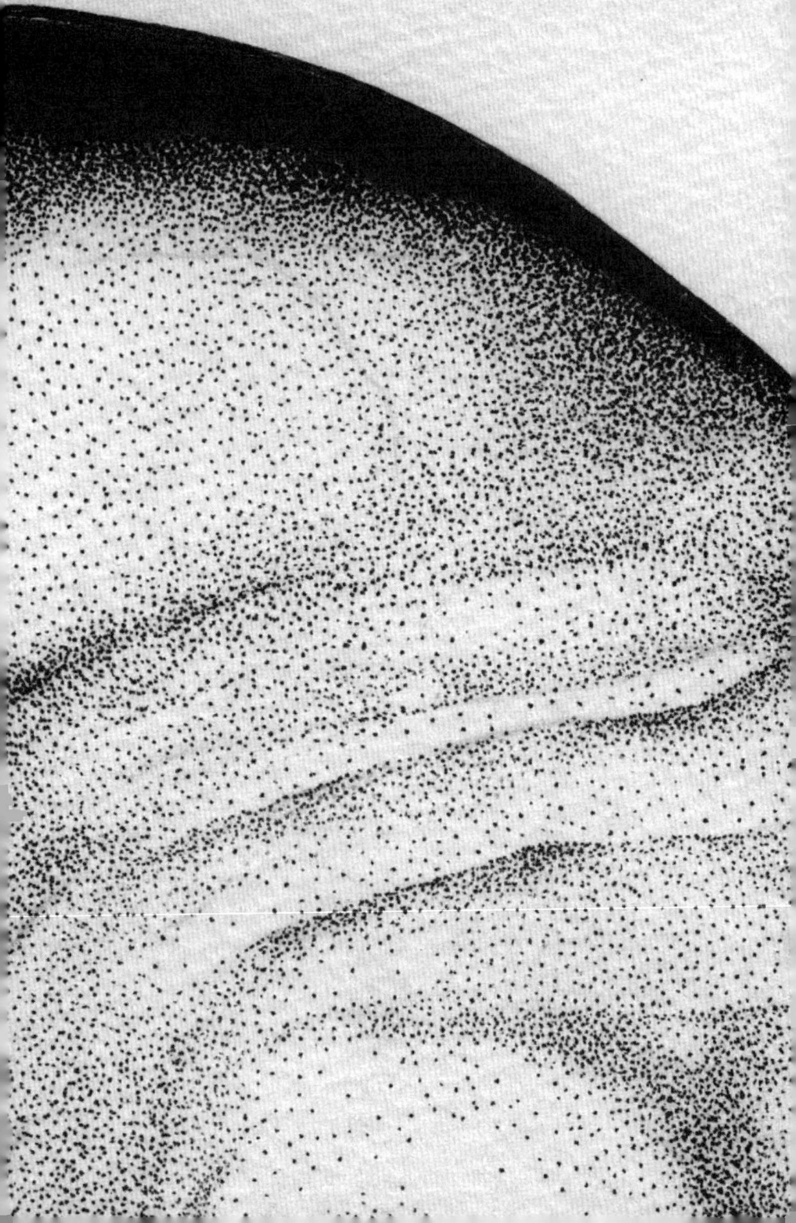

Francis D.K Ching (2009) ink on watercolor paper 9.5" x 11"

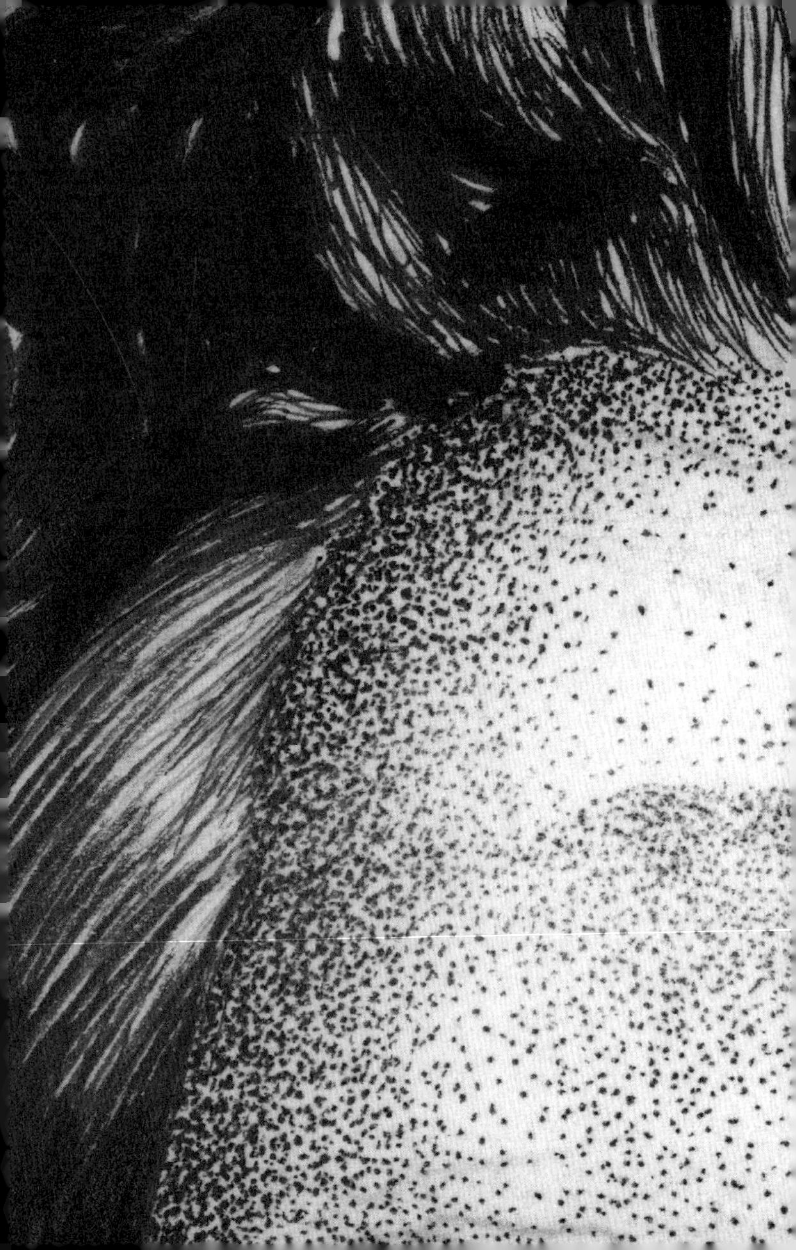

Greg Lynn (2010) ink on bristol board 9" x 10"

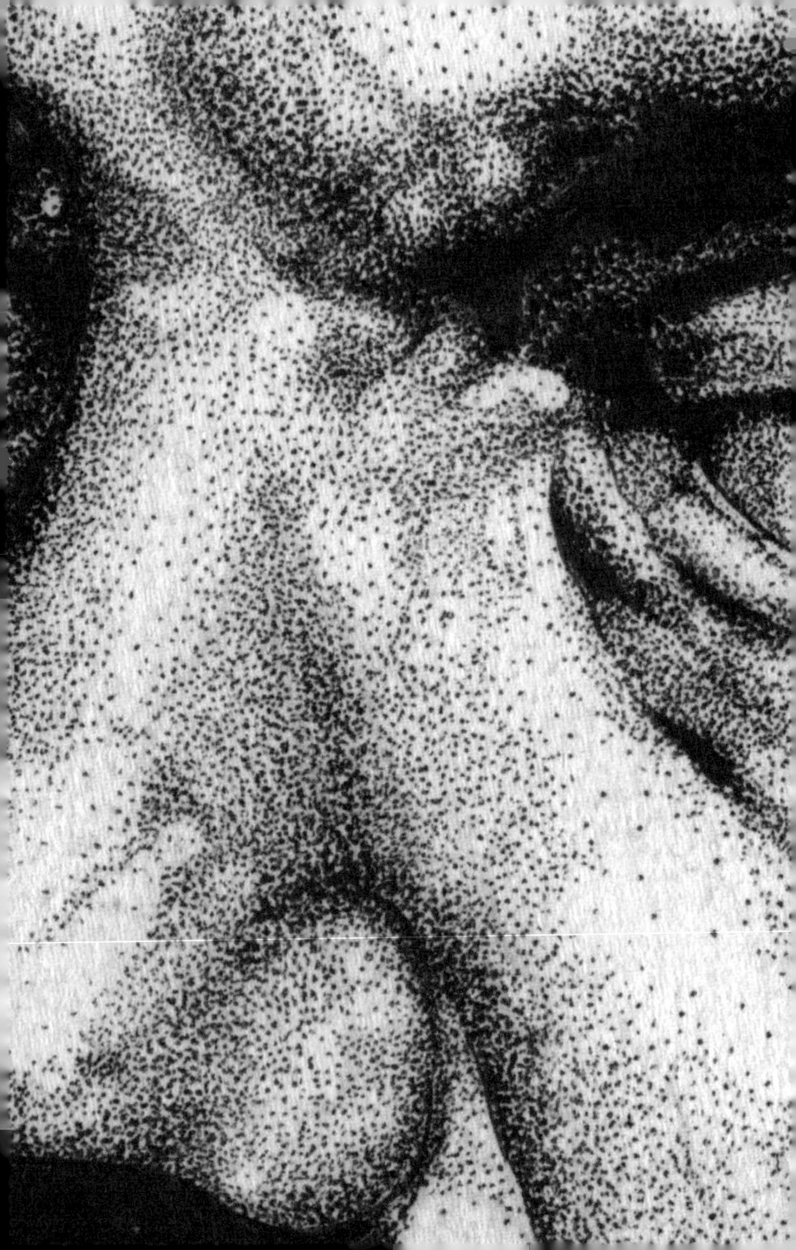

Erik Gunnar Asplund (2010) ink on watercolor paper 8.5" x 11"

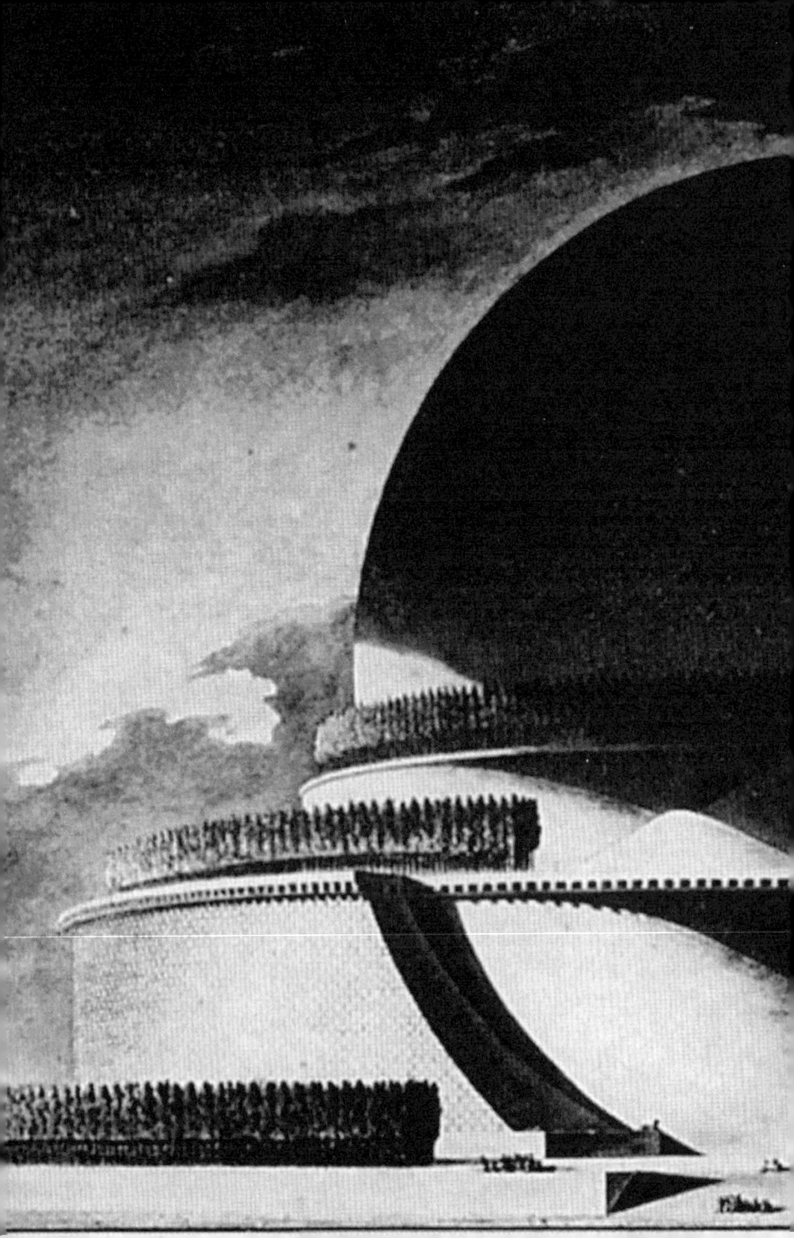

DRAWING [ON] THE SUBLIME
REPRESENTATION OF THE UNREALIZED PROJECT AND THE SUBORDINATION OF THE REAL

MARCUS CARTER

The late 18th century brought radical changes to Western thought. Often seen as the beginning of the Modern Era, this period witnessed the turn to reason and scientific method effecting social, political, and economic systems in Europe. The waning of religious and monarchical control allowed the transition into a secular society engaged in a free market. Following the Baroque and the excess of the Rococo, artists and architects sought ways to portray new ideals of the day.[1] At this time, two important philosophical works, Edmund Burke's *A Philosophical Enquiry into the Sublime and Beautiful* (1757) and Immanuel Kant's *Critique of Judgment* (1790), sought to dissect our experiences of the beautiful and the sublime in both nature and art. As architects, we are caught between overlapping yet different views on the sublime as put forth by these two influential thinkers.

Figure 1: (left) Etienne-Louis Boullée, *Newton's Cenotaph* (1784)

Burke distinguishes between two types of affect: *pain* and *pleasure*. The later he ties to society, which he further segregates into passions of the sexes and those of general society. That which fills the mind with great pleasure, in his view, typically ties back to engagement with others, whether it is falling in love, being in the company of others, having lively conversation, or sharing a laugh. Though he concedes that pleasure can be derived from temporary solitude, such as an act of contemplation, prolonged solitude can nevertheless lead to emotional pain. In contrast, he ties pain to self-preservation; the passions concerning self-preservation include ideas of pain, sickness, horror, and death.[2] He posits that in general, pain and danger do not directly pertain to society collectively because they engage humans at the level of the individual by filling our minds with notions of horror. He explains, "Whatever is fitted in any sort to excite the ideas of pain, and danger, that is to say, whatever is in any sort terrible, or is conversant about terrible objects, or operates in a manner analogous to terror, is a source of the *sublime*; that is, it is productive of the strongest emotion which the mind is capable of feeling."[3]

Kant, however, offers two definitions of the sublime.[4] On the one hand, Kant's mathematical sublime can be defined as the state of mind whereby the mind attempts to grasp something "that in comparison with which everything else is small."[5] The mathematical sublime results from that which is absolutely great — or absolutely miniscule — in comparison to the norm. This always implies a relationship with something other, whereby the greatness is relative to something else.[6] The mathematical sublime is the feeling produced by the struggle for reconciliation of the irreconcilable disjunction between the imagination and our own rationality.

The dynamical sublime, on the other hand, results from that which strains our imagination because of its might over the mind—this is best represented for Kant by nature. Much like Burke, Kant believes that nature has the power to annihilate causing us to fear for our lives. This could be extended to other things that cause our resistance to remain insignificant to their might, including God or a tyrannical power.[7] Even as this state of mind grapples with the boundless and infinite, we realize that absolute freedom is even more resistant and unbounded than anything else we encounter, including the forces of nature.

It is this sense of boundless freedom that informed works of art and architecture that were contemporaneous with Burke and Kant. Whereas some artists and architects of the time returned to neoclassical examples as an appeal to science and reason, others sought to delve into the imagination in hopes of reaching a higher level of experience. Similarly, Etienne-Louis Boullée (1728-1799) and Giovanni Battista Piranesi (1720-1778) both elicit the sublime in their work. Here, I pay special attention to unrealized projects by both architects. Boullée's cenotaphs and Piranesi's *Carceri* (prisons) will be examined for their ability to demonstrate Kant and Burke's varying principles of the sublime.

UNREALIZED PROJECTS OF BOULLÉE AND PIRANESI

Boullée and Piranesi both intended to evoke monumentality and grandeur for their respective audiences. If they could be erected, Boullée's proposals would stand taller than any historic structure with the exception of the Egyptian pyramids. His renderings are initially deceptive, presenting an ambiguity of scale. Only when one realizes that the tiny specks near the bottom of the frame are people does one understand the enormity of the buildings. The effects of similar overscaling have been well known: the grandest buildings worked to glorify overriding ideals or power structures of their time. Egyptian pyramids protected the bodies of pharaohs for

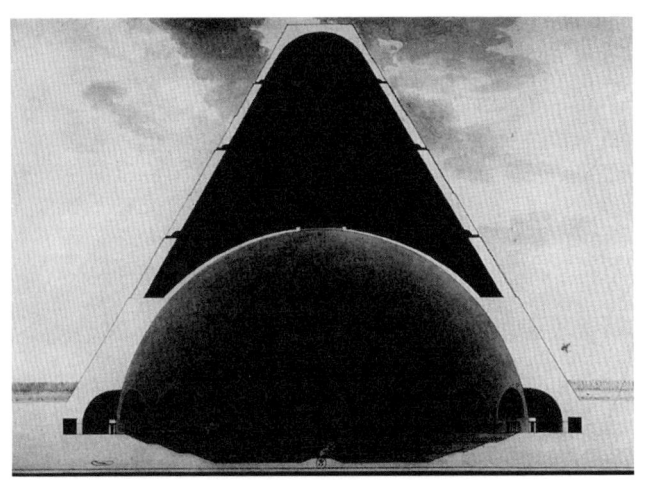

FIGURE 2: Boullée, *Conical Cenotaph* (date unknown)
FIGURE 3: Boullée, *Entrance to a Cemetery* (date unknown)
FIGURE 4: Boullée, *Monumental Cemetery* (date unknown)

eternity, Greek and Roman temples deified their various gods, and Gothic cathedrals soared to reach the Christian heavens. But with his cenotaphs, Boullée presents the viewer with temples to Reason: architecture that not only diminishes the individual man, but that also exceeds the logic of religion.[FIG. 1]

Boullée saw more possibilities of evoking sublimity in painting than in the realization of architecture, making representation all the more critical, regardless of a project's practicability. Unlike his contemporary Ledoux, who was interested in social reform, Boullée focused on more idealized programs illustrating to what architectural form can aspire.[8] For example, the cross-section of the *Conical Cenotaph* reveals a cavernous dome with an improbable thickness that technology of this time, using stone masonry, would likely not have been able to structure.[FIG. 2]

Boullée "hewed" his cenotaphs from stereometrically pure forms such as the pyramid and the sphere, their simplicity a curious contradiction to the enormity of the forms.[9] These basic geometrical solids serve as symbols for a return to Reason as well as to principles free from mortal desires. The contradiction of scale to form subverts reason, especially because the scale is initially so ambiguous in all of the projects. While the forms appear rational to our mind, we mentally place ourselves within the scene imagining the affective nature of these immense spaces bearing down on us. What at first appears overbearing and threatening in the end celebrates unbounded human reason once we are able "to get our heads around it."[10]

It is surely not by coincidence that most of Boullée's theoretical projects are for cenotaphs, funerary structures, and cemeteries, often associated with monumentality. He surrounded many of his edifices with rings of cypress trees, symbolic of mourning. These projects strive to leave the viewer in a mood of anxiety and somberness as Boullée used harsh lighting to dramatize the scene and accentuate the austerity of his forms. In many cases, the rendering casts the building in a blanket of shadow and emphasizes an imposing eeriness in contrast to its surroundings. He continued these effects inside where he used dark and gloomy renderings for the interiors.[12]

Presented primarily in frontal view, Boullée's projects often are composed symmetrically with a large structure on center with flanking lower walls extending out to the edge of the drawings.[FIG. 3] This horizontal extension perhaps serves to suggest that the building is only part of a much larger complex. In addition, the lower extensions help to heighten the scale of the all-consuming central piece that appears within the frame. Some projects, such as the *Monumental Cemetery*, sprawl out horizontally across the landscape implying an infinite repetition of forms, or at least more forms than can be seen in one view.[FIG. 4] Yet another tactic of extension occurs in Boullée's concept of 'sunken architecture' whereby a form appears as the implied tip of a much larger edifice underground.[13]

The basic formal vocabulary also resists the burdens of previous architectural languages, whether they are classical or Gothic, and the associative baggage that comes with them. Again, the only dominant metaphor is that of Reason. A sense of timelessness pervades Boullée's projects. They produce severe temporal dislocation causing one to wonder if the structures are supposed to be ancient or futuristic. This infinite extension back and forward into time may serve to make us aware of our own limited time as mortals, merely glimpsing an instant of the life of these buildings.[14]

In different ways, each architect undermines the viewer's understanding of space to further exalt the architecture over the human inhabitants. Architects normally employ two-dimensional drawings (plans, sections, and elevations) as objective representations of measurement and use perspective to illustrate atmosphere. Though Boullée used elevations and sections in most representations, he rendered them to accentuate dramatic atmosphere while challenging our perception of scale by contrasting architectural form with miniscule inhabitants not perceived at first glance.

Piranesi, on the other hand, worked exclusively through perspective, a convention thought to be "truthful" because it approximates reality as experienced through human vision. Perspective has the effect of presenting a work of art as finite and within the control of established rules. Karsten Harries states "Perspective reveals a world which has its measure in the spectator and leaves no room for the transcendence of the sublime. Yet perspective also can be used to negate the spectator's point of view and the finite world which has its foundation in it."[16] Piranesi plays with our ability to reason as the interior perspectives effectively pull the viewer into the space. Instead of looking at an abstraction, such as an elevation, with detached distance, Piranesi's technique draws one into an immense, overwhelming spatial labyrinth. Here too the minute humans scattered throughout the space serve only to contrast the overscaled architecture. People remain sketchy and inarticulate in relation to the architecture, which Piranesi renders with highly detailed architectural effects. Going far beyond the improbability of constructing a prison of such scale, Piranesi increases the anxiety by incorporating a series of perspective deceptions not apparent at first glance. He intentionally subverts our perception by creating images using multiple viewpoints that fragment the linearity of perspective representation.[17] Instead of using perspective to present an objective, highly rationalized view of space, Piranesi deploys it as a mechanism for subverting this view of the world.

FIGURE 5: Giovanni Battista Piranesi, Carcere VII: *'The Drawbridge'* (State V, mid-1770s)

An example of this occurs in *Carceri*, Plate VII, where Piranesi composes a perspective using objects rendered from slightly different vantage point.[FIG. 5] In later states, his addition of bridges betrays planimetric logic. The lower bridge and the drawbridge appear to be aligned on the stone wall centered over the arch. But as one traces each towards the left, the drawbridge remains in front of the column, while the lower bridge passes directly through it. Horizontal section cuts at different heights would indicate the different locations of the column in relation to the various bridges. Plate XIV provides the viewer with another of the more perceptible examples of intentional deception.[FIG. 6] If one analyzes the first and second pier, at the top where they meet the pointed arch, they appear to lie within the same plane. As the eye moves down the bases seem to lie in different but parallel planes with the grand stair protruding between. In each case Piranesi defies the laws of perspective and of statics, forcing one into a game of mental reconstruction in attempt to reframe the coherence of the structure.

The suggested labyrinthine quality of the Carceri exacerbates our perception of monumentality in each plate. By layering a series of successive spaces, Piranesi implies an infinite spatial repetition. Under each arch, glimpses of more arches beyond extend the space further and further back. As one is never granted views to the exterior, much less given any plans, one never realizes the scale of the overall complex. The mind perceives the prisons as an unbounded space beyond comprehension. In addition, one imagines the anxiety created by walking through this space and not ever having sight of an exit or the perimeter of the structure.[18] In terms of representational techniques, the interior perspective serves to break the frame of the etchings, suggesting that the spaces not only extend infinitely into the background, but also project out from the picture plane. Piranesi resists the time of his present in a different way by returning

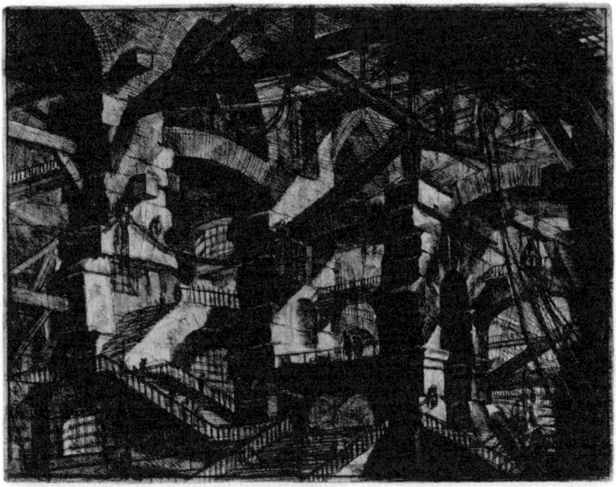

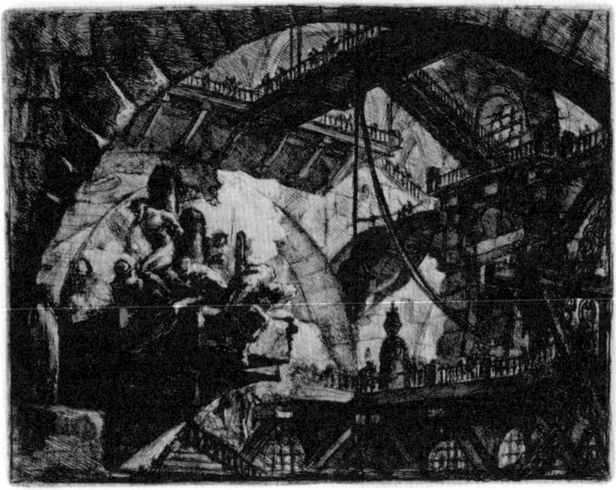

FIGURE 6: (top left) Piranesi, Carcere XIV: *'The Gothic Arch'* (State III, 1761)
FIGURE 7: (bottom left) Piranesi, Carcere X: *'Prisoners on a Projecting Platform'* (State V, mid 1770s)
FIGURE 8: (above) Piranesi, Carcere II: *'The Man in the Rack'* (State V, mid 1770s)

to a formal vocabulary similar to that of ancient Rome. Inadequacies he may have seen in his time are put up to comparison with the splendor of the Roman Empire.

Piranesi carries the anxiety and somberness to an even higher level than Boullée invoking terror and the grotesque in his prison etchings. A decade after their original release, the *Carceri* series underwent a series of revisions in which the artist reworked the original copper plates to both add more elements and make the compositions increasingly dark and gloomy. As he made a second, third, and fourth pass, the increased the density of the etched strokes made the scenes more ominous. Additions include chains, spikes, and other torture devices suggestive of malevolent activities. In Plate X, we see prisoners shackled on poles, slumped over as if they have been tortured.[FIG. 7] In the later state, Piranesi added a timber beam with chains, leaving it up to our imagination to think about what type of brutalities could occur with these props. Plate II of the second addition becomes more explicit, presenting a man in the process of being tortured on the rack.[FIG. 8] This series reach the sublime, as described by Burke, by presenting scenes of terror in much the same way as the opening pages of Michel Foucault's *Discipline and Punish*. Foucault's description of a prisoner undergoing torture and then execution by being drawn and quartered affects one through association as the mind attempts to imagine the unbearable happening to one's own body.

The selection of a prison as the setting for the architectural fantasies in the *Carceri* is not insignificant and operates on various levels. In addition to projecting an eerie, somber setting for the sublime – as described by Burke – Piranesi intentionally uses the prison as a symbol for a higher, omnipresent authority. The subject remains in a state of alienation in respect to this authority. This could be seen as a critique on existing state authorities at the time. The critical theorist Manfredo Tafuri points out how "as early as the *Carceri* the affirmation of the need for domination clashes with the affirmation of the rights of the subject. The result of the clash – represented epically in plates II and X, which depict surreal scenes of torture – is that not men but only things become truly 'liberated'."[19] In both plates, men are bound for torture, yet remain subservient to the architectural games around.

The etchings could also create awareness of the authority of reason that had become predominant during the Enlightenment. Similarly, by situating the viewer within the penal system, Piranesi demonstrates how we are all imprisoned by the limits of our own finite understanding. Or, going even further, he may be pointing – through his perspectival distortions – to the limitations of reason.[20]

The power of Boullée's and Piranesi's projects lies in their perpetual state of unrealization. Realization would only subvert their sense of the sublime, their attempt to defy the real and finite. In addition, the cenotaphs and *Carceri* fluctuate between reason and subversion. Piranesi probably comes closer to realizing the sublime in the Kantian sense. Working with perspectival trickery, he subverts the easy application of reason, forcing viewers to stretch their imagination by mentally reconstructing the impossible structure of the compositions. Boullée, at first sight, appears to present the more monumental projects when one looks at the overall size in relation to the humans below. But, another look should convince us that Piranesi comes closer to presenting the "absolute great." Interior perspectives as a representational technique effectively deprive us of any understanding of the whole. The labyrinthine quality also alludes to the endless oppositions in Piranesi's work which puts meaning into question.[21] The Boullée projects may be enormous in comparison to the norm, but as presented in most cases, we still understand them as clear and finite.

Though his scenes have a somber tone, Boullée mainly strives for the monumental while Piranesi, the more sinister architect, attempts to create anxiety and terror that Burke speaks about.[22] By actually pulling the viewer into the scenes, one becomes more of a silent voyeur witnessing an incident from behind a corner than a detached patron looking at a piece of art work. Both artists put reason and/or authority into question while seeming to exalt it through the rendered edifices. In both cases, one could argue that the images remained confined by the frame, but in fact, the frame *enabled* the representation of the sublime by suggesting something further beyond.

NOTES

1   The architectural historian Emil Kaufmann sought to explicate a link between the "revolutionary architects" in France at this time (especially Boullée, Ledoux, & Lequeu) and those of the Modern Movement via their use of self-sufficient, isolated (autonomous) form that defied Baroque unity. He justifies this interpretation when he articulates the changing role of the historian from one of simply restating facts to one with the responsibility to investigate and analyze architectural form. See Emil Kaufmann, "Claude-Nicolas Ledoux, Inaugurator of a new Architectural System" *The Journal of the American Society of Architectural Historians*, Vol. 3, no. 3 (Jul., 1943), pp. 12-20, and Kaufmann, *Three Revolutionary Architects, Boullée, Ledoux, & Lequeu* (Philadelphia: The American Philosophical Society, 1952). Even as he refers to it as a "myth," Anthony Vidler explicitly supports Kaufmann's position in his own interests of the late eighteenth century, especially his focus on Claude-Nicolas Ledoux. See the introduction to Anthony Vidler, *Claude-Nicolas Ledoux* (Cambridge, MIT Press, 1990), pp. x-xv. Also see Vidler, *Histories of the Immediate Present* (Cambridge: MIT Press, 2008), pp. xiv, 11-13. Other contemporary historians, such as Kenneth Frampton and William Curtis, to varying degrees, acknowledge this period's role in the formation of modernism without explicitly endorsing Kaufmann's narrative of formal autonomy. See Kenneth Frampton, *Modern Architecture: A Critical History* (New York: Thames

and Hudson, 1992), pp. 13-16 and William J. R. Curtis, *Modern Architecture Since 1900* (London: Phaidon Press Limited, 1996), pp. 28-29, 371.

2   Edmund Burke, *A Philosophical Enquiry into the Sublime and Beautiful* (New York: Penguin, 1998), pp. 85-7, 90.

3   *Ibid.*, p. 86.

4   Kant distinguishes between beauty and the sublime. For Kant, the beautiful is that which pleases only our judgment, remaining disinterested in conceptual thought, or an idea. Contrasted to the idea, Kant says the ideal (of the beautiful) cannot be explained through concepts, but rests on presentation serving as the archetype of taste which must be produced within ourselves by which we judge every object of taste. This view invalidates much art, such as that with religious affiliations, because a concept can be assumed to lie behind most creative acts. But, at the same time, Kant did not support an art that only created beautiful objects. The beautiful for Kant resides in the forms of nature. Those that take an interest in the contemplation of natural beauty demonstrate cultivation for moral feeling. Immanuel Kant, *Critique of Judgment*, trans. J.H. Bernard (New York: Hafner Press, 1951), pp. 68-9.

5   *Ibid.*, p. 88.

6   Kant elaborates on this idea of the mathematical sublime, stating how "The feeling of the sublime is therefore a feeling of pain arising from the want of accordance between the aesthetical estimation of magnitude formed by the imagination and the estimation of the same formed by reason." *Ibid.*, p. 96.

7   Kant noted how with the dynamical sublime, "We find our own limitation, although at the same time in our rational faculty we find a different, nonsensuous standard, which has that infinity itself under it as a unity, in comparison with which everything in nature is small, and thus in our mind we find a superiority to nature even in its immensity." *Ibid.*, p. 101.

8   Vidler, *Claude-Nicolas Ledoux*, p. 390.

9   Simple forms can acquire impressiveness by imbuing them with colossal dimensions and an extreme sparseness of detail only adds to the impression of grandiosity. For Boullée, the overall composition remained paramount since he believed 'character' depended on the artful arrangement of masses more so than from details. Kaufmann, *Three Revolutionary Architects*, p. 472.

10 Kant's notion of freedom knows no limits, yet human understanding is finite in the face of the threatening sublime. But to acknowledge limits is to understand them and when we understand our limitations, we transcend them so human reason cannot be contained. Karsten Harries, *The Meaning of Modern Art* (Evanston: Northwestern University Press, 1968), pp. 40-1.

11 Even projects with more mundane programs such as the *Museum at Whose Center is a Temple of Fame for Statues of Great Men* or the *Municipal Palace for the Capital of a Great Empire* instill a sense of grandeur in their title to further the representation of monumentality.

12 Kaufmann notes, "The artist declared himself to be the 'inventor of architecture of shades and shadows.' i.e. disposing masses so that their contrasting forms produce attractive lighting effects." Kaufmann, *Three Revolutionary Architects*, p. 472.

13 Jean-Marie Pérouse de Montclos, *Etienne-Louis Boullée, 1728-1799: Theoretician of Revolutionary Architecture* (New York: George Braziller, 1974), p. 36. This impression arises from our knowledge of complete forms in traditional architecture. *The Funerary Monument*, like similar triangular compositions, is an example of "sunken architecture" as it implies a pediment devoid of its portico. In many of the projects, the verticals supporting an entry arch are reduced or even eliminated to exacerbate this effect.

14 Harries explains: "The megalomaniacal, inhuman scale of so many of these designs – their sublime, time-defying, archaic, or 'Egyptian' quality – answers to modern individualism and its dread of death, which is always also a dread of individual life, answers the dread of individual dying by glorifying death in the service of some abstract collective, be it humanity or the nation, that dwarfs the individual with its importance." Harries, *The Ethical Function of Architecture*, 307.

15 Filippo Brunelleschi conducted his notorious experiment in linear perspective on the Florence Baptistery in 1413. Leon Battista Alberti formalized the rules for perspective shortly after in his treatises for painting and architecture.

16 Harries, *The Meaning of Modern Art*, p. 41.

17 Alberto Perez-Gomez and Louise Pelletier, *Architectural Representation and the Perspective Hinge* (Cambridge: MIT Press, 2000), pp. 216-7.

18 Critic Manfredo Tafuri states, "In the Carceri, the constriction comes not from the absence of space, but from an opening toward the infinite." Manfredo Tafuri, *The Sphere and the Labyrinth: Avant-Gardes and Architecture from Piranesi to the 1970s* (Cambridge: The MIT Press, 1995), p. 31.

19 *Ibid.*, p. 32.

20 "Piranesi's heterotopia lies precisely in giving voice, in an absolute and evident manner, to this contradiction: the principle of Reason is shown to be an instrument capable of anticipating... the monsters of the irrational." *Ibid.*, p. 46.

21 Piranesi operates on endless oppositions: republican justice vs. imperial cruelty, the need for domination vs. the need for rights of the subject, architectural signs vs. signifieds, language vs. non-language, reason vs. irrationality, new vs established. Tafuri believes Piranesi understood contradiction as reality. "The loss of meaning, of its univocity, is fully explained: the Piranesian heterotopia consistently uses infinite dialectics." He adds, "The greatness of his 'negative utopia' lies in his refusal to establish, after such a discovery, alternative possibilities: in the crisis, Piranesi seems to want to show, we are all powerless, and the true 'magnificence' is to welcome freely this destiny." *Ibid.*, p. 54.

22 It is important to note that Kaufmann did not see Piranesi as being as important as Boullée and Ledoux. He states, "We should of course keep in mind that Piranesi did not go beyond the old system. The time was not yet rip for the next step." Perhaps Kaufmann's evaluation of Piranesi was premature or it didn't fit his thesis about autonomous form. Piranesi gained considerable stock during the postmodern debates when discourse returned to language and a de-centered space in reaction to Modernism's austere forms. Piranesi's influence shows in projects by contemporary architects such as Peter Eisenman and Rem Koolhaas. See Kaufmann, *Architecture in the Age of Reason* (New York: Dover, 1968), p. 110.

96
97

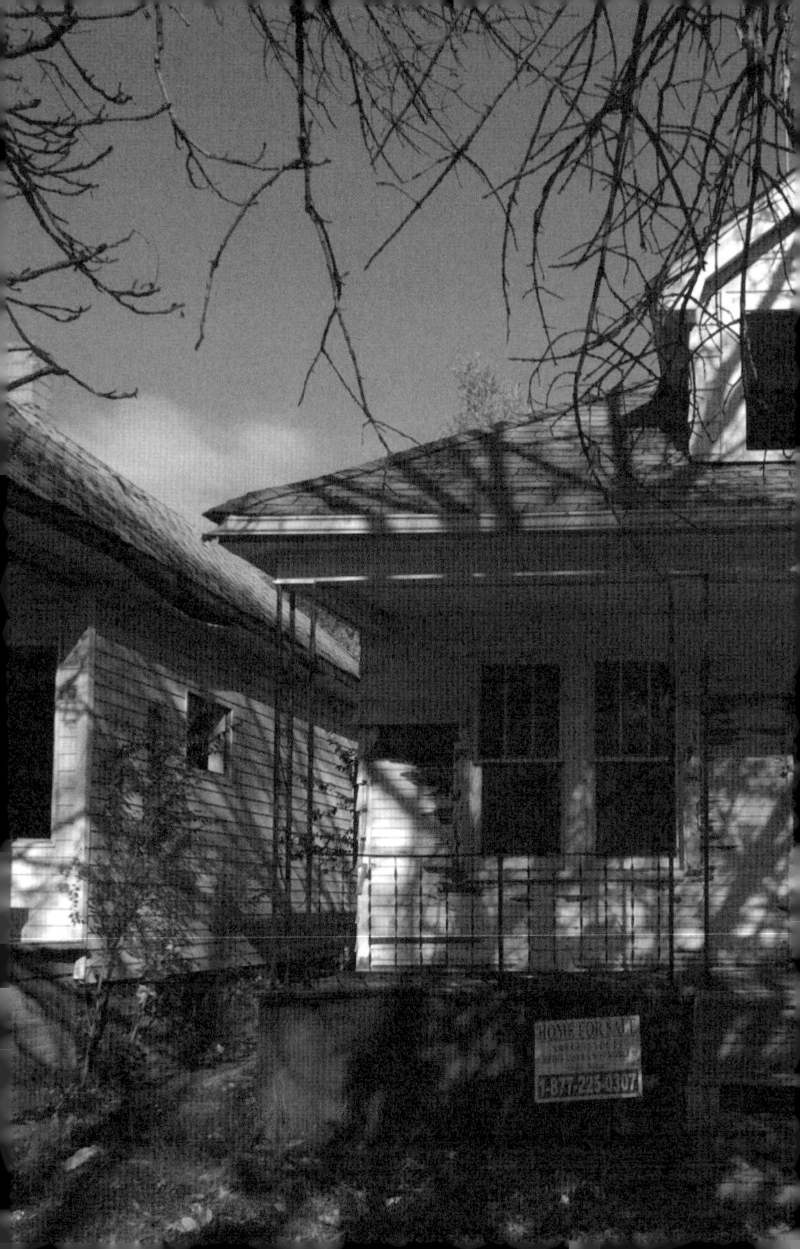
HOME FOR SALE
1-877-225-0307

[*] FIVE FELLOWS: FULL SCALE is one project in five parts - five discrete interventions designed and fabricated by five individuals, all sharing the activating medium of a 1072 sf house in Detroit. The project opened to the public in April 2010.

[†] Ellie Abrons, Meredith Miller, Thom Moran, Catie Newell, and Rosalyne Shieh

FULL DISCLOSURE[*]

FIVE FELLOWS[†]

Landing in Ann Arbor for one-year stints as teaching fellows at Taubman College, The University of Michigan, the five of us all found our interests drawn to the city 45 minutes to the east. Detroit seemed a vital but opaque place: that elusive city stalked by our Michigan predecessors and the frequent paradigm of American cities in decline. But the canary-in-the-coalmine role that's often assigned to Detroit can promote a passive engagement with the city: stand back, track patterns and monitor demographics... and perhaps wait for the inevitable.

For us, architecture provided a way in, a process of finding opportunity in an uncertain situation and making a constructive adjustment. Rather than apply our fellowship grants to five independent research efforts, we pooled our resources to buy and alter a single-family house in northeast Detroit.

WHAT FOLLOWS IS A FULL DISCLOSURE.*

*This list records the steps involved in buying the house at 13178 Moran Street as the space and material for five design experiments.**

It's not meant to be a confession of illicit acts nor does it constitute a recipe for repetition, but rather it describes the circumstances we negotiated* over the rapid course of 7 months - the lack of infrastructure, the slipping population, and the unreliable civic services — conditions that did not prevent work, but really facilitated it.

As a catalogue of the non-standard operations and logistical maneuvering that the process demanded, the following could be read as a supplement to the 'best practices' of architectural job-speak. It suggests situational agility as a way of working, a willingness to redirect expectations, and a preference to operational knowledge collected on-the-ground* over that imported from the outside.

****This document then constitutes what we know now of today's Detroit, a city we've grown quite attached to. Consider it not just a disclosure of actions rendered into words, but a dispatch to other agents in the field.

> **PROCEDURAL CATEGORY**
> *The way it's typically done.*
> **The way we did it.**
> Expanded version.

> key

SHOPPING FOR REAL ESTATE

A real estate agent serves as guide and broker. Selection criteria may include size, amenities, affordability & neighborhood.

Two artists 'brokered' their neighborhood and became mentors & neighbors. Selection criteria included relative lack of damage by fire or theft, affordability and good neighbors. Setting out to test the waters of Detroit real estate, we landed at the steps of the Power House, an off-grid project by the artist/architect duo Gina Reichert and Mitch Cope, who collaborate as Design 99. They showed us their neighborhood just north of Hamtramck, where their domestic and artistic lives are closely intertwined, and their ambitions have set the groundwork for a series of house projects by others, including an art collective from Chicago, a German curator, and a graduate architecture student from Cranbrook. Other than a vacant house for us to alter, this neighborhood offered the chance to participate in this community, a constellation of experimental houses drawn together by the affordable properties and by interest and support for each other.

By some marvel of timing, this first visit to the neighborhood happened just before Wayne County's annual tax auction, where thousands of foreclosed properties are sold to the highest bidder. It's a public event, but without the tip-off from Mitch and Gina, we would have missed this once-a-year chance. A handful of properties in their neighborhood were listed in the phone-book-thick publication available to buyers beforehand. With only four days intervening, we expedited the shopping — it was time to buy.

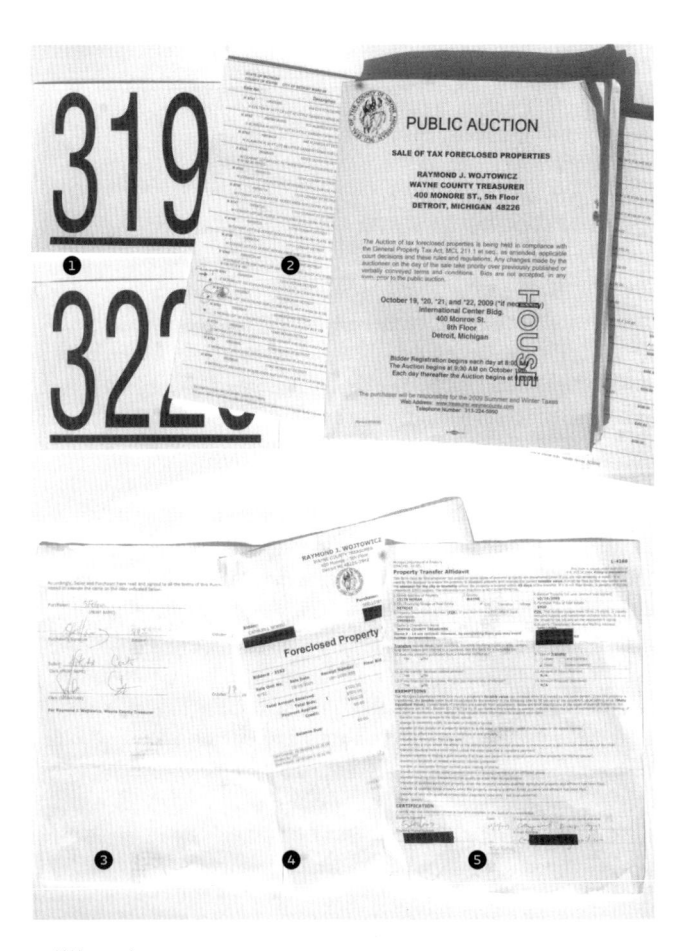

1. bidders numbers. *anonymous*
2. bidders book. 554 pages. *8864 plots*
3. purchase agreement. *5fellows signature*
4. receipt. $500
5. property affidavit. *officially filed immediately*

COSTS

$140,900 (average home price in the Midwest region)

$500 was the starting bid for every plot of property in the auction. To gain access to the auction, each attendee had to present a cashier's check equivalent to this base bid, one check for each property intended to purchase. With 5 of us splitting this investment, a nominal contribution of $100 each presented little risk. Property taxes would increase the actual cost of home ownership (and the amount would inevitability be a multiple of the purchase price)

DEED

A document that gives the grantee the legal capacity to receive property from the grantor.

5Fellows, the LLC that never existed, was the legal grantor. With the prospect of home ownership suddenly imminent, the name that would go on the title became of particular importance. None of us had been homeowners. We were acting as a collaborative but individually tied to the University of Michigan, which came with potential conflicts of interest. Following premature advice from a lawyer, we intended to form an LLC for the purchase as well as for the sharing of future operational costs like insurance. This process remained unfinished at the time of the auction, so the fellows who made the bid essentially acted as purchasing agents for the unformed entity. At the end of the sale "5fellows," a never-to-exist LLC, signed the dotted line.

MOVING IN

Steps may include uprooting the FOR SALE sign and changing locks to secure the new property.

Steps included uprooting the for sale sign, climbing through a missing window, then breaking the padlock. 13178 Moran Street had been transferred to our ownership from the county government,

6. deed. *instant transfer from Treasurer to 5fellows*
7. legal documents. *on paper*
8. keys. house keys still valid. *garage lock broken*
9. business cards. *local resources*
10. tax valuation. *property values declining*
11. quit claim deed. *transfer to Design.99*

a sale immediately processed in the casino/convention hall hosting the auction downtown. The physical house was a reality displaced from the paper document that entitled us to occupy it. Adding to this sense of displacement was the fact that the previous owners — whoever held the keys to the padlock on the front door and hopefully placed a FOR SALE sign in the lawn — would remain anonymous.

In order to exercise our new ownership, we climbed on a discarded TV cabinet, breaking in to our own house through a side window. Evidence of recent occupants — human, animal, and vegetable — gave an incomplete picture of a stalled DIY renovation and the subsequent intruders that had won out. In a sense, we were the next wave of intrusion; the window entrance and TV-step was our means of access until we boarded and secured the entire house.

KEYS

Owners typically have access to properties; keys to deadbolts and locksets materialize this right.

3 keys came with the Masterlock padlock. We were 5. (See Moving In). While we could have balanced this ratio by getting extra keys from the manufacturer or a hardware store, we somehow put it off as a low priority. But the shortage of keys afforded constant grounds for coordination and keeping invested in each other's progress. Consequently, we learned ways to keep breaking in to our own house, always aware that this meant anyone had this same capability.

UTILITIES

New homeowners contact the utility company to transfer account names.

5 months passed before the house had electrical services: we replaced the destroyed meter, waited for electrical company to inspect it, then waded through the process of removing a hold on the account (due to service theft at our address) before Detroit Ed-

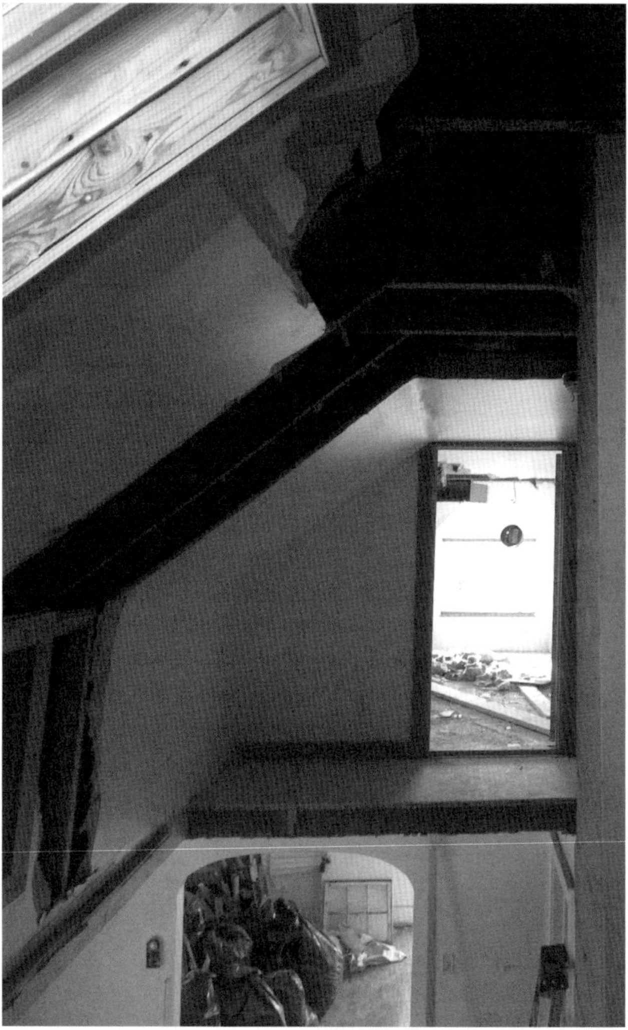

ison could connect the house to the utility pole in the back alley. **Water was deemed a non-necessity.** Getting electricity provided us with an early introduction to Detroit's deficient infrastructure. Like many unoccupied houses in the city, ours had no electrical service. Luckily, the wiring throughout the walls and ceilings had only been largely spared from copper looters.

The house next door was also disconnected from the power lines, and the couple living there used a generator. The jarring lawn-mower sound of its motor became a familiar signal that our neighbors were home.

Without plumbing or fixtures, we established our own methods of toilet, washing, and drinking. Much later in the project's calendar, we discovered an unexpected and unmetered water source in the basement.

PERMITS
Owners acquire authorized documents approving construction.
No permits were filed at any stage of the project. Work commenced according to our own impulses and schedules, without any permit procedures being initiated. While we never submitted descriptions of our intentions to any authorities, we produced drawings and models primarily to aid with our own internal communications, decision-making and construction. No formal CDs exist.

DEMOLITION
Contractor demos as needed according to architect's demo plans.
Demo as a means of research. Unfamiliar with the specifics of the construction systems for 1930s midwestern house typologies, we performed research through demolition. Initial design moves were folded into the discoveries and accidents that resulted from this

method, while a better understanding of the material and structural composition of the house informed the development of each of the five interventions.

TRASH REMOVAL

In Detroit, the city provides trash bins for weekly pick-ups.

City-issued trash bin was requested but never delivered; we transferred the debris from demolition into 2 dumpsters, paying $280 each (in cash) to have them haul away whatever divers didn't take.

STRUCTURE

Architect hires a structural consultant

The structure was incrementally challenged by multiple holes and partial removals of ceiling, floors and exterior walls (see Insurance), and monitored with advice from local contractors.

TRANSFER OF TITLE

Two parties agree on a monetary exchange and transfer the deed.

$1 and a quitclaim deed were exchanged between 5Fellows and Design 99. In order to resolve funding issues (research money cannot be applied to 'improving' personal property), we needed a third party to take ownership of the house. In the interest of moving our project forward as well as ensuring the house's creative use after our fellowships had ended, we deeded our property over to Design 99, for a sum of $1.00 (yet to be exchanged) and the transfer of a homemade quitclaim deed. .

INSURANCE

Contractors have protection for potential liabilities. Owners buy coverage property.

Through the University of Michigan, we were protected even in our moonlighting as builders. Property insurance was acquired

by Design.99. Covered in the case of injury by our shared employer, each of us could carry out our work without worry. But given the intention to create a venue for a larger public to occupy and interact with the installations, we had to consider the project's implications for those outside our 'family' unit. According to the university's policy, liability coverage extends to any worker or visitor who was an invited guest. An official guest list for the two school-sponsored 'public' openings generated a paper trail should anything go awry, but the friends and passers-by that stopped in to check on our progress fell outside this legal designation.

The distinction measured by the 38 miles between the architecture school and the house carried over into the dual roles we negotiated daily — between acting as responsible agents of the university and simply being good neighbors.

WORKING HOURS
Contractors comply to local noise codes and generally respect neighbors.
Anytime not spent teaching.

CONSTRUCTION METHODS
Design-build practices merge the roles of architect and contractor, relying on expertise in both areas.
Our mode of operating: make it full-scale.
The five projects varied in fabrication techniques, but always the evaluation of expense versus time tended to favor a DIY approach. Materials, like siding and steel struts, were foraged from nearby vacants. Laptops replaced drawing sets for reference and to test the inevitable on-site adjustments.

CERTIFICATE OF OCCUPANCY
After an inspection a C.ofO. states the building is suitable for occupancy.
None.

OCCUPATION
The area is zoned for single-family houses.
A new interpretation of use prompted architectural invention.
Detroit's single-family housing stock exceeds its demand. Simply stated, this fact has played out with complex variations and effects on the urban landscape. By working on one of countless unoccupied homes across the city, we frequently confronted questions of whether the motivation was to rehabilitate the house as a home. Were we 'fixing up' its broken condition to live there?

Restoring the original program seemed an ineffective route with a predetermined course, especially given the state of the house and its context. Stripped of the infrastructure or comforts of a home, the house made room for a new mode of occupation: architectural research. The work projected new spatial and programmatic agendas into this vacancy.

While the five projects modified the house in different ways, its typological identity wasn't wholly erased. The fundamental qualities of the building—its faded domesticity, outmoded construction, and vulnerability to the aggression of both climate and intruders—endure as the medium that connect the projects and inflect the designs themselves. Repurposing the house was an act of design that had material consequences, but none that would permanently keep the house from returning to domestic use in the future.

With some hindsight, we have come to learn that staging an occupation by architecture is admittedly a temporary invasion, an interim strategy for engage one vacancy out of many. Ultimately, the house at 13178 Moran is rooted in its city and its neighborhood, both comprised of many small acts of inhabitation.

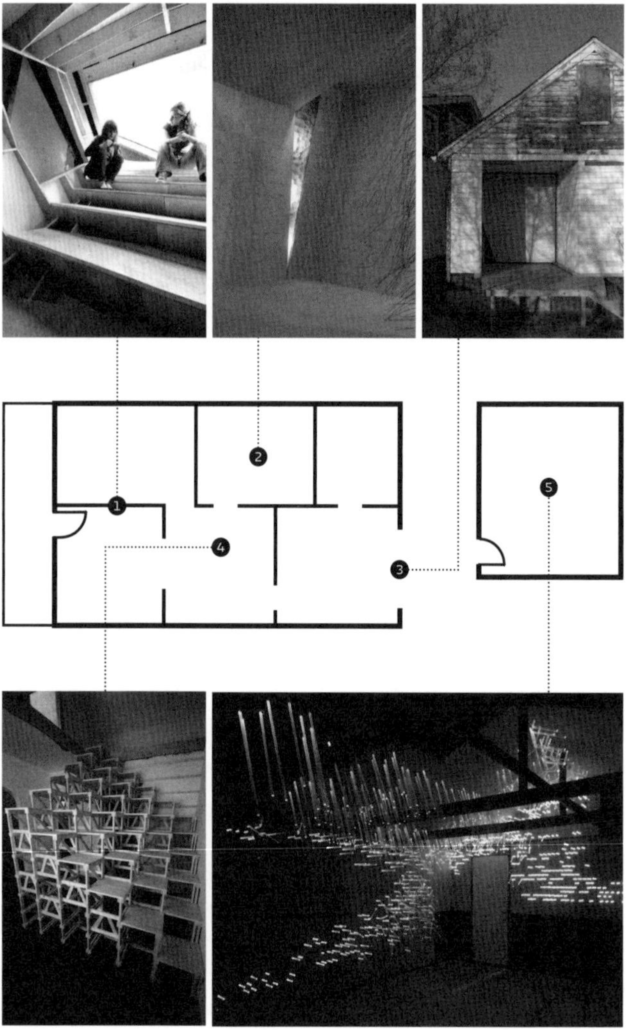
1
2
3
4
5

1. Rosalyne Shieh | Room Addition | This diagonal volume cuts a path for light, illuminating the northern side yard and anticipates the removal of the adjacent fire-damaged house, suggesting the future re-orientation of the entire block.
2. Ellie Abrons | Tingle Room | Transforms the otherwise taut surfaces of floor, wall and ceiling it into a deep volume, unloocking a space within the thickness of the wall, and ultimately moving architecture from blank backdrop to active participant.
3. Meredith Miller | R.O. | Reformatting the separation between public and private domains, an operable element slides between two positions: one secures the interior while giving over space to the exterior and the other creates an entry through a third space.
4. Thom Moran | Table and Chairs | A bleecher-like stair realized with minimal means and standard 1x2 boards and nails. Somewhere between a shelf and a ladder; a room and circulation
5. Catie Newell | *Weatherizing* | Punctuating the barrier between the atmospheres of the interior and the exterior, the nearly one thousand glass tubes spatialize and amplify light conditions, both natural and artificial.

Simon Crubellier (photographer), *Westway*, (2006).

SCENES FROM THE LATE 20TH CENTURY AUTOGEDDON

PATRICK CICCONE

VA-VA-VOOM ... POW!
(LOS ANGELES, CALABASAS, MALIBU, CALIFORNIA, CA. 1955)

The 1955 film noir, *Kiss Me Deadly*, opens to a highway at night, with a woman, naked save for her trench coat, attempting to hitchhike. Failing to attract attention from the side of the road, she moves directly into the path of traffic. Detective Mike Hammer's car swerves and barely misses the woman, but he decides to pick her up anyway. The engine of doom set in motion by this highway near-miss leads to an explosive ending, two hours of screen time later, when a nuclear device explodes in a California beach house.

Kiss Me Deadly, directed by Robert Aldrich and written by A.I. Bezzerides, is the greatest movie ever made about the car.[1] The plot and twisted, baroque *mise en scène* combine to form the definitive view of the automobile, linking Los Angeles, the highway, sex, and atomic power together into one apocalyptic vision, best summed up by Hammer's mechanic: "Va-va-voom ..POW!"

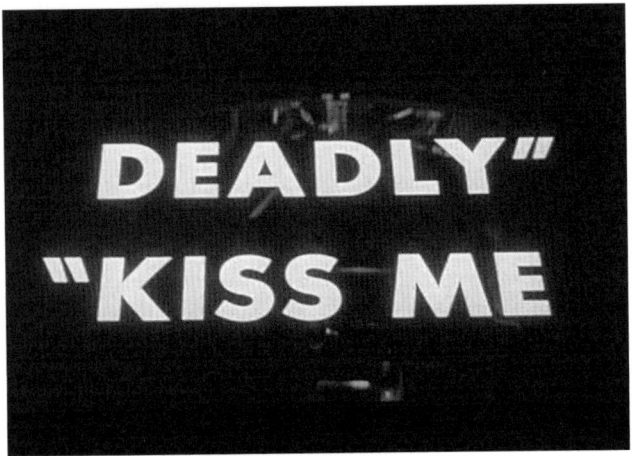

Opening credits to *Kiss Me Deadly* (dir. Robert Aldrich, 1955).

The film's plot is car-centric in the most literal sense. The film opens with Hammer nearly totaling his sports car in picking up the hitchhiker. Her pursuers attempt to kill both of them in a staged car accident. Later, the same party tries to kill Hammer by sending him a bomb-rigged convertible as a "gift." Hammer learns that a woman he is searching for has been run down been a truck. A mechanic is killed when a jack is pulled out from beneath him. The vast automotive landscape of Los Angeles transforms this labyrinthine plot into a tangled skein of sex, death, and American car culture.

Where *Kiss Me Deadly* truly excels, however, is as a work of formalism, marrying the expressive potential of cinema with the automobile into a deadly fugue of extreme violence, brutality, sex, and the coming nuclear apocalypse. Consider the film's opening sequence, a remarkable set piece that lays out all of these themes in only a couple of seconds. The first shot frames the hitchhiking woman (whom we later find out has escaped from a mental hospital) so that only her bare legs and feet are visible as she runs down the night highway. The road behind her is mostly black and the passing headlights periodically overexpose her body. The rush of oncoming automobiles creates a metallic threnody, a soundtrack whose intensity matches the woman's panicked breathing. As she rushes into the middle of the road, we first see the shot framed from behind, emphasizing the approaching headlights. The film then cuts to a medium shot of Mike Hammer through the windshield as his convertible screeches toward her. When Hammer finally swerves away and comes to a stop, an astonishing tracking shot moves forward into the dust of the near-accident and ends by framing Hammer in the drivers' seat. He says, "You almost wrecked my car!" A pause. "Well, get in." A Nat King Cole tune is playing on the radio. The music continues during the credits (which are read in the same backward manner as road surface markings) as they roll over the forward view from Hammer's car. The woman's frenzied breathing now dominates the soundtrack as the car moves through the night.

Kiss Me Deadly is violence by design. Or, rather, by the designed-in dangers of the automobile. Cars, in the film's formulation, are engines of creativity, which in bursts of movement and violence create the world anew. Recall the famous shot where a gas station materializes out of the darkness as Hammer drives toward it. The car, however, is far more than a device that creates space through the windshield lens, it is an organizing principle in the most general sense, the origin of human identity. Hammer and his car are conflated with each other, encapsulated in this exchange:

> CHRISTINA: You're angry with me aren't you? Sorry I nearly wrecked your pretty little car. I was just thinking how much you can tell about a person from such simple things. Your car, for instance.

> HAMMER: Now what kind of message does it send you?
>
> CHRISTINA: You have only one real lasting love.
>
> HAMMER: Now who could that be?
>
> CHRISTINA: You. You're one of those self-indulgent males who thinks about nothing but his clothes, his car, himself. Bet you do push-ups every morning to keep your belly hard.

Such narcissism is the symptom of a culture in grave decline, painted in Aldrich's tones of a "mood befitting the Decline of the West."[2] Cars are mechanized death, harbingers of a wholly modern apocalypse. In one of *Kiss Me Deadly's* key lines, a police detective informs Hammer of the gravity of what he has discovered in three terse phrases: "Manhattan Project, Los Alamos, Trinity." Three more could have been added: General Motors, Ford, and Chrysler.

OUTER SPACE/INNER SPACE
(BETWEEN WESTWAY FLYOVER AND M4 MOTORWAY, LONDON, CA. 1974)

"Soon after three o'clock on the afternoon of April 22nd 1973, a 35-year-old architect named Robert Maitland was driving down the high-speed exit lane of the Westway interchange in central London. Six hundred yards from the junction with the newly built spur of the M4 motorway, when the Jaguar had already passed the 70 m.p.h. speed limit, a blow-out collapsed the front nearside tyre."[3] With these words, the opening sentences to *Concrete Island* (1974), J.G. Ballard ushers in his readers into 20th century roadspace. The novel is *Robinson Crusoe* recast into the blank anonymous space of the modern freeway. Robert Maitland crashes his vehicle off the highway and finds himself trapped in a triangular reservation between three express routes, the title's concrete island. The narrative first follows his failed attempts to escape; two other castaways then appear, and the novel shifts to a conflict of wills. In the end Maitland again thinks of escape, but it becomes clear that he will never leave the island.

Concrete Island is less a work about the car than a caustic analysis of a culture where cars define the landscape and test the limits of human consciousness. Ballard describes a strange, alien world that is in fact the one that we inhabit. It is a world that elides distinctions between familiar and unfamiliar, ordinary and fantastic, body and car.

Technology is the agent of this elision. The car, in Ballard's vision, is an instrument that allows a latent human irrationality to surface: "Once inside a car some rogue gene, a strain of rashness, overran the rest of [Maitland's] usually cautious and clear-minded character."[4] The car extends and perverts both human consciousness and the body itself: "In the polished panels of the rear-wheel housing Maitland stared at the distorted reflection of himself," revealing a "madman's grimace."[5] Like Aldrich, Ballard uses automotive language to describe people and vice versa. Whereas the front end of his Jaguar "was punched into itself like a collapsed face", Maitland's face becomes a constellation of "silver scar tissue" after the accident.[6]

More important than the actual physical junction between flesh and metal is the human mind's need to project itself outward through technology, through the car and its supporting infrastructure. By making Maitland an architect, Ballard can employ his protagonist literally and metaphorically; he is the designer of both the real and psychological space he inhabits. His instinct for survival is in fact the need to conquer space: "As he was already well aware, it was this will to survive, to dominate the island and harness its limited resources, that now seemed a more important goal than escaping."[7] The same impulse that drives people to identify with their cars, to project themselves onto the machine, makes them project themselves across the exterior space of the world.

Are Maitland, his car, and the world around him fused together, or is this union merely a grand delusion? When describing Maitland's delirium, Ballard does not allow his protagonist to answer the question himself: "He looked round wildly at the island and its deserted motorway embankments. Was he still trapped inside his car? Was the entire island an extension of the Jaguar, its windshield and windows transformed by his delirium into these embankments?"[8] Such inquisitiveness lapses into a need for total control of the island and its resources, a desire that Ballard identifies as the need "to rove for ever within the empty city of his own mind."[9]

This empty city of the mind is filled with the remnants of a lost civilization only several decades old. Maitland identifies "the outlines of building foundations, the ground-plans of Edwardian terraced houses" as well as "the entrance to a World War II air raid shelter, half-buried by the earth and gravel brought in to fill motorway embankments."[10] Maitland appropriates these structures because in his mind, they were created for his own use. The new highway landscape is thus a world constructed solely for himself: "Below the span were the approach roads to the Westway interchange, a labyrinth of ascent ramps and feeder lanes. Maitland felt himself alone on an alien planet abandoned by its inhabitants, a race of motorway builders who had long since vanished but had bequeathed to him this concrete wilderness."[11] Maitland feels no need to leave the island at the novel's end because there is in fact nothing to escape from: "In some ways the task he had set himself was meaningless. Already he felt no real need to leave the island, and this alone confirmed that he had established his dominion over it."[12]

AUTO-EROTICISM
(LONDON AIRPORT FLYOVER, CA. 1973)

Ballard's 1973 novel *Crash* is a bleak narrative set in and around

London's Heathrow airport. It is also a technological romance, a meditation that investigates and conflates interest in technological disasters and celebrity culture. The narrator (also named J.G. Ballard) interacts with and becomes part of a community of car-accident re-enactors and crash survivors. In *Crash*, escape from the modern technological universe is possible through the erotic embrace of death in a car crash, crystallized in Ballard's description of Seagrave, a car-accident re-enactor, who has just survived yet another deliberate crash: "Seagrave's slim and exhausted face was covered with shattered safety glass, as if his body were already crystallizing, at last escaping out of this uneasy set of dimensions into a more beautiful universe."[13]

Characters in *Crash* attempt to reunite themselves with the machines that are, in a sense, already part of themselves. The union is impossible as long as the characters remain alive, though the marks of such attempts are left visible everywhere on their bodies. In one of *Crash*'s most extreme passages, Ballard describes photographs of genitalia mutilated by car wrecks: "In several of the photographs the source of the wound was indicated by a detail of that portion of the car which had caused the injury: beside a casualty ward photograph of a bifurcated penis was an inset of a handbrake unit; above a close-up of a massively bruised vulva was a steering-wheel boss and its manufacturer's medallion."[14] This language demonstrates how *Crash* is first and foremost automotive work, a portrayal of a world where human eroticism is linked to the desire to die, and where death is made easy by the fatal logic of the automobile.

Ballard's writing, stated crudely, is a literary mode not far removed from the "va-va-voom...POW!" of *Kiss Me Deadly*. That is, his characters have melded the two meanings of the phrase—the sexual act and the car crash—into one. The symmetry of this union is inescapable, at least within the context of *Crash*: the automobile is simultaneously the great technological symbol of sexuality and one of the most efficient means of destruction and self-destruction available to modern society. The thrillseekers of *Crash* merely use the car to its fullest possible expression: "In our wounds we celebrated the re-birth of the traffic-slain dead, the deaths and injuries of those we had seen dying by the roadside and the imaginary wounds and postures of the millions yet to die."[15]

Ballard's moral stance toward his characters is never clear, but their self-destructive impulses are tied to the larger threat of a culture about to be subsumed by "abandoned technology left to its own devices."[16] The world of *Concrete Island* is, metaphorically at least, post-apocalyptic, and in *Crash*, the threat of a massive catastrophe hangs over the air of every event and landscape. As the narrator describes, "I felt an undefined sense of extreme danger, almost as if an accident was about to take place involving all these cars. The passengers in the airliners lifting away from the airport were fleeing the disaster area, escaping from this coming autogeddon."[17] The individual's desire for fulfilling one's own self-destruction is replicated across all society and imprinted in its technology: the narrator watches "for the first signs of this end of the world by automobile, for which the accident had my own private rehearsal."[18] This personal end of the world takes on the dimensions of a global catastrophe as *Crash* ends with the narrator's thrill at planning his own fatal car crash and imagining the gruesome fates of millions of other automobile passengers.

DESIGNED-IN DANGERS
(THE U.S. INTERSTATE HIGHWAY SYSTEM, 1965)

Vaughn, the mastermind of the car crashing enterprise in *Crash*, is an archivist of technical literature: "The shelves and walls were packed with scientific textbooks, incomplete runs of technical journals, science-fiction paperbacks and reprints of his own papers."[19] Vaughn's program, moreover, seems nothing less than a inverse mirror of the design process of automotive stylists described in Ralph Nader's *Unsafe at Any Speed* (1965) of "spectacular dangers" in their encrustation of American cars with useless and deadly chromium ornament.[20] Indeed, Nader appears in one of Ballard's short stories, "Plan for the Assassination of Jacqueline Kennedy" (1970), where the narrator imagines a "film of automobile accidents devised as a cinematic version of Nader's *Unsafe at Any Speed*."[21]

Unsafe at Any Speed was likely the first popular work to view the car itself as a weapon, as a killing machine. Nader's book is a masterpiece of hyperbole: it opens with the lines, "For over half a century the automobile has brought death, injury, and the most inestimable sorrow and deprivation to millions of people. With Medea-like intensity, this mass trauma began rising sharply four years ago, reflecting new and unexpected ravages by the motor vehicle."[22] Nader approaches the car as a machine designed not to ensure its occupants safety but to guarantee their gruesome demise. He casts his entire argument with puritanical fire: "Something happened to men's rationality when they placed themselves in vehicles—chariots, wagons, carriages, boats, trains, automobiles and aircraft. Death and injury from crash impacts in these carriers were called 'acts of God' or 'bad luck;' escape from casualties in accidents was called 'a miracle.'"[23]

Unsafe at Any Speed helped launch automotive safety as a viable movement, leading to the passage of the 1967 National Traffic and Motor Vehicle Safety Act. The subsequent four decades have seen the continued improvement of automotive safety design and a massive per capita decline in automotive fatalities in the U.S. However, these improvements have only masked the dangers inherent in the automobile without removing them: automobiles remain machines of death. Ballard's vision of autogeddon is thus perhaps slightly obsolete since the automobile has been emasculated through safety, but his vision of technology remains prescient. Indeed, in his foreword to *Crash*, Ballard maps out a wider framework for the novel: "The marriage of reason and nightmare which has dominated the 20th century has given birth to an ever more ambiguous world. Across the communications landscape move specters of sinister technologies and the dreams that money can buy."[24] The 21st century is no different. Human consciousness continues to reproduce itself in technology, and there are as many possible *–geddons* as there are machines.

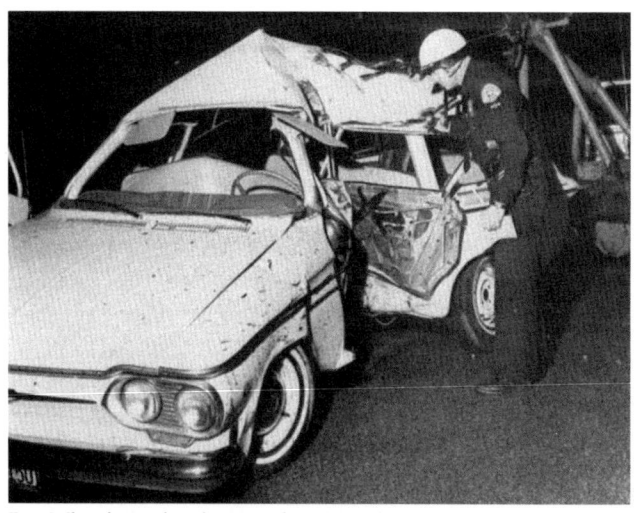

The 1961 Chevrolet Corvair station wagon of comedian Ernie Kovacs at the intersection of Santa Monica Boulevard and South Beverly Glen Drive, Los Angeles, California, January 13, 1962, shortly after the car skidded out of control into a light pole, killing Kovacs instantly.

NOTES

1. The title of this essay was adapted from the Mickey Spillane novel of the same name (save for comma), *Kiss Me, Deadly* (New York: Dutton, 1952). Also deserving of mention in the film's credits is cinematographer Ernest Laszlo, a frequent Aldrich collaborator in the 1950s.
2. Andrew Sarris, *The American Cinema: Directors and Directions 1929-1968* (New York: Dutton, 1968), p. 85.
3. J.G. Ballard, *Concrete Island* (New York: Farrar, Straus, and Giroux, 1974), p. 7.
4. *Ibid.*, p. 9.
5. *Ibid.*, p. 13.
6. *Ibid.*, pp. 10, 87..
7. *Ibid.*, p. 65.
8. *Ibid.*, p. 67.
9. *Ibid.*, p. 142.
10. *Ibid.*, p. 38.
11. *Ibid.*, p. 149.
12. *Ibid.*, p. 176.
13. Ballard, *Crash* (New York: Vintage, 1974), p. 185
14. *Ibid.*, p. 134.
15. *Ibid.*, p. 203.
16. *Ibid.*, p. 212.
17. *Ibid.*, p. 50.
18. *Ibid.*, p. 50.
19. *Ibid.*, p. 167.
20. Ralph Nader, *Unsafe At Any Speed: The Designed-In Dangers of the American Automobile* (New York: Pocket, 1965), p. 77.
21. Ballard, "Plan for the Assassination of Jacqueline Kennedy" in *The Best Short Stories of J.G. Ballard* (New York: Henry Holt, 1978), p. 297.
22. Nader, *Unsafe at Any Speed*, p. v.
23. *Ibid.*, p. 64.
24. *Crash*, p. 1.

Secretariat Building, Le Corbusier, Chandigarh, Punjab, India

*Students in Beatriz Colomina and Esther de Costa Meyer's seminar, "Modernist Dilemmas: Brasília and Chandigarh Turn 50" traveled to Chandigarh, India to study the modernist city's legacy. These photographs, taken by Frankfurt-based architect Ragunath Vasudevan, and a co-traveler with the students, represent the first recordings of an ongoing project about the present state of Chandigarh's unique urban project.

CHANDIGARH AT 50*
MODERNISM REVISITED

PHOTOS BY RAGUNATH VASUDEVAN

During the twentieth century, several new capitals were built from scratch, for economic and political reasons. Two of these — Brasília and Chandigarh — share several traits, partly due to the impact of Le Corbusier. The full force of modern architecture was put to the test. Today's renewed emphasis on city-building and on the development of post-colonial nations has cast these mid-century urban experiments in a new light. The monumentality of Chandigarh, the new capital of East Punjab after the territorial split of Pakistan and India, seems altogether brutal and unforgiving when compared to today's emphasis on transparency, informality, and temporality. The ongoing collaboration between the *Princeton School of Architecture* and the *Chandigarh College of Architecture* will attempt to analyze the contemporary condition of the city, which, as these pictures show, is not so clearly construed as many journals and essays might claim. Chandigarh's urban project continues, just as its architectural legacy will still serve to inspire future generations of designers and planners.

Hindustan Motors "Ambassador" car in front of the entrance to Le Corbusier's Secretariat building. Despite its British origins, this car is considered to be the "King of the Indian roads."

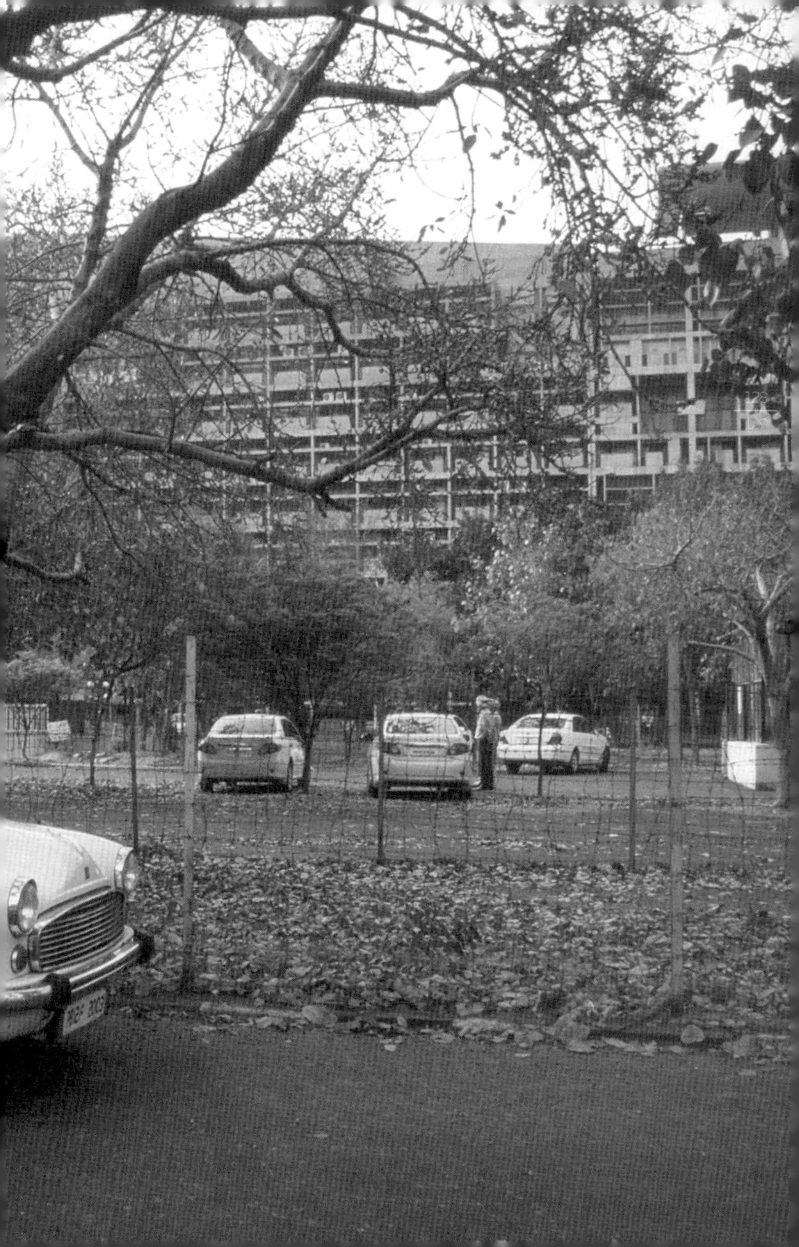

Sector 17, the central quadrant in Chandigarh's historic core, plays host to much of the city's commerical and social core.

The Government Museum and Art Gallery, Le Corbusier, 1968, view from the Chandigarh City Museum.

Secretariat's roof.

The brise-soleil of the Assembly Building parking garage serves an informal resting place for goverment workers.

Le Corbusier's Secretariat Building as seen from the attached access ramp. Note the contrast between the more stable concrete and the informal appropriation of space by the bureaucrats and service workers of the Punjab government.

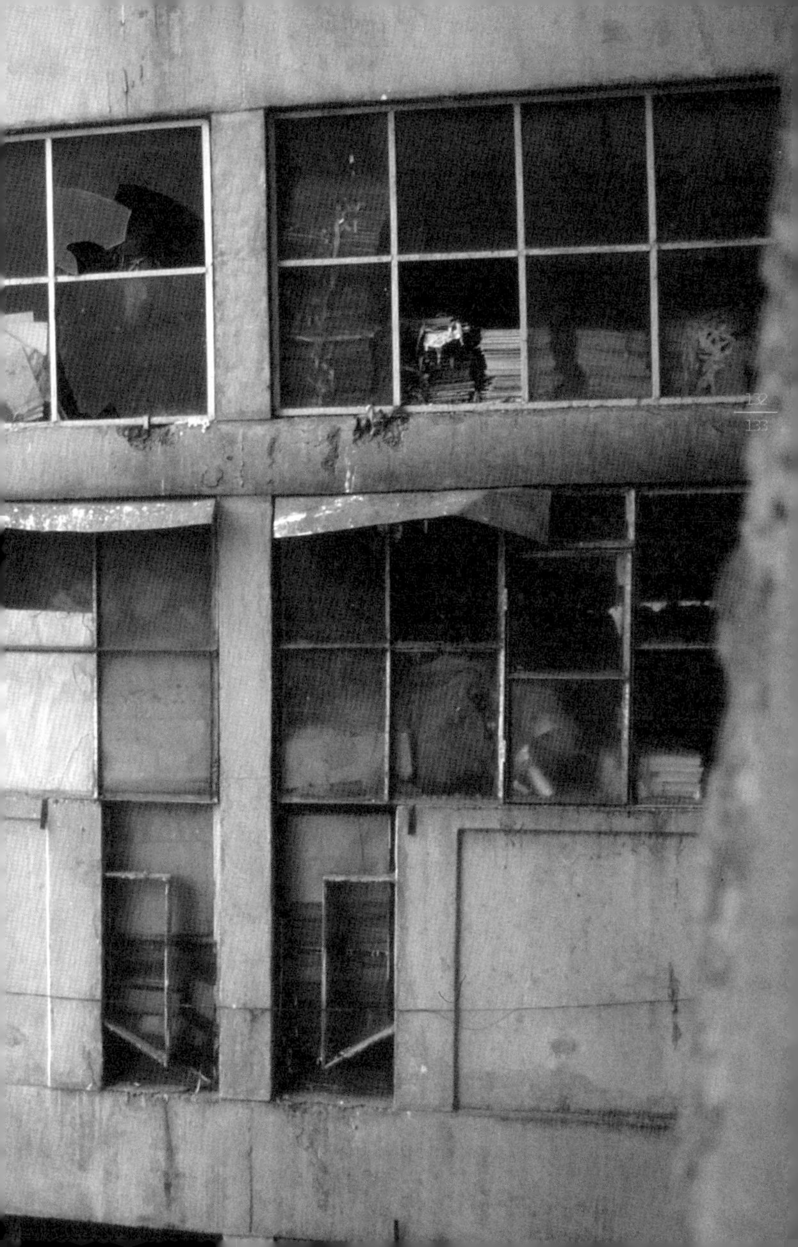

Typical housing, Sector 22.

The canopy of the High Assembly is filled with official vehicles awaiting the barristers and judges inside.

The rear of the High Assembly overlooks a courtyard where members of the court assembly to prepare for trials and meet other colleagues.

Parking garage near the Assembly building.

Chandigarh College of Architecture; 'Esther da Costa-Meyer (left); Professor Vikram Prakash (far right), University of Washington-Seattle, son of Aditya Prakash who worked with Le Corbusier in Chandigarh; and S.D. Sharma (second from the right), who worked for Le Corbusier and Jeanneret in Chandigarh; with local students.'
[Photograph by Matthew Clarke]

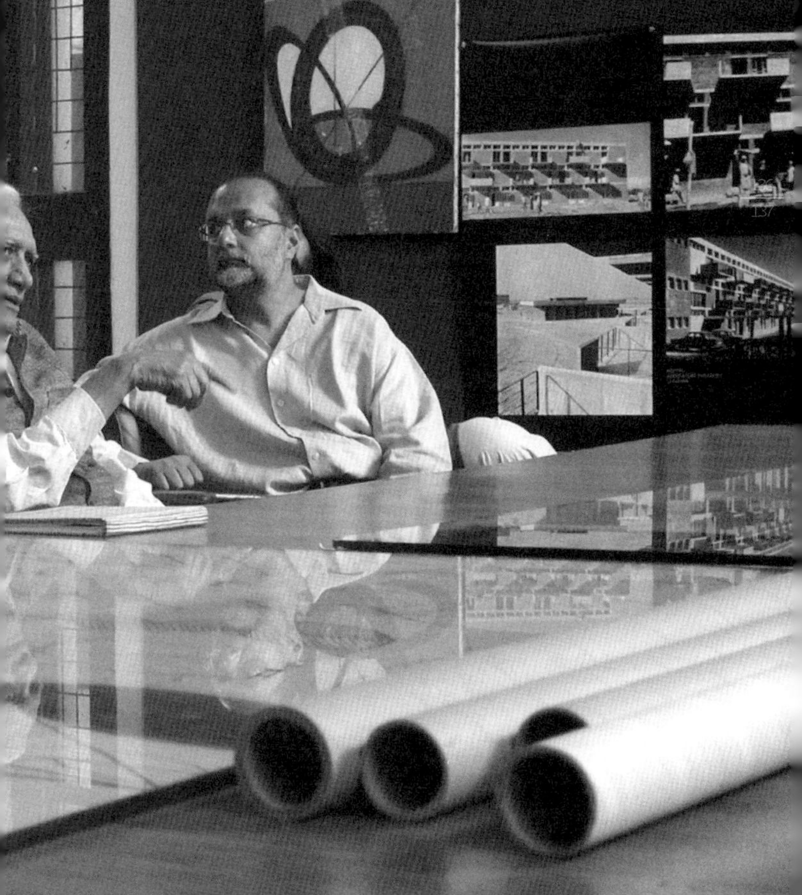

Isa Genzken, *"Sie sind mein Glück"*, Installation view Kunstverein Braunschweig, 2000.

"IM ANFANG WAR DIE BEKLEIDUNG":
ISA GENZKEN'S CLAD COLUMNS

LISA LEE

With only a few exceptions—the square, marble tiles of *Lawrence* (2000), for instance, or the alternating panels of wood veneer and perforated metal that comprise *Wolfgang* (1998)—Isa Genzken's series of *Columns*, some three dozen works realized between 1998 and 2003, feature a motley array of claddings: a high-low mix of copper, marble, glass, aluminum, alloy, wood, mirror, reflective foil, tape, and, occasionally, photographs or other printed matter. Intrinsic differences in material properties are intensified with additional treatment, either in the manufacturing process or by the artist's hand. Metal plates come matte, polished, perforated, or textured (gridded or hammered). Wood panels and particleboards may be stained, painted, lacquered, or veneered. Add to the mix the reflective properties of mirror and glass (often tinted) and the optical pizzazz of metallic foil (holographic, gridded, and color-saturated), and you have the elements for an exuberant play in polychromy and surface effects.

The *Columns* are highly allusive, by way of synecdoche and pun. The gridded, mirrored foil, darkened glass, and metal cladding of *Untitled* (1998), *Christopher* (1998), and *Layout* (2001) evoke the steely façades of corporate high-rises. (*Untitled* also features black and white photographs of the towers of the World Trade Center.) *Lawrence*'s white marble veined in grey and hints of brown calls to mind hushed lobbies. Wood panels lacquered blue with tufts of white—featured in *A*, *B*, and *C* (each from 2002/2003)—make permanent (and opaque) the fleeting reflections of the sky on glass curtain walls. (Four smaller *Columns*, each titled *Vom Himmel Zurück* (2003), are entirely lacquered in this manner—Magritte-esque mind-benders if one thinks of them as architectural models.) Anomalous-seeming at first, *Aquarium* and *Kleine Fischsäule* (both of 2001) are entirely covered with collaged images of tropical fish. Never one to resist a visual pun, Genzken highlights and mimics the natural cladding (and ornament) of fish scales in the medium of collage—so many paper scales. She draws a sly analogy between the denizens of glass architecture and those of a fish tank. The *Columns* that feature a punchy mix of holographic foil and metallic tape evoke an urban stroll, where digital billboards, illuminated marquees, and colored awnings jam the visual field.

Art historical references accrue as well. One face of *Lehmbruck* (2000) is painted silver with a central, red stripe. A polished metal plate covers its lower quarter. At its middle Genzken has attached four identical postcard reproductions of expressionist sculptor Wilhelm Lehmbruck's *Standing Youth*, also known as *Ascending Youth* (*Emporsteigender Jüngling*), of 1913. Arguably the last significant German sculptor to have practiced figuration in the neoclassical vein, Lehmbruck was invested in presenting an essential image of man, even when, after the First World War, that essence necessarily involved trauma. However attenuated his sculptural physiques then became (*The Fallen Man*, 1915; *Seated Youth*, 1916), the human figure remained intact. Genzken

Isa Genzken, *"Aquarium"*, 2001. Wood, collaged paper. 281 x 32 x 34cm.

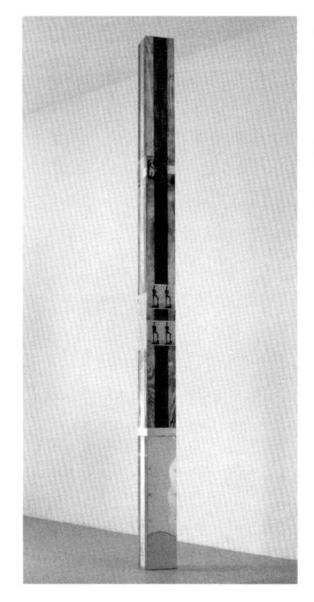

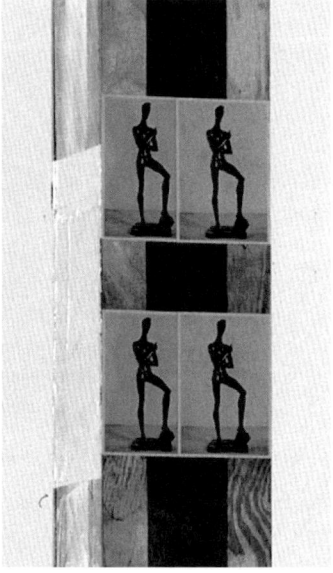

Isa Genzken, "Lehmbruck", 2000. Wood, metal, aluminium roil, postcards. 320 x 19,5 x 18cm.

punctures the profundity of Lehmbruck's image of introspection in *Standing Youth* by affixing above it an image of a puppy. This characteristic levity aside, I would argue that Lehmbruck raises an issue crucial to Genzken's *Columns* as a body of work, namely the place of the human figure in contemporary sculpture after Minimalism— i.e. emphatically not in the vein of monumental Neo-Expressionist figuration in hewn wood daubed with paint. Or, put another way, with this series Genzken tests the possibility of abstract statuary, though it would seem an oxymoron. For if, with their architectural claddings and small footprints relative to their height, the *Columns* evoke skyscrapers, as so many critics have noted, I wish to propose that they also have the bearing of personages.

In their simple, geometric forms, the *Columns* are minimalist gestalts. In "Art and Objecthood," Michael Fried criticized the sculptural volumes of so-called literalist art for their latent anthropomorphism. Of Tony Smith's cubic *Die* (1962), for example, he writes:

> One way of describing what Smith was making might be something like a surrogate person—that is, a kind of statue.... [T]he apparent hollowness of most literalist work—the quality of having an inside—is almost blatantly anthropomorphic. It is, as numerous commentators have remarked approvingly, as though the work in question has an inner, even secret, life....[1]

One might recall in this context that Robert Morris's first sculptural work, *Column* (1960), was a plywood box in the hollow center of which the artist could stand.[2] What Fried perceives to be a great weakness of literalist forms Genzken courts explicitly. Yet there are important distinctions to be made. If the quintessential minimalist form is a geometric volume rendered in some impervious industrial material by industrial means, Genzken breaks the surface of the forms with a myriad of surface treatments, the application of which is so idiosyncratic as to render the far side of the gestalt unknowable. Even the most colorful of minimalist works—Donald Judd's use of tinted Plexiglas and anodized aluminum come to mind—have nothing on Genzken's off-kilter chromatic sensibility. While Genzken's *Columns* are hollow, any "inner life" is lived on the surface.

A large number of the *Columns* bear the names of Genzken's coterie of friends and fellow artists. *Wolfgang* refers to the photographer Wolfgang Tillmans, Genzken's occasional collaborator, and *Lawrence* can boast a namesake in conceptual artist Lawrence Weiner. *Kai* (2000), fraternal twin to *Isa* (2000), is named after contemporary artist Kai Althoff. (Both don yellow-on-black racing stripes that double as homage to Barnett Newman's "zips.") The *Columns* are manifestly handmade, an important quality that is lost in photographic reproduction. Excess glue seeps from edges; painted panels show streaks and air pockets; materials are often overlapped rather than set seamlessly one alongside another, producing a subtle dimensionality. In a section of *Dan* (1999), for instance—that's Dan Graham to you—a wood core is covered with a mirror, then a marble tile, followed by a tinted mirror. Contrary to the one-thing-after-another nature of minimalist seriality, each of the *Columns* is unique, not just in terms of surface treatment, but in dimension—the columns range in height from 215 to 324 centimeters, with square or rectangular bases

Isa Genzken, Installation view Kunsthalle Zürich, 2003.

the sides of which vary in length from 18 to 38 centimeters. (Crucial to the *Columns*' allusiveness is that, unlike Morris's *Column* or his *Box for Standing* (1961), their dimensions do not approximate those of the human being.) Genzken's *Columns* embody individuality exteriorized as surface, as cladding. Or, changing the emphasis, one might say that the *Columns* present surface decoration as constitutive of individuality.

"Im Anfang war die Bekleidung [In the beginning was cladding]," writes Adolf Loos in his 1898 essay, "Das Prinzip der Bekleidung."[3] The principle promised in the essay's title dictates that cladding must not be imitative of the underlying structure but call attention to itself qua cladding. In the formulation of this principle, Loos refers to the work of Gottfried Semper, for whom architecture's origins and essence are to be found in woven coverings that demarcate space. Semper asserts that the basic woven pen served "as a means of dividing the 'home,' the *inner life* from the *outer life*, as a formal construct of a spatial idea."[4] Once interiority and exteriority are visualized and actualized, the inner life *of the subject* also becomes thinkable.

Both Semper and Loos put great store in the fact that the term *Bekleidung* has as its root *kleiden*, "to clothe, to dress," thereby establishing the textile origins of architecture. Similarly, the German words for wall [*Wand*] and garment [*Gewand*] share the same root. Cladding's etymological and anthropological relationships to the body and to dressing resonate in Genzken's *Columns*, on the surfaces of which cladding and clothing converge and where the creation of the subject follows fast on the creation of space. On this point one might note that in the same year that Genzken made her first *Columns*, 1998, she also produced a series of some thirty paint-slashed and spray-painted shirts. Violent and exuberant, expressing the freedom of personalization and the aggressiveness of vandalism, these altered garments have as much to say about abstraction in painting as about the sculptural readymade. "The evolution of skin, the surface with which spatiality is produced, is the evolution of the social. The social subject, like the body with which it is associated, is a product of decorative surfaces," Mark Wigley writes in his discussion of Semper's theories of *Bekleidung*. "Interiority is not simply physical. It is a social effect marked on the newly constituted body of the individual."[5] If the clad body can be a mark of extreme alienation, as is evoked by the Vorticist imaginary of segmented and armored monsters, Genzken's *Columns* suggest subjects that, though hardened, have reclaimed the surface for the possibility of sociality. They render physiognomy as architectural skin, with none of the dissimulation that "façade" implies.

The research and writing of this essay was supported by the Center for Advanced Study in the Visual Arts, National Gallery of Art, and by the Spears Fund, Princeton University.

NOTES

1 Michael Fried, "Art and Objecthood," *Art and Objecthood: Essays and Reviews* (Chicago: University of Chicago Press, 1998), p. 156.

2 Morris's *Column* (1960) was conceived for a performance of the Living Theater in New York, during which the upright box was tipped over after three and a half minutes and allowed to lie flat for an equal length of time. The toppling, triggered by the tug of a string from offstage, would have appeared to the audience as if animated by the "inner, even secret, life" of the *Column*. Initially, Morris planned to stand in the *Column* during the performance and to topple the structure from within it. See *Robert Morris: The Mind/Body Problem* (New York: Solomon R. Guggenheim Foundation, 1994), p. 90.

3 Adolf Loos, "The Principle of Cladding," *Spoken into the Void: Collected Essays 1897-1900* (Cambridge, Mass. and London: MIT Press, 1982), pp. 66-69.

4 Gottfried Semper, *Style in the Technical and Tectonic Arts, or, Practical Aesthetics* (Los Angeles: Getty Research Institute, 2004), p. 248.

5 Mark Wigley, *White Walls, Designer Dresses: The Fashioning of Modern Architecture* (Cambridge, Mass.: MIT Press, 1995), pp. 12-13.

Isa Genzken, *"Sie sind mein Glück,"* Installation view Kunstverein Braunschweig, 2000

146 / 147

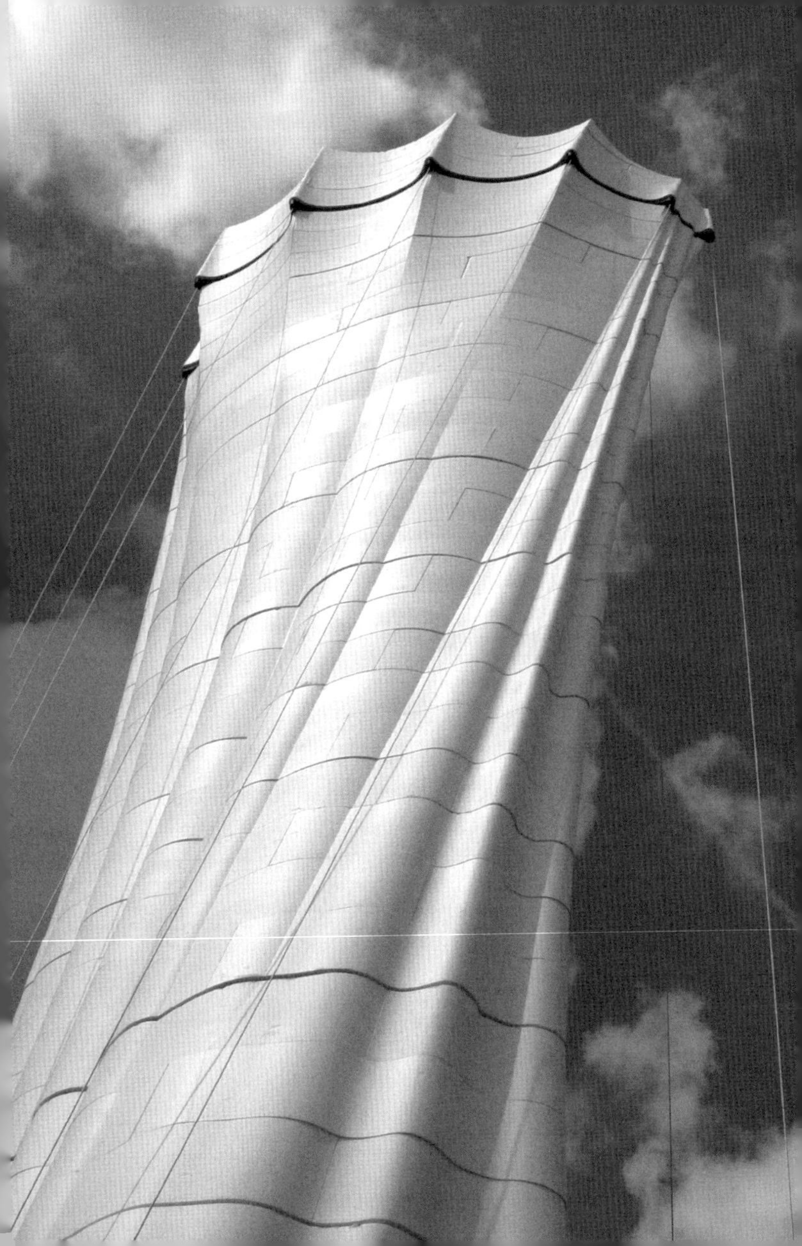

(left) Matter Design, *Periscope: Foam Tower* National 10UP! Competition Winning Entry (2010)

FOAM ADVOCATES
FROM SURFACE TO VOLUME

BRANDON CLIFFORD + WES MCGEE

Periscope is the winning entry in the national 10UP! competition, but it is also an experiment derived from our ~~obsession~~ ongoing research into foam as a building material.

In recent years, the boom in digital fabrication has empowered architects. By directly engaging the fabrication process architects have been able to regain control over practices and techniques previously relegated to the construction industry. Unfortunately, industrialized construction materials have been compressed into economically-friendly, paper-thin sheets. Industry, driven by economies of production and manufacturing, attempts to provide better building materials at an efficient price. Composite woods are covered in luxurious veneers, stone construction is reduced to wafer thin cladding on stacked CMU, and walls are rendered as thin as possible. These well intentioned innovations have had a parallel effect on architecture -- collapsing depth and favoring thin over thick. The catalog of sheet materials grow and contemporary digital fabrication methods

EPS FOAM UNIT
HEIGHT: 8'-0"
WIDTH: 4'-0"
DEPTH: 12"
WEIGHT: **32 LBS**

STANDARD CMU
HEIGHT: 8"
WIDTH: 16"
DEPTH: 8"
WEIGHT: **32 LBS**

continue to produced a plethora of folded, notched, bent, perforated and otherwise surface-driven projects.

In order to resist that tendency, we advocate a material with depth, though one that might still compete with the economic logic of sheets. Cheap and thick, expanded polystyrene (EPS) foam is inherently volumetric (98% air) and at around $1 per cubic foot, one of the cheapest building materials available. Perhaps because of this fact, it has a certain stigma and is usually relegated to fill material. The Federal Highway Administration currently uses large blocks as earth fill under highways (EPS foam is literally cheaper than dirt!). But there are a number of other advantages to the material that have perhaps been underappreciated. It contains no CFC's and is 100% recyclable (manufacturers that supply stock material will also pick up scraps from the fabrication process to toss back into their next batch). These material properties in conjunction with advanced fabrication methods provided a solid platform to revert back to a stereotomic logic of construction.

150 / 151

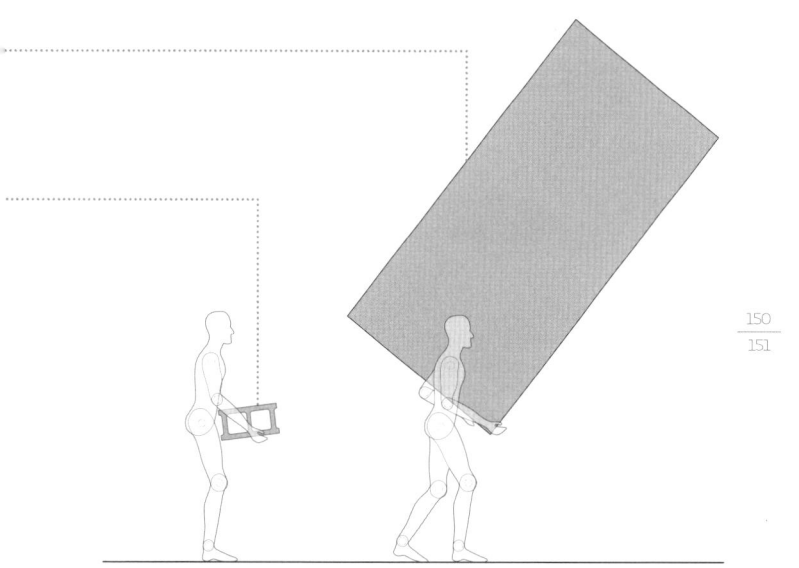

Foam sub-assemblies are designed to be carried by two people.

WIND+FOAM=COLLAPSE

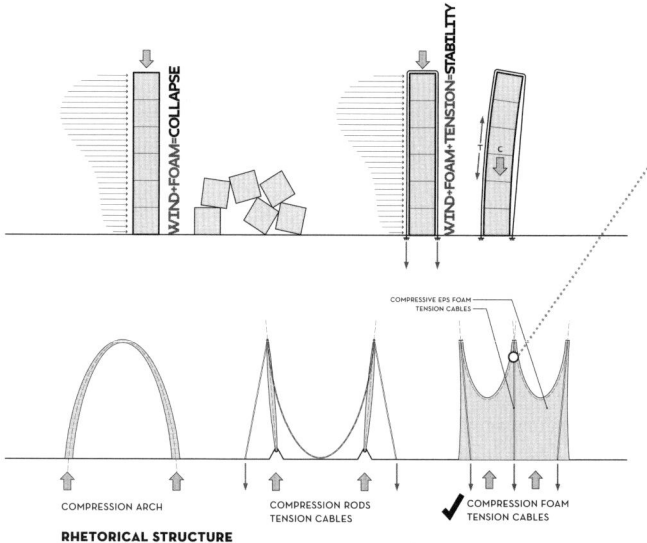

WIND+FOAM+TENSION=STABILITY

COMPRESSIVE EPS FOAM
TENSION CABLES

COMPRESSION ARCH

COMPRESSION RODS
TENSION CABLES

✓ COMPRESSION FOAM
TENSION CABLES

RHETORICAL STRUCTURE

TENSION CABLES
7/16" DIAMETER CABLE

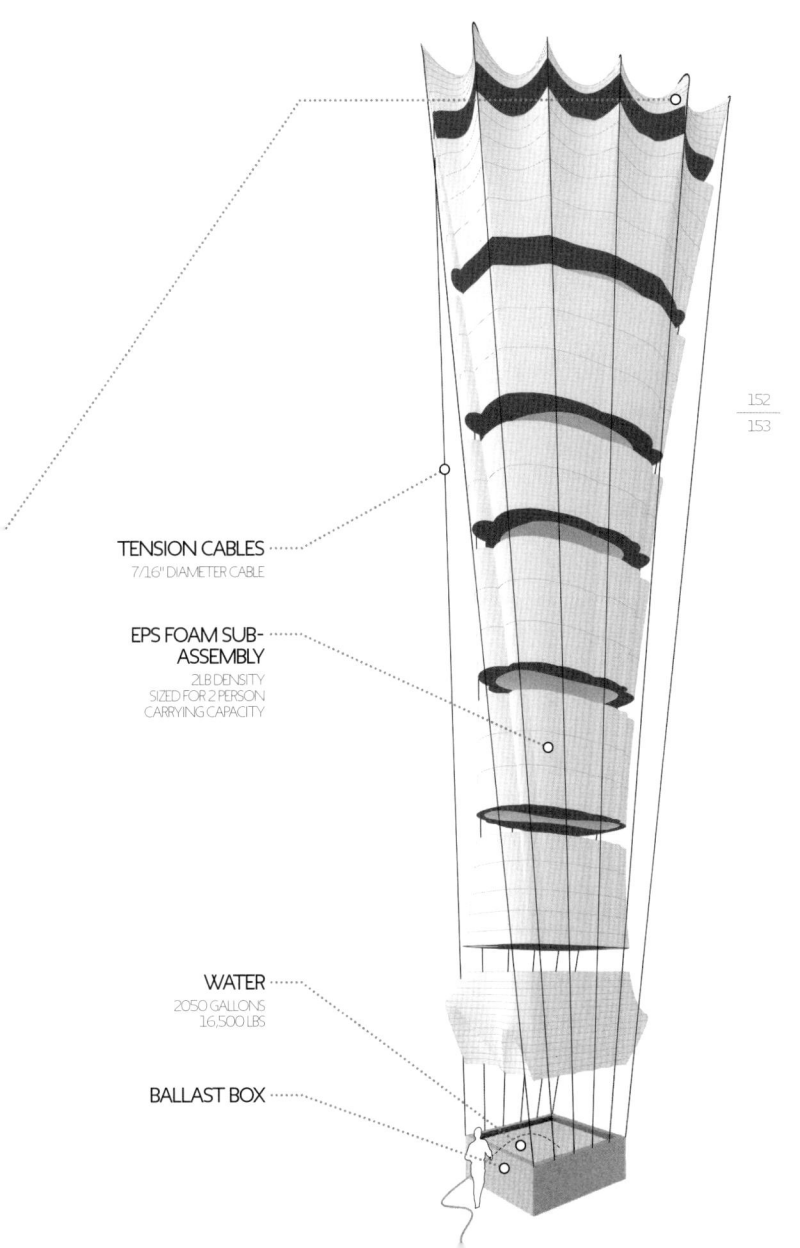

EPS FOAM SUB-ASSEMBLY
2LB DENSITY
SIZED FOR 2 PERSON
CARRYING CAPACITY

WATER
2050 GALLONS
16,500 LBS

BALLAST BOX

152
153

In an effort to test this theory we searched for a competition that would allow us to control the process of fabrication and assembly. The 10up competition called for large-scale installation proposal to serve as signage for the week-long *'Modern Atlanta'* event while addressing contemporary architectural concerns. More to the point, a series of stringent parameters needed to be addressed.
- Fabrication in less than 1 month
- Completion for less than $5,000
- 10'x10' maximum footprint.
- Installation on-site in less than 24 hrs.

There was a strange omission from these regulations -- a height restriction. As one might suspect, other entries remained in a 10' cube volume setting. at 50', 'Periscope' stood out as one of the most ambitious of proposals.

At first glance, the tower appears to be a tensile fabric pulled vertically by compressive rods, similar perhaps to a deployable tent. In fact, the tower functions in opposition to that initial reading. Where the eye reads tensile fabric, the tower is in fact compressive foam, and the rods in fact perform as tensile cables. This rhetorical inversion invites spectators in for closer inspection to find the tower is not constructed of thin surfaces at all, but rather carved from solid blocks of EPS foam. Upon discovering this illusion, the spectator is offered a glimpse into the means and methods of fabrication that make the tower possible. Though it has been cut by a robotic hotwire, the logic of this installation is in fact closer to stone masonry than to laser cut panels. The 500+ custom carved foam blocks stack in a running bond. The interior and exterior surface of the volume kiss at a minimum of 4" in the center of the tower but are free to expand and depart from each other via an internal poché that no-one minds. After all it is just foam!

TOP OF TOWER
ELEVATION 50' - 0"

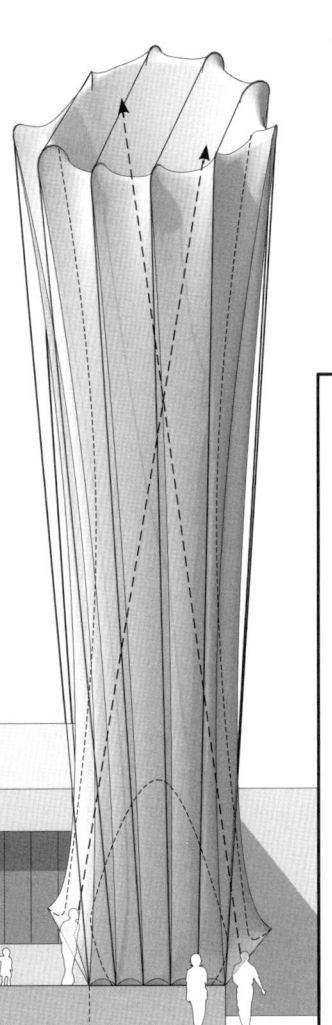

154
155

TOP OF BALLAST
ELEVATION 3' - 6"

GROUND
ELEVATION 0' - 0"

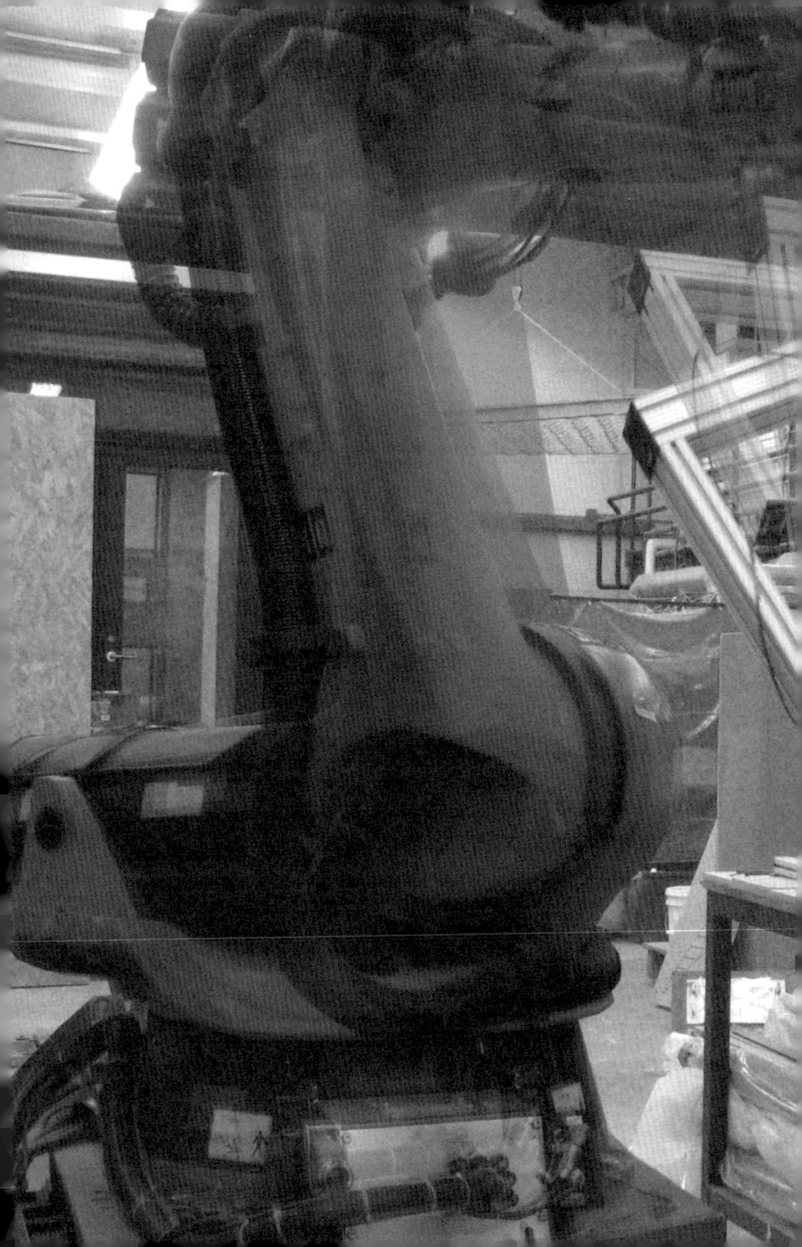

Custom 7-axis Robotic Hot-wire Cutter

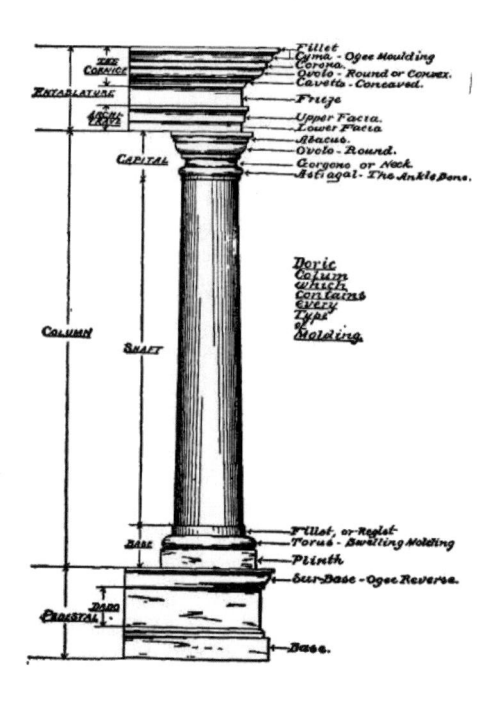

The tower was installed in just 6 hours and remained in place for a full week of events. Afterward the structure was dismantled and now awaits its next manifestation.

CREDITS

Design Team: Brandon Clifford, Wes McGee, Dave Pigram

Structural: Matthew Johnson

Build Team: Brandon Clifford, Wes McGee, Maciej Kaczynski, Johanna Lobdell, Deniz McGee, Kris Walters

158 / 159

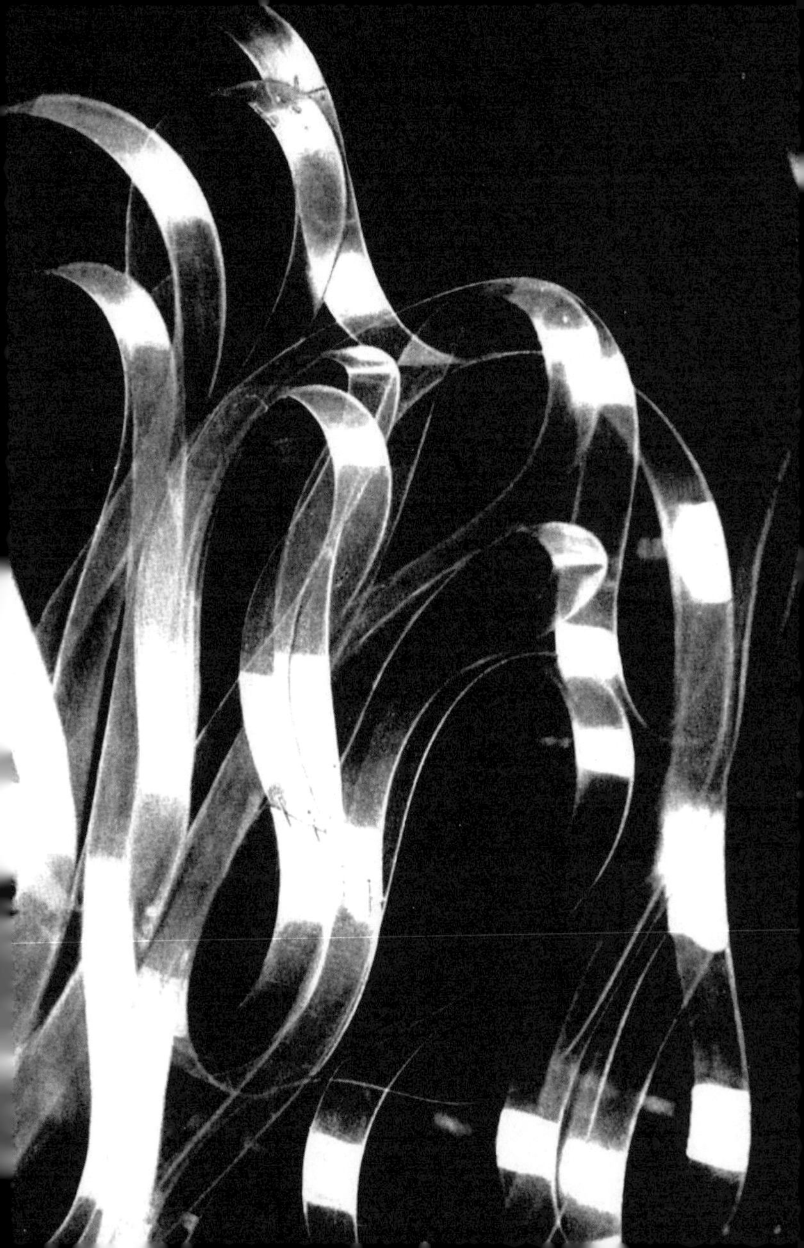

Almanacco Letterario Bompiani: Le applicazioni dei calcolatori elettronici alle scienze morali e alla letteratura, (1962) 175-188.

THE FORM OF DISORDER*
(LA FORMA DEL DISORDINE)

UMBERTO ECO
TRANSLATED, WITH NOTES AND INTRODUCTION, BY BRITT EVERSOLE [1]

Whereas Abraham Moles said it more succinctly — "Permutational art is inscribed in filigree on the technological era"[2] — Umberto Eco's theories regarding the effects of industry, communication and computation on cultural forms were among the most influential of the 1960s. His seminal book Opera Aperta (Open Work) *highlights predilections for indeterminacy in modern literature, music and the visual arts, granting artists and audiences increasing autonomy in performing and consuming works of art. Observing that much postwar experimentation precluded determinate form, he theorized that neo-avant-garde practices undermine singular meaning and foreground participation, yielding incompletion and multiplicity: techniques such as seriality, discontinuity, and interaction destabilize a work's permanence and objecthood, forging between audience and text a dialectic grounded less in semantics than in communicating and receiving information.[3]*

For the 1962 exhibition Arte Programmata (Programmed Art), *Bruno Munari and Eco brought together Italian artists of this "new tendency," such as Enzo Mari and the collectives Gruppo N and Gruppo T. The show celebrated practices that were "beyond the Informal": artwork that employed kinetics, interaction and the aleatory*

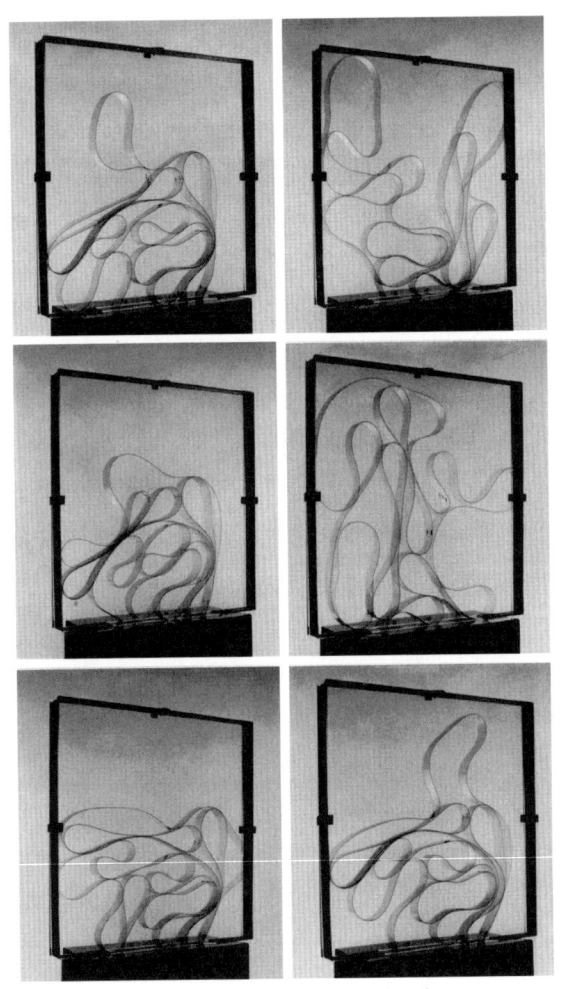

FIGURE 1: Gianni Colombo, "*strutturazione fluida.*" A long ribbon of transparent plastic constantly changes shape under the influence of a motor-driven pulley in the sculpture's base.

that demonstrated, rather than simulated, transformation and entropy.[4] *Neither a style nor a movement,* Arte Programmata *implied an operation: "Art can be programmed: from precise programming arises a multitude of similar forms."*[5] *The efficacy of the painter's capricious hand to represent or interpret reality was waning; conjuring statistics, particle physics and popular science, the artist now delimits parameters for potential form:*[6]

> We see reality as a continuous becoming of "phenomena" that we perceive in variation. Because a reality understood in these terms has replaced a fixed and immutable reality in the consciousness of man (or only in his intuition), we recognize in the arts a new tendency to express reality in terms of its becoming.[7]

Programmed works do not transliterate nature; creatively soliciting science's images, they are interactive inscription devices which problematically figure an expanding, dynamic extra-visual reality even as they change it.

Eco's "The Form of Disorder" was his contribution to the 1962 Almanacco Letterario Bompiani, *the theme of which was "Applications of electronic calculating machines in the moral sciences and literature."*[8] *Other contributors considered topics regarding how computer "brains" work, how computation aids translation and textual analysis, histories of automation and computation, hopes for efficient data retrieval in "electronic libraries," and Italian perspectives on "the two cultures."*[9] *Also included was Nanni Balestrini's "Tape Mark," the first serial poem created with computer algorithms.*

Form and disorder have particular meaning for Eco. Form is a reflection of cultural and material processes; this is why he sometimes prefers the phrase modo di formare: *ways of forming, or "artistic technique as vision of reality."*[10] *Programmed form derives from forces and operations whose open structure implies "less a prediction of the expected than an expectation of the unpredictable."*[11]

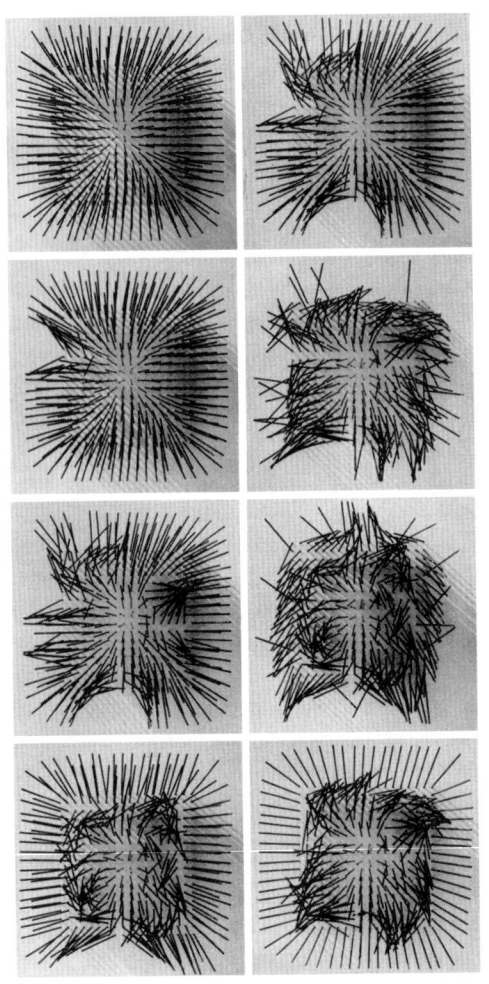

FIGURE 2: Gruppo N, *"relievo ottico-dinamico."* This piece was composed of graduated lengths of metal rods embedded in a base. The piece encourages the public to move the free ends of the rods and to change the overall composition, progressing from order to disorder.

Embodying entropy and probability, artistic research that mobilizes disorder neither signifies nor symbolizes, but communicates. "[Within] the richness of disorder, chance...[and] random processes" lie the potential of material and mathematical experimentation to elucidate the "formal possibilities of the informal, seeking to give a form, a new form, to that which was usually considered pure disorder."[12] Open works express intent but are not "easy:" apprehending information is a durational endeavor that denies the receiver the comfort of passive assumptions. Furthermore, Eco is not imposing new ideologies: his observations regarding Euclidian geometry's use-value suggest that if programmed art exhibits operative value for figuring new realities, traditional and representational forms are nonetheless relevant for explaining other aspects of human reality. There is no cultural or scientific determinism as regards art: it is always a contingent choice.

Though Opera Aperta, Arte Programmata, and "The Form of Disorder" address similar subjects, the latter presumes a general, yet literate audience. The essay exhibits Eco's trademark wordplay and agility at combining diverse discourses, from science to mythology. Like the interactive works illustrating the text, Eco invites the reader to become immersed in twisted grammar, arcane citations and unexpected imagery. Open/programmed works make one demand of spectators: play. *They provoke pleasure — even laughter. Certainly, they are "critical" —engaging popular science and mass communication, displacing privileged worldviews and disrupting perceptual and social habits.[13] Yet they refuse the polarity of either an estranged, resistant art work or a general deference to popular taste. These open and programmed works proffered a dialectic of enjoyment enveloping audiences in a quotidian and universal "field effect"[14] — in the pleasure of an open, changeable, socially revolutionary future.*

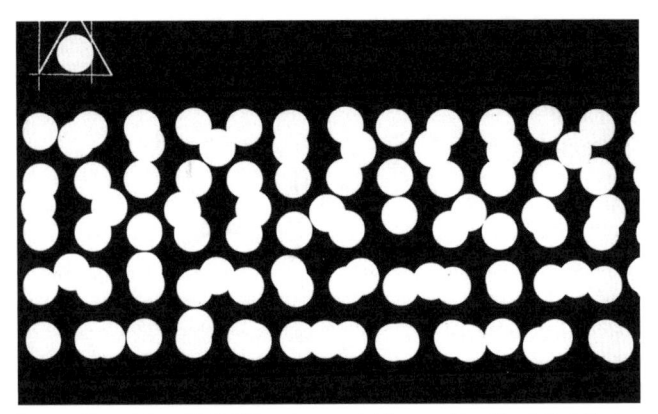

FIGURE 3: Giovanni Anceschi, *"Reticiolo complesso generata dalla sovrapposizione di due reticoli semplici, uno quadrato e una triangolare equilatero."*

FIGURE 4: Gianni Colombo, *"Superficie pulsante, N. 11"* An electric motor set the aluminum flaps of this piece in constant motion, creating changing waves and patterns.

THE FORM OF DISORDER

In the beginning there was order. And the earth was formless [*informe*] and empty. Then the spirit of God exhaled over the waters and there was Chaos. And with Chaos there was life, the immensity of possibilities, and the youthfulness of perpetual novelty and of perennial creation.

So the new cosmology (were it not distrustful of all metaphysics and had it wisely not endeavored to disown its own cosmology by identifying itself as methodology) would have to organize its creation myth, proffered such that it might find converts among the masses of simple persons and that it might carve the histories of creation on the tympani of great buildings housing electronic calculating machines. But the technicians of the new statistical cosmology remain demure and silent in the great sterile monasteries erected by the Industrial Church; and, almost out of spite toward the world, the binary signals of their great cybernetic *summae* are punched on cards. They are the Bit Generation.

And art? With great attention, outstretched antennae confusedly gather up the form of the new world in which man is dwelling and try to express it as he can and as he must through images [*figure*].[15]

Does science discover Chance? Art throws itself a *corpo morto* on Chance, and makes it its own.[16]

There is a romanticism of Chance. One madly sprays tubes of colored paint onto the canvas laid on the ground, one beats on the piano with a hammer. Chance designs its figures and the painter gathers them and identifies them as his own. Chance directs its sounds and the musician, without prejudice, welcomes them into his scales. In truth, the more he is an artist, the more he seeks aid in Chance but ultimately domesticates it, directs it, and solicits it; but he also

FIGURE 5: Bruno Munari, *"Struttura continua N. 018 smontabile e componibile in modi diversi."* As with many of Munari's pieces, this sculpture consisted of interchangeable elements to be playfully reassembled.

makes choices within it, accepts it but rejects some of it. The more he does this, the more the artist does not make his forms by chance [but instead] gives form to Chance. But even if one makes romanticism from Chance — such as in abstract expressionism, action painting, neo-dada musicals — one can, however, also get at Chance in the opposite manner: forecasting it, programming it, not choosing the products of Chance after it has happened but letting Chance play its course according to unbreakable rules of statistical probability in which maximum randomness coincides with maximum predictability.

This is a second stage of the marriage between art and Chance and we should be able to see the manifestations of it in various arts. That is, if the proposals made in these images by a group of painters (or are they painters? or programmers? or planners of form?) were not leading us to a more delimited discourse that takes its cues from their exercises in order to risk hypotheses that, however, go beyond the exercises themselves.

These artists, as one can see, assume for the most part a basic geometric formation and they subject it to rotations and permutations (just as is done in certain kinds of serial music), programming all the necessary variations and arraying all of them without discrimination. The result is a not a form, but a film of a form in motion, or, the complementary choice from among various forms.

The beginning is most rigorous: the starting point has the perfect immobility of classical forms that with mathematical dizziness drove mad the theoreticians of Divine Proportion — nothing more distant from the irresponsible freedom of informal painting. Order and geometry — they are the starting point. The point of arrival,

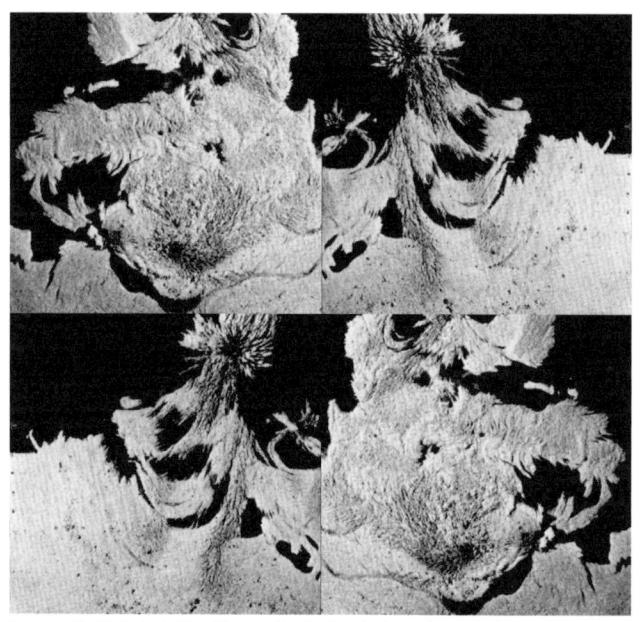

FIGURE 6: Davide Boriani, "*Superficie magnetica, N. 19.*" Boriani experimented with magnetic works, using motors to create changing patterns with metal filings.

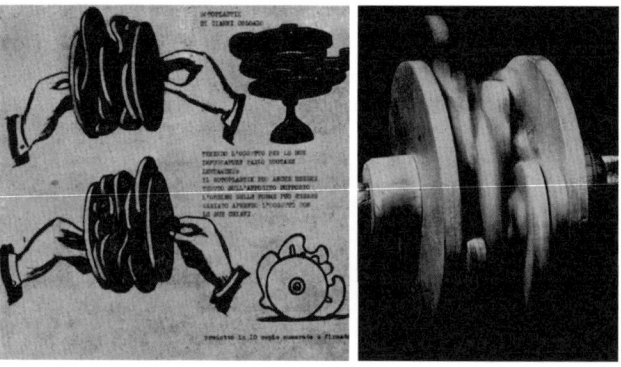

FIGURE 7: Gianni Colombo, "*Rotoplastik.*" Another of Colombo's toy-like artworks, loose pieces of wood or plastic were animated by hand.

however, no longer depends on the programmer, but belongs to that zone of freedom in which the subatomic world moves, that of statistical equiprobability. This is not only true for the subatomic world: heat passes from a body at a higher temperature to a body at a lower temperature because molecules that move at a faster speed transfer part of their velocity when they hit slower molecules. Though it is not impossible that slower molecules transfer what little velocity remains in them to faster molecules, it is statistically very improbable. Therefore molecules tend toward a state of elementary disorder that is none other than equiprobability, and that, at its limit, is mistaken for the greatest order.

The statistical programming of Chance can offer us an almost absolute regularity that arises, however, from a decision opposite to those of Pythagorean builders who sought the most optimal proportions and modules.

Thus in the experiments of these programmers we have a proportion achieved through negation, an inverted renaissance, an Unholy Disproportion, or to be more precise, a Plutonic Section. Boltzmann replaces Luca Pacioli.[17]

It is an unholy disproportion because it suspends within the indeterminate the choice of possibilities: having fixed the basic element and having programmed the permutations, the work of art lies not in the most successful element chosen from among all others, but precisely in the co-presence of all thinkable elements.

[Take for example…] the electronic poems of Nanni Balestrini.[18] With the complicity of a poet and an engineer-programmer, the IBM brain fired off more than three thousand variations of the same group of verses, trying all the possible combinations that the initial

```
MENTRE LA MOLTITUDINE    DELLE COSE    ACCADE    I CAPELLI    TRA LE LABBRA  TRENTA VOLTE  PIU
LUMINOSO   DEL SOLE   GIACQUERO     IMMOBILI  SENZA PARLARE  MALGRADO  CHE LE COSE     FIORISCANO
SI ESPANDE    RAPIDAMENTE  FINCHE NON MOSSE    LE DITA   LENTAMENTE    L ACCECANTE    GLOBO
DI FUOCO  CERCANDO  DI AFFERRARE   LA SOMMITA    DELLA NUVOLA

MENTRE LA MOLTITUDINE    DELLE COSE    ACCADE    I CAPELLI    TRA LE LABBRA  ESSE TORNANO  TUTT
E   ALLA LORO RADICE    L ACCECANTE    GLOBO   DI FUOCO   GIACQUERO    IMMOBILI   SENZA PARLARE
TRENTA VOLTE   PIU LUMINOSO   DEL SOLE  FINCHE NON MOSSE   LE DITA   LENTAMENTE    SI ESPANDE
RAPIDAMENTE   CERCANDO  DI AFFERRARE   LA SOMMITA    DELLA NUVOLA

MENTRE LA MOLTITUDINE    DELLE COSE    ACCADE   L ACCECANTE    GLOBO   DI FUOCO  ESSE TORNANO
TUTTE    ALLA LORO RADICE    SI ESPANDE    RAPIDAMENTE  FINCHE NON MOSSE     LE DITA   LENTAMENT
E    QUANDO  RAGGIUNGE  LA STRATOSFERA   GIACQUERO    IMMOBILI  SENZA PARLARE  TRENTA VOLTE  PIU
LUMINOSO   DEL SOLE  CERCANDO  DI AFFERRARE   ASSUME    LA BEN NOTA FORMA   DI FUNGO

MENTRE LA MOLTITUDINE    DELLE COSE    ACCADE   L ACCECANTE    GLOBO   DI FUOCO   GIACQUERO    IMMOBILI   SENZA PARLARE
E   ALLA LORO RADICE   L ACCECANTE   GLOBO   DI FUOCO   GIACQUERO    IMMOBILI   SENZA PARLARE
TRENTA VOLTE   PIU LUMINOSO   DEL SOLE  FINCHE NON MOSSE   LE DITA   LENTAMENTE    SI ESPANDE
RAPIDAMENTE   CERCANDO  DI AFFERRARE   LA SOMMITA    DELLA NUVOLA

MENTRE LA MOLTITUDINE    DELLE COSE    ACCADE   L ACCECANTE    GLOBO   DI FUOCO  ESSE TORNANO
TUTTE    ALLA LORO RADICE    SI ESPANDE    RAPIDAMENTE  FINCHE NON MOSSE     LE DITA   LENTAMENT
E    QUANDO  RAGGIUNGE  LA STRATOSFERA   GIACQUERO    IMMOBILI  SENZA PARLARE  TRENTA VOLTE  PIU
LUMINOSO   DEL SOLE  CERCANDO  DI AFFERRARE   ASSUME    LA BEN NOTA FORMA   DI FUNGO

LA TESTA  PREMUTA    SULLA SPALLA   TRENTA VOLTE    PIU LUMINOSO   DEL SOLE   GIACQUERO    IMMOBILI
SENZA PARLARE  ASSUME    LA BEN NOTA FORMA   DI FUNGO  FINCHE NON MOSSE     LE DITA   LENTAMENTE
L ACCECANTE     GLOBO   DI FUOCO  CERCANDO  DI AFFERRARE   SI ESPANDE    RAPIDAMENTE   I CAPELL
I    TRA LE LABBRA  QUANDO  RAGGIUNGE  LA STRATOSFERA

IO CONTEMPLO    IL LORO RITORNO    FINCHE NON MOSSE    LE DITA   LENTAMENTE    L ACCECANTE     GLO
BO   DI FUOCO  ESSE TORNANO  TUTTE     ALLA LORO RADICE    LA TESTA  PREMUTA    SULLA SPALLA   TREN
TA VOLTE    PIU LUMINOSO   DEL SOLE   GIACQUERO    IMMOBILI   SENZA PARLARE  ASSUME    LA BEN NOTA FO
RMA   DI FUNGO  I CAPELLI    TRA LE LABBRA  SI ESPANDE   RAPIDAMENTE

IO CONTEMPLO    IL LORO RITORNO    FINCHE NON MOSSE    LE DITA   LENTAMENTE    L ACCECANTE     GLO
BO   DI FUOCO  ESSE TORNANO  TUTTE     ALLA LORO RADICE    I CAPELLI    TRA LE LABBRA  TRENTA VO
LTE    PIU LUMINOSO   DEL SOLE   GIACQUERO    IMMOBILI   SENZA PARLARE  SI ESPANDE    RAPIDAMENTE
CERCANDO  DI AFFERRARE   LA SOMMITA    DELLA NUVOLA

IO CONTEMPLO    IL LORO RITORNO    FINCHE NON MOSSE    LE DITA   LENTAMENTE    L ACCECANTE     GLO
BO   DI FUOCO  ESSE TORNANO  TUTTE     ALLA LORO RADICE    I CAPELLI    TRA LE LABBRA  TRENTA VO
LTE    PIU LUMINOSO   DEL SOLE   GIACQUERO    'IMMOBILI   SENZA PARLARE  SI ESPANDE    RAPIDAMENTE
CERCANDO  DI AFFERRARE   LA SOMMITA    DELLA NUVOLA

TAPE MARK
```

FIGURE 8: (top) Nanni Balestrini, *"Tape Mark I"* - Computer punch card used for generating poem
FIGURE 9: (bottom) Nanni Balestrini, *"Tape Mark I"* - Iterations of serial poem

parameters allowed. If we go looking among the three thousand results we will find some silly ones and others (but few, it seems to me) of the highest lyrical temperature,[19] which we would not have hesitated to attribute to a human brain. But herein is precisely the error: sitting at the table by himself, Balestrini would probably have been capable of obtaining these few, highly selective results. Having chosen the verses, little stops us from putting them together in the most organized manner, "in the manner of," or in harmony with certain currents of taste. The work of the electronic brain and the validity of that work (which is, if nothing else, experimental and provocative), consist precisely in the fact that there are three thousand poems and it is necessary to read all of them together. The whole work resides in its variations, or rather, in its variability. The electronic brain has made an attempt at creating an "open work". . . the work of art resides not in one of its variants but in the co-presence of all variants.

As such these experiments are aligned with many others, and through all of them contemporary art realizes one of its principle functions: providing for contemporary man imaginative translations of the natural reality that science explains to him.

In this world that has learned to vortically free itself in the heart of those same atomic nuclei according to non-laws susceptible to hypotheses only through methodological models of indeterminacy and complementarity (or imaginable by default through paradoxes of topology), contemporary man is still constrained to "imagine" in Aristotelian terms, because in this way they refer him to the illustrated pages of *La Domenica del Corriere* or of comics, or films and commercial novels. He is aware that under his feet is an unimaginable microcosm but he must still think of it in macrocosmic terms. Nor is it bad that he does this, because if I have to measure my bedroom for a new dresser, it is still useful to refer to the canon of Euclidian

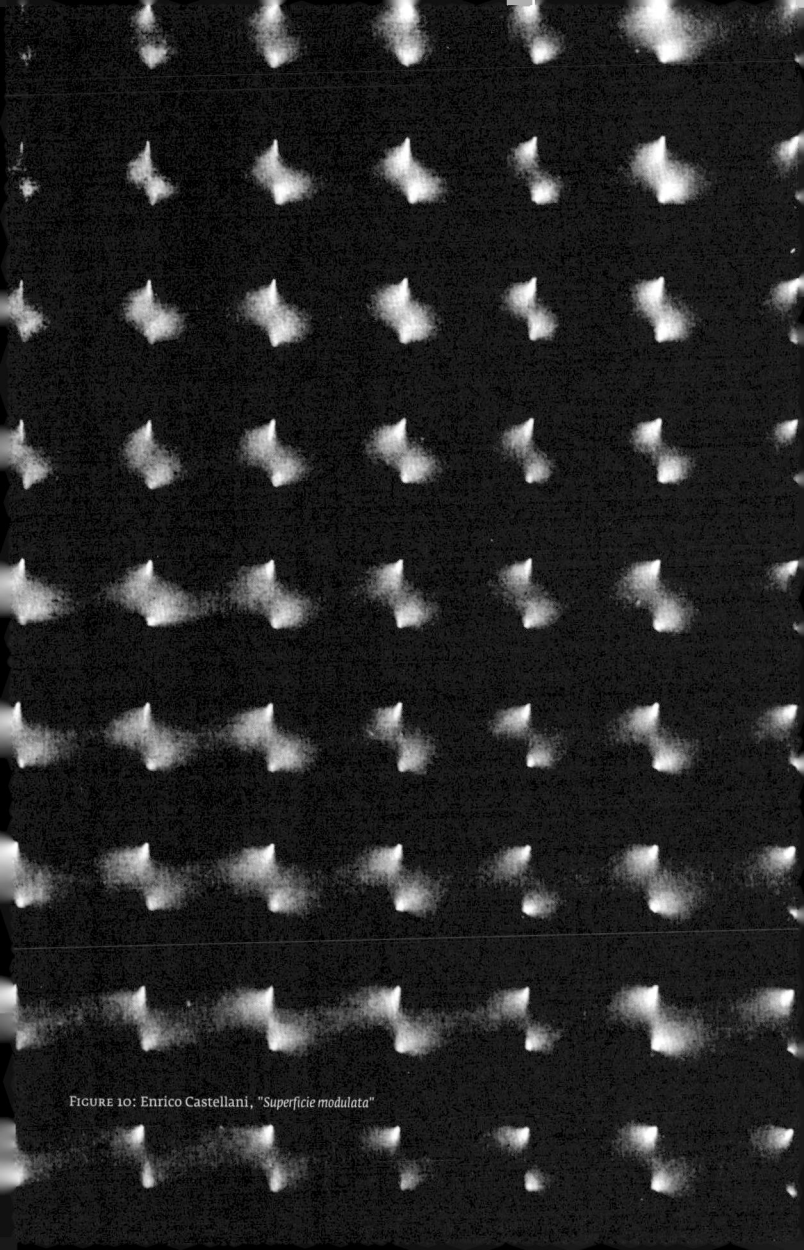

FIGURE 10: Enrico Castellani, *"Superficie modulata"*

geometry even if I know all too well that it is no more true or false than non-Euclidian geometries. Nevertheless, I still must be capable of "seeing" the universe that is growing within me as very different from the universe of yesterday.

Today the punctilious and impeccable exercises of these arithmetic mystics try to furnish us the imaginative structures with which to conceive the world that contemporary reason built long ago and that is described in the propositional functions of symbolic logic or in the differential equations with which one expresses the changing perspectivalisms of our measurements in space-time.

Oh, we know it well! Space-time and the universe are very important things, whereas these [works of art] are games, not always but often made for play, and ultimately at a certain point they change the realities they wish to express (or don't wish to express, or don't know how to express). But what does this have to do with anything? We are not making a critique of art here, we are taking the pulse of the era. The lucid folly of Bruno Munari's[20] "Cybernetic Perturbation" has, in the end, one incontrovertible justification, unsuspected because it "grows well." It justifies itself with the formula: *art imitates nature*. Except that in this case art does not imitate the nature that through our perceptive habits we see every day, but that which conceptually we define in a laboratory. And therefore "nature" is meant in the only correct sense possible: art imitates not nature, but our modes of determining and defining nature. It imitates our operative relation to nature, it imitates nature as a possible object of our definition that knows how to define non-definitively.

Turn your eyes to "Cybernetic Perturbation:" allow them to slowly flow [over the work], begin the game of these rotating rods,[21] let yourself be captivated by this perfect graphic symbol just like that

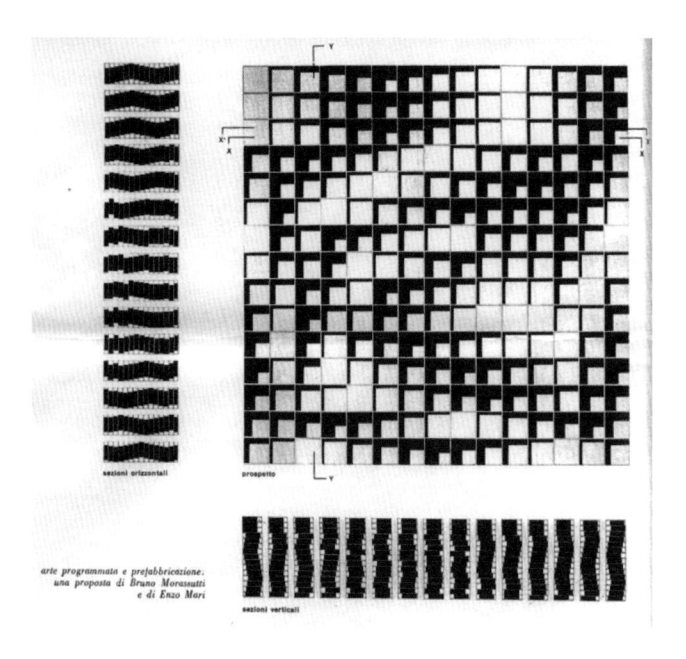

FIGURE 11: Bruno Morassutti and Enzo Mari, *"Arte programmata e prefabbricazione."* Architect Morassutti collaborated with Mari to apply the sculptor's mathematical patterns to the design of a building with a constantly varied envelope condition, to be built from prefabricated components.

symbol of the serpent that chews its own tail, given that the final position coincides with the beginning and the word with which the graphic discourse begins joins itself with that with which it terminates. Enter into this finite and limitless space curve. And now try to look away, to rest your gaze on a single detail. You will no longer succeed; you will be swept into the dance of the provisional and the relative; you will accumulate information that does not correlate to a singular meaning but to the totality of possible meanings; you will not receive a message but the possibility of many co-present messages. And you will no longer find reassuring coordinates that show you the high and the low, the right and the left. The cosmos explodes, expands, expands . . . and where will it come to an end? The observer of the renaissance perspective was a good Cyclops who put his only eye up to the slot of a magic box in which he saw the world from the only point of view possible. The man of Munari is forced to have a thousand eyes on the nose, the neck, the shoulders, the fingers and the buttocks. And thus he turns restless in a world that bombards him with stimuli assaulting him from all sides.

Through the programmatic wisdom of the exact sciences an unquiet dweller of an *expanding universe* reveals himself.

I am not saying that this is a beautiful history. It is History.

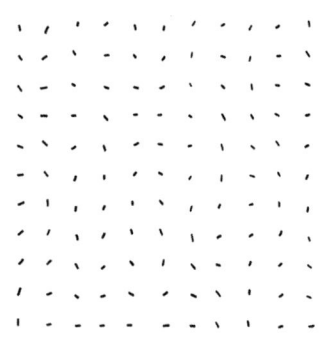

FIGURE 12: Bruno Munari, *"Perturbazione cibernetica"*

NOTES

1 I thank Daria Ricchi and Alicia Imperiale for their suggestions, criticism and assistance with the translation.

2 Abraham A. Moles, "Vasarely and the Triumph of Structuralism," *Form*, No.7, (1968) 25. See also Abraham Moles. *Information Theory and Aesthetic Perception*. (Urbana: University of Illinois Press, 1966) (first published in French in 1958). Primarily associated with the *Hochschule für Gestaltung*, Ulm, Moles was one of the leading theorists of intersections between the graphic arts, aesthetics and information theory.

3 Umberto Eco, *Opera Aperta*. (Milano: Casa Editrice Valentino Bompiani, 1962) English translation: *The Open Work*. (Cambridge: Harvard University Press, 1989). The thinking in *Opera Aperta* is a product of Eco's engagement with contemporary art practices, and information theory, communication theory and cybernetics; it precedes his semiotic phase. *Opera Aperta* became the theoretical manifesto of the neo-avant-garde *Gruppo '63*, a loose knit collective of writers and artists who sought new forms of textual expression and social engagement, drawing influence from communication theory, structuralism and Marxism.

4 Bruno Munari and Umberto Eco, *Arte Programmata*. (Milano: La Direzione Pubblicità della Società Olivetti, 1962). Munari curated the show and Eco intellectualized the work. The emphasis on kinetic, interactive and durational art pieces was a Continental phenomenon, inconceivable without cross-border dialogues. The roots of *Arte Programmata* pass through generations of European Constructivism as well as interwar *Astrattismo* and postwar *Arte Concreta*. The primary contacts around 1960 were the German group Zero (especially Hans Haacke, Heinz Mack and Otto Piene) and the Parisian GRAV (especially Julio Le Parc). The terms "l'oltre informale" and "dopo l'informale" demonstrate that in the early 60s, this work was seen in contradistinction to Art Informel, Tachism, and Abstract Expressionism. See the catalog to the San Marino Biennale of 1963 "L'oltre l'informale." See also Lea

Vergine. *Arte Programmata e cinetica: l'ultima avanguardia*. (Milano: Mazzotta, 1983). The work of Italian artists was also called "Nuova Tendenza" (the New Tendency). Gruppo N: Alberto Biasi, Ennio Chiggio, Toni Costa, Edoardo Landi and Manfredo Massironi; Gruppo T: Gianni Anceschi, Davide Boriani, Gianni Colombo, Gabriele Devecchi, and Grazia Varisco).

5 Eco, *Arte Programmata*, n.p.

6 It is not surprising that one finds references at this very moment to "parametric design" in architecture, such as in the work of Luigi Moretti and his Institute for Mathematical and Operative Research on Urbanism.

7 Gruppo T, "Dichiarazione del Gruppo T," *Arte Programmata*, n.p.

8 The *Almanacco Letterario Bompiani* was founded in the 'thirties, discontinued during the war and reissued in the late 'fifties. Postwar issues were edited by Valentino Bompiani and film theorist and writer Cesare Zavattini.

9 See C. P. Snow, *The Two Cultures and the Scientific Revolution: The Rede Lecture*. (Cambridge: The Cambridge University Press, 1959). Snow's text posits a divide between the scientific discourses and the arts and literature.

10 Umberto Eco, "Del modo di formare come impegno sulla realtà," *Il menabò*, No. 5, (1962) 198.

11 Eco, *Opera Aperta*, 125; *The Open Work*, 80 -- Italics Eco's. We are maintaining the English translation's use of expected and unexpected. The original terms are *previsione* and *imprevisto*: foresight and the unforeseeable.

12 Eco, *Arte Programmata*, n.p.

13 "gruppo n gruppo t ed enzo mari," *Marcatrè*, No. 1 (November 1963) 29-30.

14 Paolo Bonaiuto, "L'esperienza estetica come 'effetto di campo,'" *Lineastruttura*, No. 1 (1966) 58-60.

15 We have translated *figura*, depending on the context, as either *figure* or *image*; *figura* also can mean *representation*, *illustration* or *shape*. By using figura, Eco solicits all these meanings to point to *Arte Programmata's* problematic representation of nature.

16 *A corpo morto*: literally a dead body, but the meaning here suggests that art plops down, like a heavy body on a sofa.

17 Ludwig Boltzmann [1844-1906], physicist and statistical mathematician best known for his theories of gasses according to the second law of thermodynamics. Luca Pacioli [1446?-1517] mathematician and monk, known for teaching math to Da Vinci.

18 Nanni Balestrini [1935-] - artist, poet and author, member of *Gruppo '63*.

19 Eco's choice of temperatura is likely a poetic gesture to his earlier discussion regarding the loss of thermodynamic heat.

20 Bruno Munari [1907-1998] - Italian artist and writer. Best known in America for his children's books, mobiles and toys, Munari, a former second generation Futurist, was also associated with *Arte Concreta*. His interest in constructivism and kinetic art ranks him among the most influential Italian artists of the twentieth century.

21 Eco uses the word *bastoncello*, which means *rods* as in rods and cones, the eye's photoreceptors. *Bastoncello* is also a stick-fighting game.

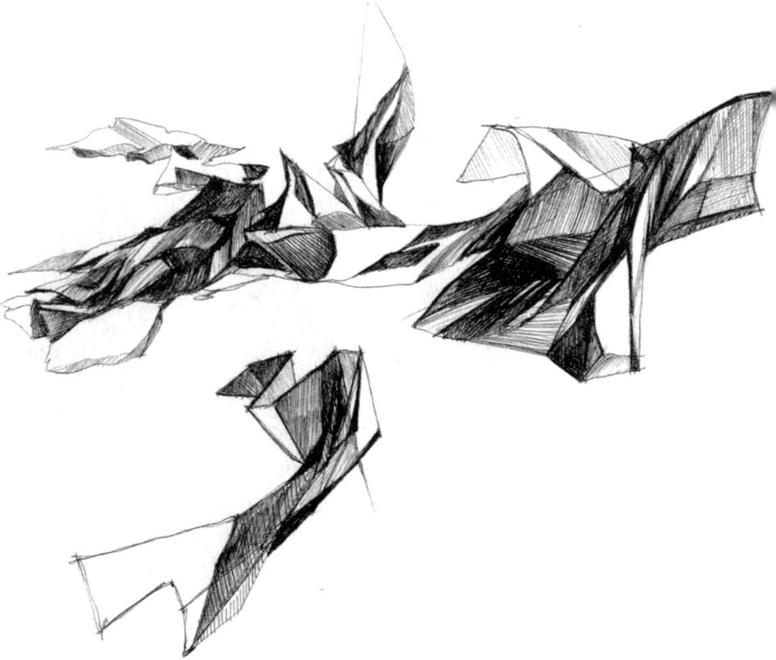

UNTITLED

BRYONY ROBERTS

These drawings are an attempt to imagine space outside of architectural practice. Rather than originating in a techtonic, programmatic, or contextual framework, they emerge one line at a time. Each line creates a tension with the one before, and these lines build local oscillations in light and depth. The local tensions generate the overall organization, rather than an a priori composition. With this process, I can discover spaces that turn themselves inside out in ways that I could not have predicted. In the end, the forms often resemble storm clouds, water, or rock formations, but only accidentally - perhaps because these natural occurrances offer a kind of varied spatial organization that is easier to discover intuitively than rationally.

182
183

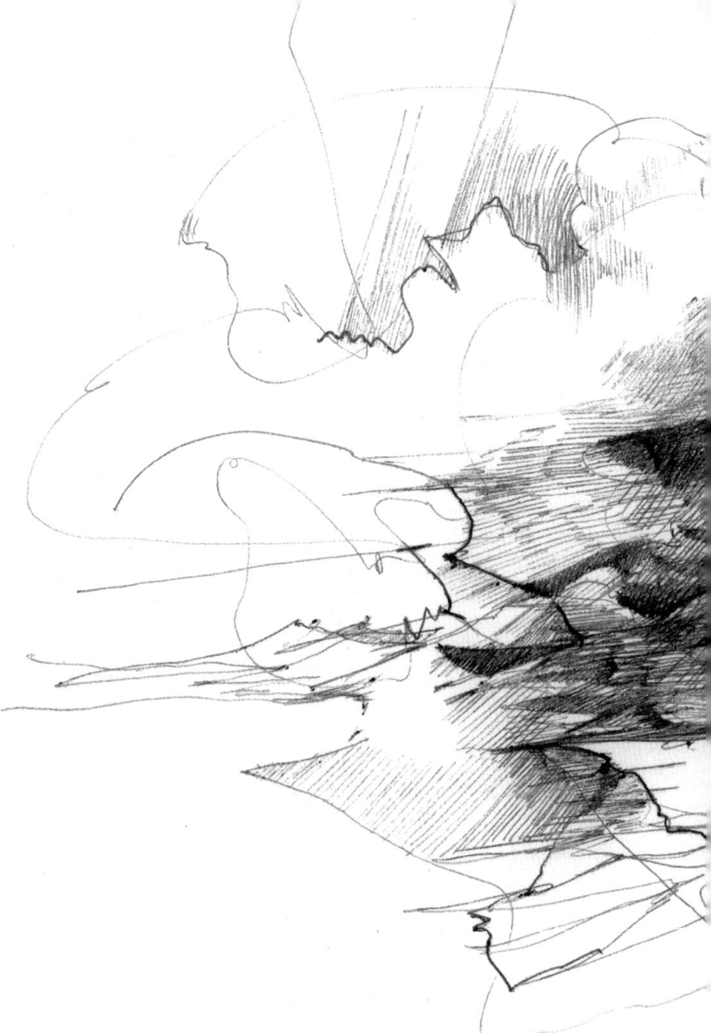

184
185

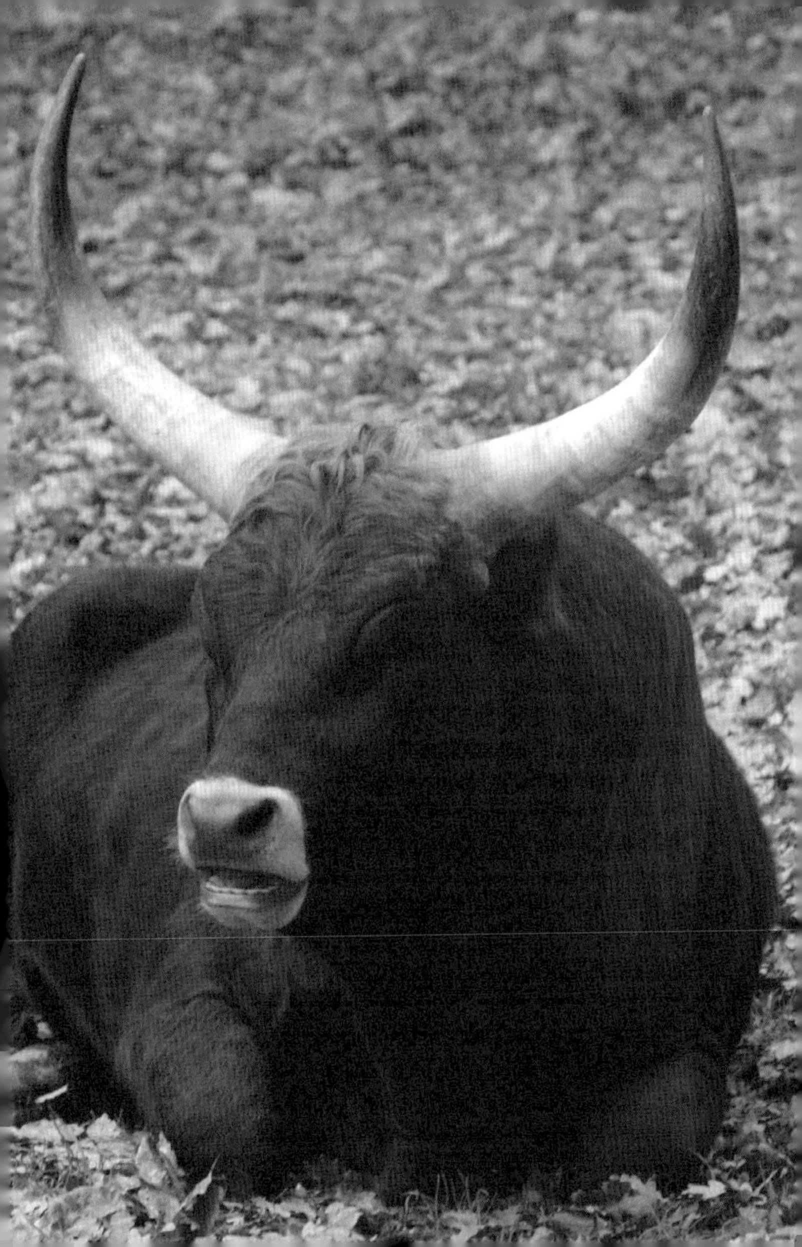

(left) Image of the modern Heck Cattle.

RE-CREATING THE PRIMEVAL WILDERNESS
THE CASE OF THE AUROCHS

JOSEPH CLAGHORN

A few miles to the west of the new Dutch town of Almere is a 30 square kilometer nature preserve known as the Oostvaardersplassen, home to the largest worldwide population of Heck cattle, an obscure bovine breed. Upon observing this large herbivore in its strange habitat, one could be forgiven if the image conjured is of primeval wilderness, perhaps of the Serengeti, and not of a recently contrived animal on newly constructed ground. Nevertheless, far from being a remnant of a former age, this animal and the landscape it shapes are both products of the ideology and science of the 20th century while illuminating the potentials, challenges, and ethical concerns of ecological planning and landscape design in the 21st.

The Heck cattle's story goes back to the year 1627, when the last recorded aurochs, the fearsome ancestor to the docile domestic cow, died in Poland's Jaktorów forest. The aurochs was a creature of legend, found in the ancient cave paintings of Magdalenian, Lascaux and Altamira and associated with 𐤁 (the second character in the

Germanic runic alphabet). It was admired by Caesar as a dangerous animal just below the elephant in size, encountered only on the wild fringes of civilization and empire. The beast's extinction in some ways marked the end of the primordial European wilderness and signaled the consolidation of human domination of the European continent. The effort to save the aurochs and the subsequent failure of the endeavor can also be regarded as one of the earliest projects and earliest disappointments of the modern conservation movement. After a centuries long preservation campaign in one of Poland's largest and most remote royal hunting preserves, the aurochs faded into memory.[1] A once noble species was lost forever—or was it?

In the 1920s, German cattle breeders began a program to breed-back the aurochs from the genes found in domestic cattle. The assumption was that while the beast itself had become extinct, pieces of its genetic makeup were still alive in the numerous strains of cattle throughout the world and could be reassembled through a careful breeding program. After years of effort, the resulting breed, known as Heck cattle, closely resembled descriptions of the aurochs in temperament, shape and coloring, but not yet in overall size. This 'reconstructed aurochs' was also able to survive quite well in the wild without human assistance, unlike many breeds of domestic cattle. The effort to re-create the aurochs, however, has not been without considerable controversy. Although conceived and initiated before the rise of the National Socialist Party, in Germany, the program was heartily endorsed and encouraged by the Nazis in the 1930s and 1940s. The project fit in all too well with the Nazi propaganda machine's goals of recreating an idealized Teutonic state cleansed of degenerate and inferior races and hearkening back to a heroic and mythologized past. The lands cleared by war, ethnic cleansing, and genocide would become the hunting grounds of the master race, and the aurochs would be their quarry.[2]

Cave Paintings of Aurochs *Lascaux Caves*.

With the defeat of the Nazis, the Heck cattle's fate appeared to be sealed as well, and many of their populations were destroyed, either intentionally or through neglect. The breed no longer served a purpose in the sociopolitical climate of postwar Europe. Within a few decades, however, the reconstructed aurochs found an ideal niche in one of the most unlikely of places. With the completion of the polder of Flevoland in the 1960s, the Netherlands completed its last major reclamation of land from the sea. The small fragment of the polder that was to become known as the Oostvaardersplassen was originally intended for housing, very much along the lines of the land around nearby Almere, but when a downturn in the real estate market halted development, nature quickly began to take over. Within a few short years, the area became an important wetland and nesting site for migratory birds, and its potential value as an ecological preserve was quickly realized. In order to continue functioning as a nesting site for birds, however, a strategy had to be developed in order to prevent natural processes of succession from occurring which would otherwise quickly convert the wetland into forest. It was here that the Heck cattle found a suitable home. Much as the ancient aurochs, the ideal ecological niche for the reconstructed aurochs was not on the dry plains of Central Europe nor in the forests of Poland, but rather in the swampy grasslands that had largely been drained and converted to agricultural use throughout the Middle Ages.[3] With the only recent reversal in the attitude that the only good swamp is a drained swamp, the wild cow could once again have a home, and through their activity, help provide a home for the millions of birds that also depend on the wetlands. The disturbance caused by the constant grazing of land by herbivores such as the Heck cattle plays a vital role in maintaining the open character of European wetlands like the Oostvaardersplassen.[4]

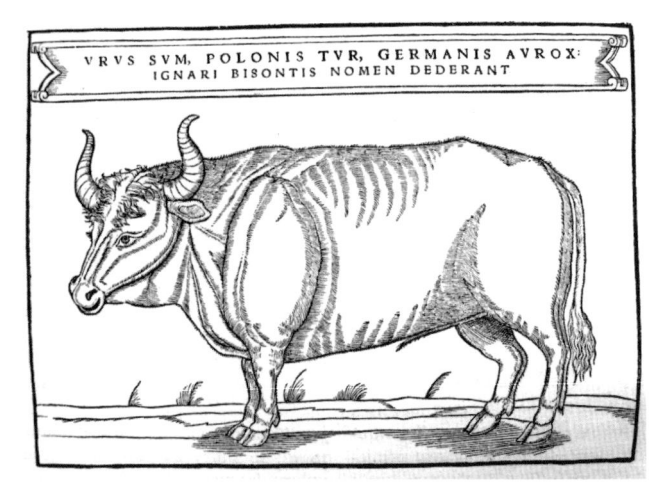

Polish woodcut from around the time of the auruchs extinction depicts a robust yet sad species much reduced in vigor and vitality from the beast depicted in Lascaux. Translation of Latin text: I'm Urus, in Polish *Tur*, in German *Aurox*. The ignorant call me bison. Sigismund von Herberstein, *Rerum Moscoviticarum Commentarii*, 1556.

Much as the efforts to save the aurochs nearly 400 years ago predate a broader and well-developed conservation movement, the efforts in Flevoland herald an incipient movement to not only conserve and protect pieces of nature from human encroachment, but to actually restore and create nature as an end in and of itself. Even as the human ecological footprint continues to expand into the planet's last wildernesses and as pristine nature fades into distant memory, ecologists, land planners, and landscape architects are becoming increasingly aware of the necessity of recreating and reconnecting the increasingly fragmented habitat of the planet's non-human species. Key to this effort have been the writings of ecologist Richard Forman, who has made a career out of analyzing ecosystems that have been severely compromised by human encroachment, rather than ecosystems in an idealized state free from human interference. Inspired by his writings, especially his book *Land Mosaics*,[5] numerous proposals have been made to link isolated islands of biodiversity known as 'patches' with corridors for species dispersal and migration. Such corridors have been demonstrated to be essential to preserve biodiversity in the long term and are essential to the long term prospects of many species, especially the mega fauna which are poster children of many conservation efforts. Despite the increased understanding of the importance of local and regional networks of connected habitat, however, most of these proposals have not been able to move forward.

To understand why such projects face a difficult future, it is useful to return once more to the Oostvaardersplassen and the reconstructed aurochs. The notion of connecting fragmented islands of habitat into a broader ecological network underlies a planned proposal to expand the Oostvaardersplassen reserve and connect it first to the nearby Horsterwold, and then to the forests of the central portion of the Netherlands and into Germany. The proposed 10 km long and 1.5 km wide link, known as the Oostvaarderswold, would first and foremost be a reserve and migratory path for animals such as Heck cattle.[6] The only problem is the land designated for the undertaking is currently owned by some 22 farmers, who have shown no willingness to sell their land back to the province, or to take farmland elsewhere as compensation for the lands they have lost to the project. This reluctance to move on the part of the farmers, despite the fact that the recently reclaimed ground that they occupy has not been in their families for countless generations, and is only maintained above the water-table through an ongoing and expensive public works investment, hints at the difficulty in realigning the bounds of human occupation in other areas where a deep generational connection to the land *is* felt, and where the landscape is maintained not as part of a broader public works effort, but through the considerable efforts of the farmer himself. In other words, if the state cannot evict a landowner from artificial ground, how can it evict a landowner from ground that has existed since time immemorial? In the past, the state has been able to justify such evictions with the logic that they serve a greater public interest. As the rights of the individual are held in ever greater regard, however, especially in the west, the burden of justifying this greater public interest with regards to property seizure has become increasingly heavy.

It is here, too, that an understanding of the dark side of the history of the auroch's extinction and subsequent reconstruction becomes useful. An oft leveled criticism of the conservation movement is that it seeks to protect resources for an elite few at the expense of progress, particularly at the lower ends of the social spectrum. A classic illustration of this point might be the injunction against hunting the wild aurochs by all excepting the king of Poland himself. In order to preserve the aurochs as game for the current and future kings (a right which the kings rarely exercised), poaching was strictly prohib-

Scale comparison of the Aurochs

ited and punishable by death. The locals were not able to graze their cattle on the royal lands, lest they interfere with the aurochs, even in times of scarcity or famine. And despite all these efforts to protect the beast as the exclusive preserve of the king himself, the effort in the end proved to be a failure.[7] In a similar vein, critics of the Endangered Species Act in the United States point to the fact that few efforts to save species have succeeded, all while personal liberties and rights have been infringed upon. Where critics of the conservation movement are most vocal in their opposition is when the right to personal property is infringed upon, especially where humans are evicted to make way for environmental conservation. The comparison between environmentalists and Nazis is often made, with the accusation that the most extreme environmentalists advocate the genocide of the whole or portions of the human race in order to make way for wilds and game parks. While such inflammatory rhetoric can hardly be considered accurate, and unfairly demeans the usually well-intentioned efforts of conservation projects, the grain of truth beneath it often dooms ecological land-planning efforts to failure.

Balancing the legitimate rights of individual landowners against what is increasingly seen as the legitimate rights of animal species is a problem which cannot be easily solved through the conventional, rigid master-plan. In order for such efforts to succeed, a much more malleable and strategic approach must be adopted. In a speculative project for restoring Buffalo habitat in Detroit Michigan, a team led by Christian Werthmann analyzed the collapsing real estate market in Detroit to devise a strategic system for filling the voids in the urban fabric with an interconnected system of Buffalo grazing habitat in the heart of the city, mediating blight with an ever-evolving game reserve that is not the province of the elite, but of the disenfranchised.[8] The proposal is not dependent on any specific lot becoming vacant, and such a network could conceivably grow and contract with local fluctuations in the cities' property market. It is here that the work of Richard Forman and ecologists meets the currently fashionable discourse surrounding parametrics in architecture and design. A digital model designed to deal with the complexity of ecological networks alongside the complexity of local real estate markets (along with other potential networks) could replace the masterplan, searching for opportunities to create a new hybrid ecology, and warning all interested parties when certain critical thresholds that threaten the overall system are being approached.

In much the same way that the aurochs was reconstructed through a managed manipulation of DNA over time for a combination of ideological and ecological reasons, we are potentially entering an era where the DNA of the human/natural ecology becomes the province of designers, where large and complex spatial systems are consciously manipulated for social, economic, or environmental ends while simultaneously preserving the rights of the individual to variance within the greater framework without endangering the whole project. Such manipulations can occur at a variety of scales, but as always, countless ethical questions will be generated at every step of the way. To put it simply, though, the question we have to answer as designers, and as a society, is if artificial ecologies and animals like the reconstructed aurochs have a place in the contemporary world, or if we should let them gracefully pass into the abyss of history?

NOTES

1   Rockosz, Mieczyslaw. "History of the Aurochs (Bos taurus primigenius) in Poland." *Animal Genetic Resources Information*, Vol. 16, (Rome: Food and Agriculture Organization of the United Nations, 1995).

2   Bruxelles, Simon de. "A shaggy cow story: how a Nazi experiment brought extinct aurochs to Devon." *The Times*, 22 April 2009.

3   Vuure, Cis van. *Retracing the Aurochs*. (Moscow: Pensoft Publishers, 2005).

4   Vera, F.W.M. *Grazing Ecology and Forest History*. (Oxford: CABI Publishing, 2000).

5   Forman, Richard T.T. *Land Mosaics*. (New York: Cambridge University Press, 1995).

6   "OostvaardersWold: Samen werken aan nieuwe natuur en recreatie in Flevoland" Provincie Flevoland, Feb. 2009.

7   Rockosz, Mieczyslaw. "History of the Aurochs (Bos taurus primigenius) in Poland." *Animal Genetic Resources Information*, Vol. 16, (Rome: Food and Agriculture Organization of the United Nations, 1995).

8   Werthmann, Christian, Leor Lovinger and Kelly Spokus. "Shrinking Cities, Detroit Michigan." International Design Comeptition, 2004.

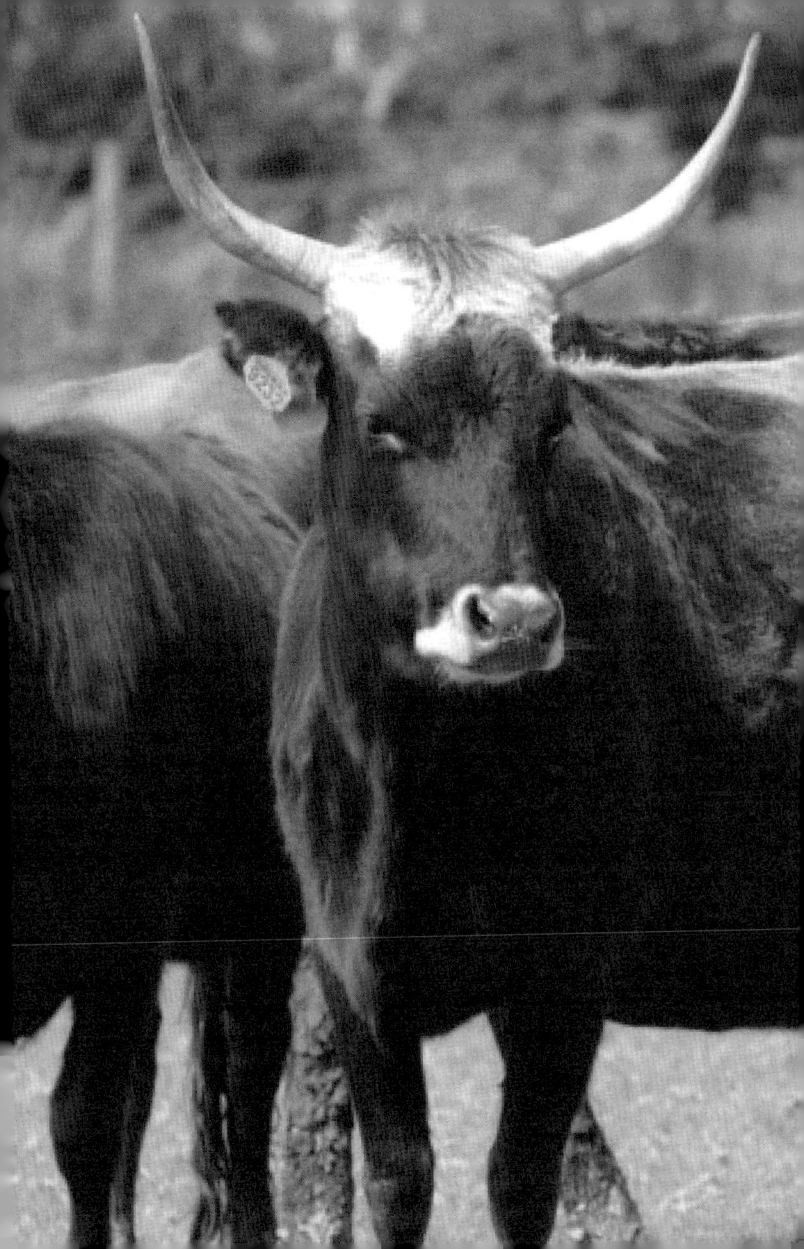

196
197

COMMERCIAL DISTRICT #1 (Noah's Ark Spaceship)

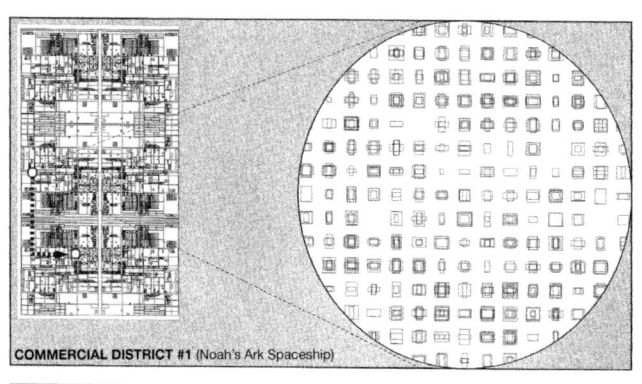

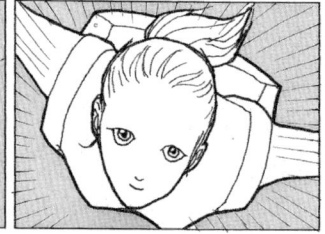

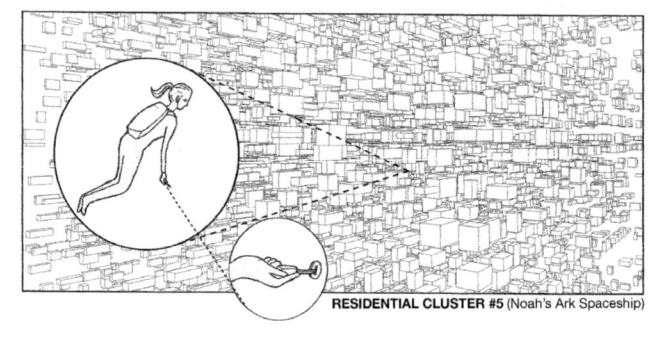

RESIDENTIAL CLUSTER #5 (Noah's Ark Spaceship)

OBSTRUCTION

JIMENEZ LAI

what are you doing?
NEW!
super-furniture
extravaganza!
fits most
homes
hey honey!
you're home!
look what I got?

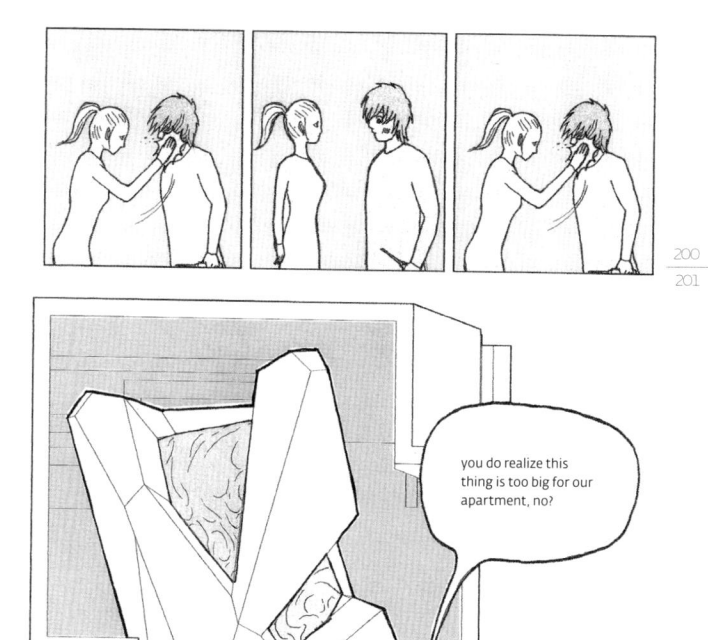

you do realize this thing is too big for our apartment, no?

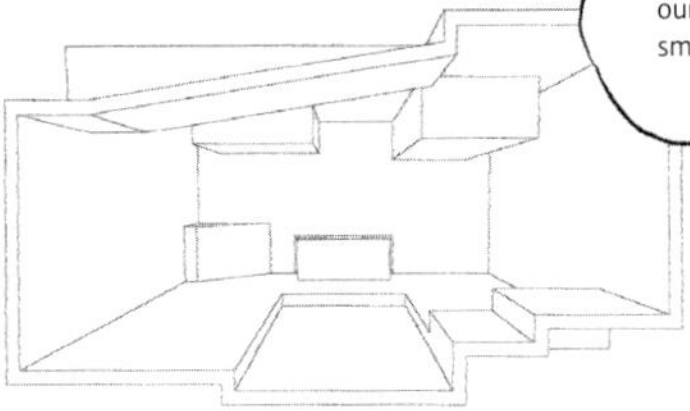

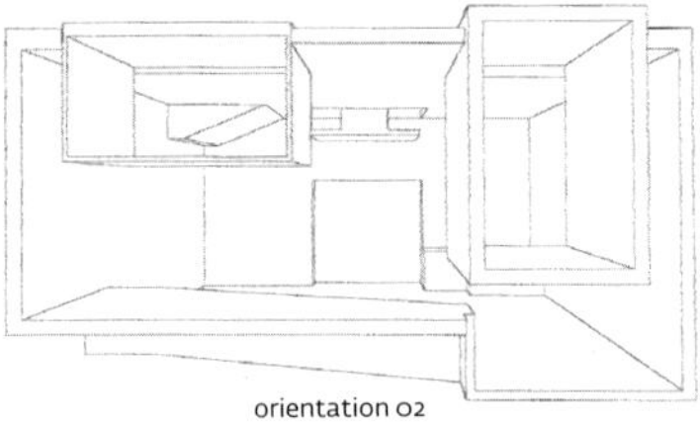

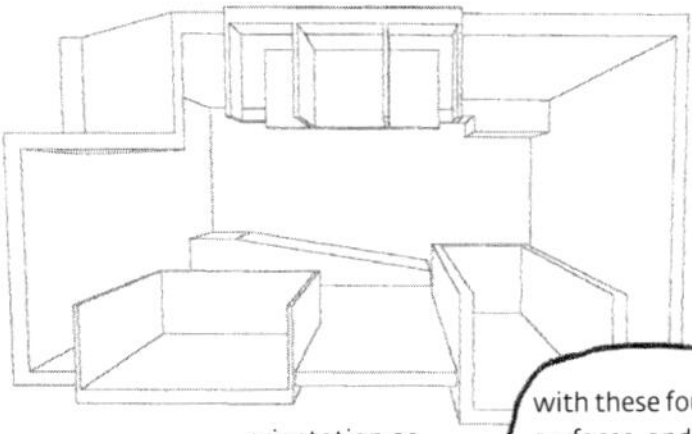

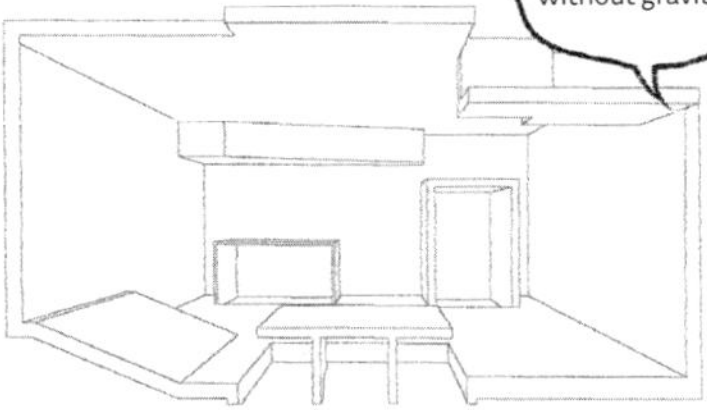

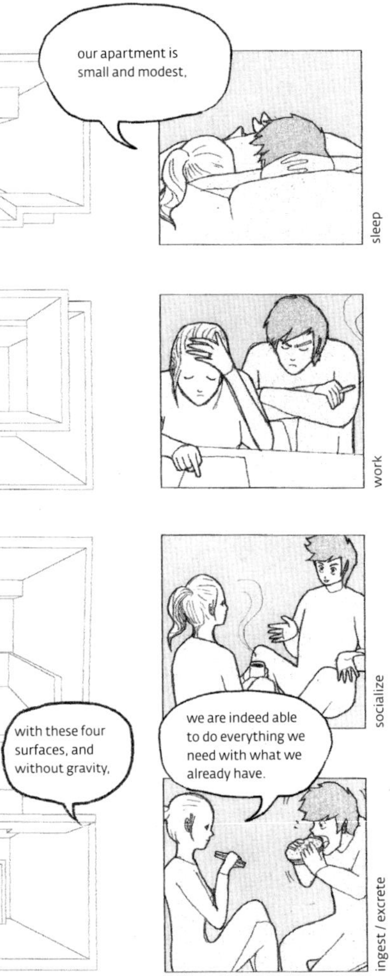

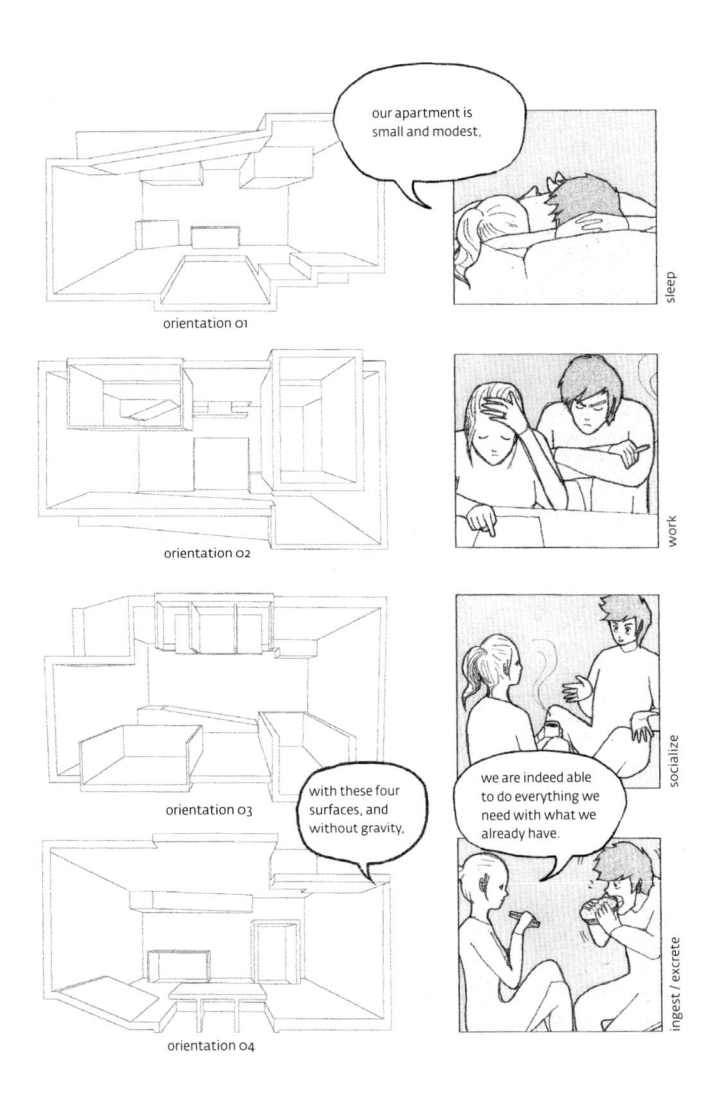

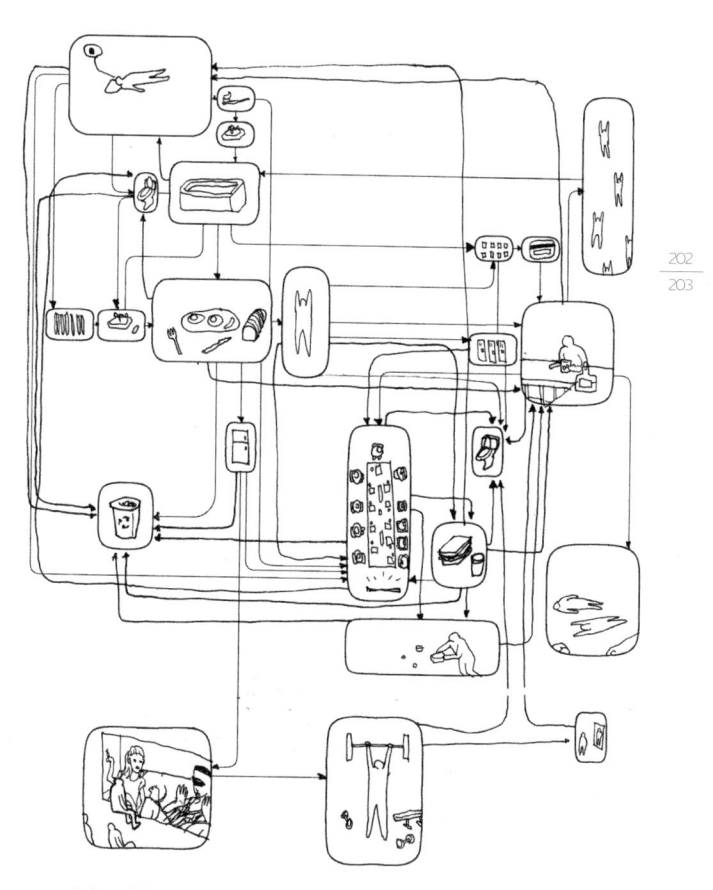

this will mess up your whole routine! and mine too!

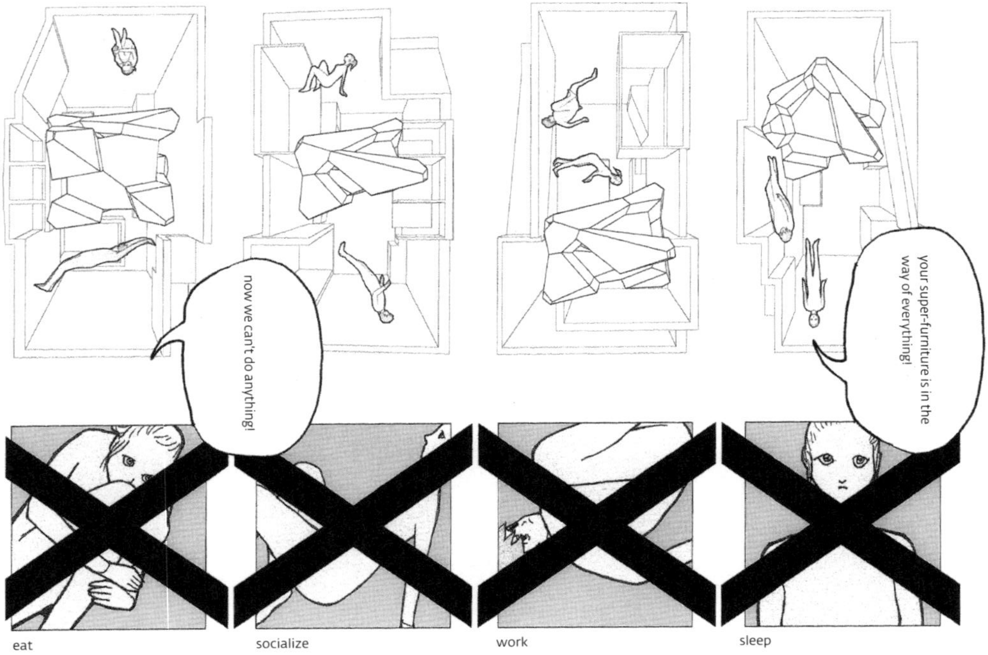
your super-furniture is in the way of everything!
now we can't do anything!
eat
socialize
work
sleep

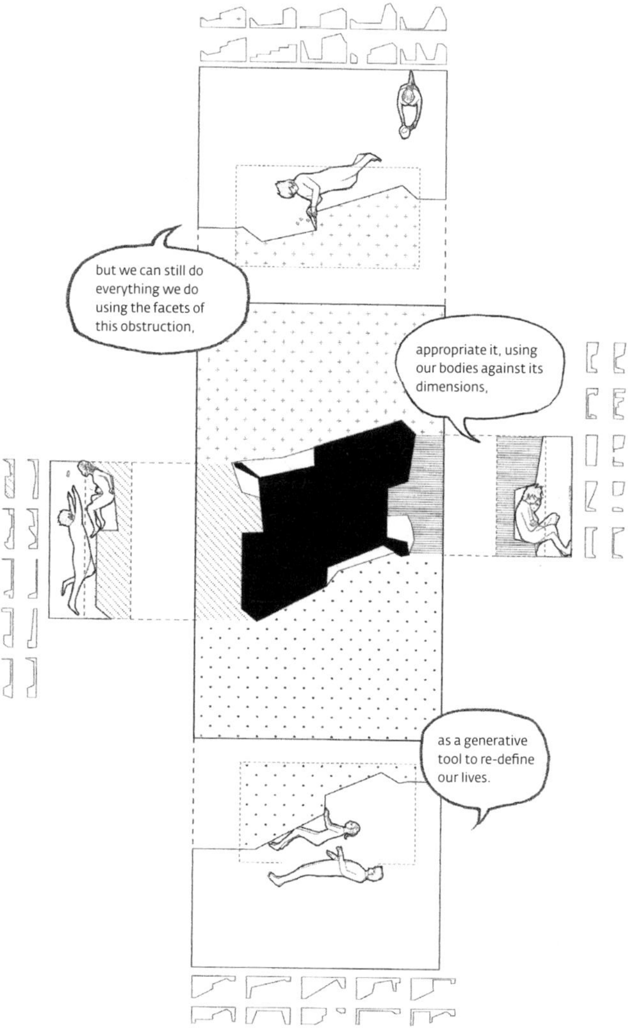
but we can still do everything we do using the facets of this obstruction,
appropriate it, using our bodies against its dimensions,
as a generative tool to re-define our lives.

we can rotate it and produce 48 different projectsion and unique perceptions... it's like cloud-watching!

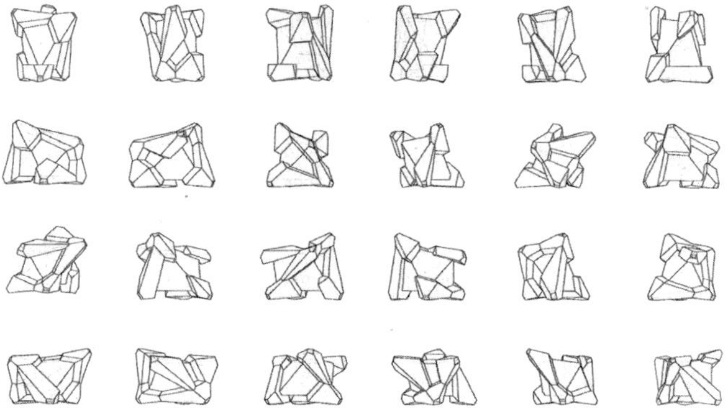

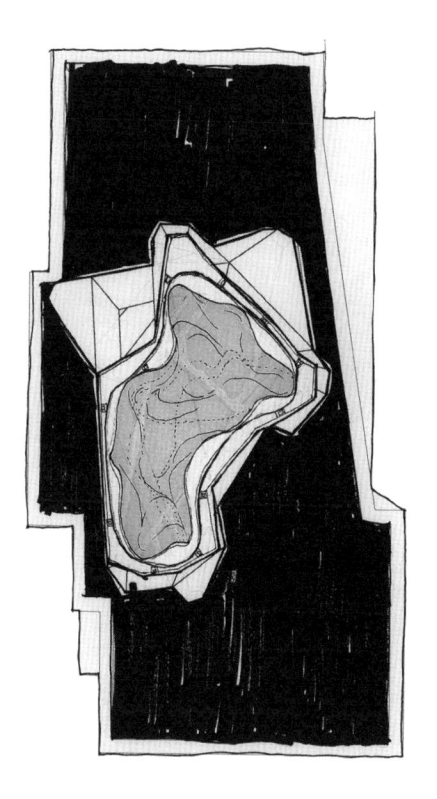

and we can do all our private things inside!

I'm sorry.
I really hate it.
please take this thing apart.
it is too late now.
our lives cannot go back to the way they were.

"a wound that does not heal is not a wound.

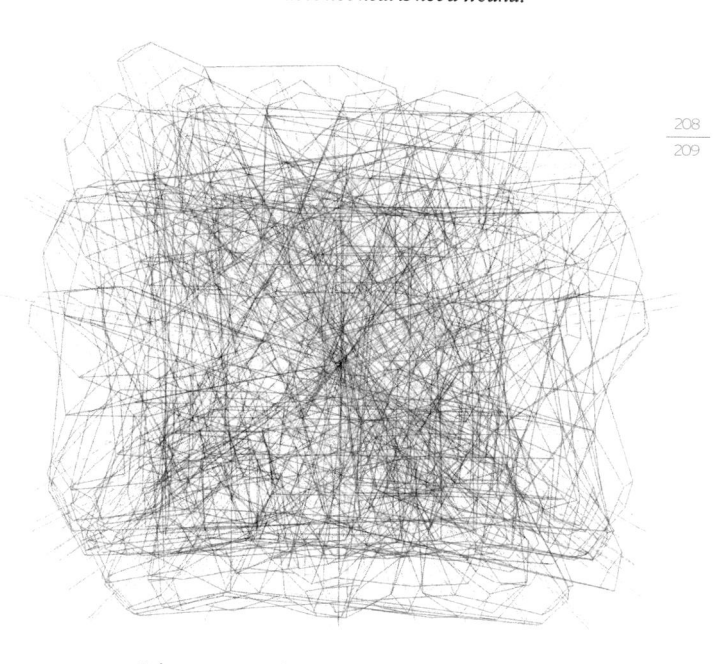

It is a new part of a new kind of healthy body."
— Jeffrey Kipnis, to Stanley Tigerman (1990)

(Top) "Cleansing of the Western Wall Plaza", Jerusalem, 1967; (Middle Left) Cover of *The renewal of The Bauhaus in Tel Aviv: The Preservation of The International Style in the White City*; (Middle Right) Special edition of *Ha'ir* (The City - Tel Aviv's local newspaper) featuring *The White City*; (Bottom) "Sprawling Monumentality," housing cluster in Gilo, Jerusalem, 1972.

NEW MONUMENTALITY
MONUMENTALITY AS A TOOL OF SOVEREIGNTY IN ISRAEL

OSNAT TADMOR

Nothing is as controversial as labeling an artifact as a "monument." This is especially the case when it is done in the name of domestic policy, for such an act has implications in the international arena. Throughout the short history of the state, the Israeli government has made tremendous efforts to emphasize its sovereignty, using monumentality as a key tool. Planning policies in Israel have lead to the creation of a dispersed built environment, comprised of significant nodes, occupying the land in a "netlike" form. Policy makers have both created and re-created monuments using preservation policies in a variety of methodologies to define and maintain this dispersed net. By reading the landscape through a monumental filter, the Israeli territory is continuously remapped according to the dynamic weight of its cultural nodes.

While monumentality is usually associated with stasis, permanence and the vertical, Israel asserts its sovereignty through a flexible set of gestures, expansions and horizontalities; monuments are interpreted as places of high cultural value.

Advertisements for Tel Aviv and Jerusalem, *Keren Ha'Yesod Yearbook*, (Jerusalem, 1932).

On the one hand stands the contemporary archeological effort of mapping the land according to biblical and historical events, disregarding finds that do not comply with the Zionist narrative. This effort serves Israeli purposes by reconstructing a history that is otherwise incomplete. On the other hand, a new type of monumentality has been appearing in recent discourse; a search for modern monuments culminating in the marking of new, pioneering Israeli enterprises, that are detached from ancient history, as culturally significant. The 'White City' of Tel Aviv is a recent example of a modern cultural node that found its way to the ever growing, intricate, Israeli net of monuments.

CULTURAL DISPERSION

An ideology of defense through dispersion is embedded in Israeli settlement patterns and in civil and military infrastructure developments.[1] But dispersion has emerged as a tool not only from defensive strategies but also from religious and nationalistic perceptions of the Holy Land, which many Israelis and Jews at large envisage as spreading from the Jordan River to the Mediterranean Sea. One of these strategies is the blurring of the border between Israel, its neighboring countries and the Palestinian entity. Eyal Weizman suggests that the geographic model of the frontier between the Israeli and the Palestinian entities is elastic and in constant transformation depending on the use of military power, barriers, "sterile" areas and security zones.[2] The same strategy is used in the cultural realm. Monumentality, in various incarnations, helps create a dispersed form of built environment, one that includes and excludes cultural nodes according to their frame of reference.

Exclusion is an intrinsic characteristic of defining a cultural heritage. By their very essence, monuments are tied to the heritage of a specific group of people. Through the dispersion of significant cultural nodes, Israel is creating an exclusive cultural realm that relies on spatial methods of control. This dynamic enterprise uses a flexible mechanism that adjusts itself to different periods and locations. This system of spatial exclusion operates horizontally (on the ground) as well as vertically (underground). David Ben Gurion's claim that the Jewish right over Palestine is based on "digging the soil with our own hands"[3] emphasizes how archeology has been the only tool in the formation of Israeli identity since the establishment of the state. The existing landscapes of Palestine were seen as a contemporary veil, which once lifted, would reveal (through digging) historic biblical landscapes, important battlegrounds and sites of worship.[4] Israel assigned a national role to archeology to remove the visible layer and expose the ancient Israelite landscape as proof for Jewish ownership. The subterranean strata were perceived as a "parallel geography akin to a national monument."[5]

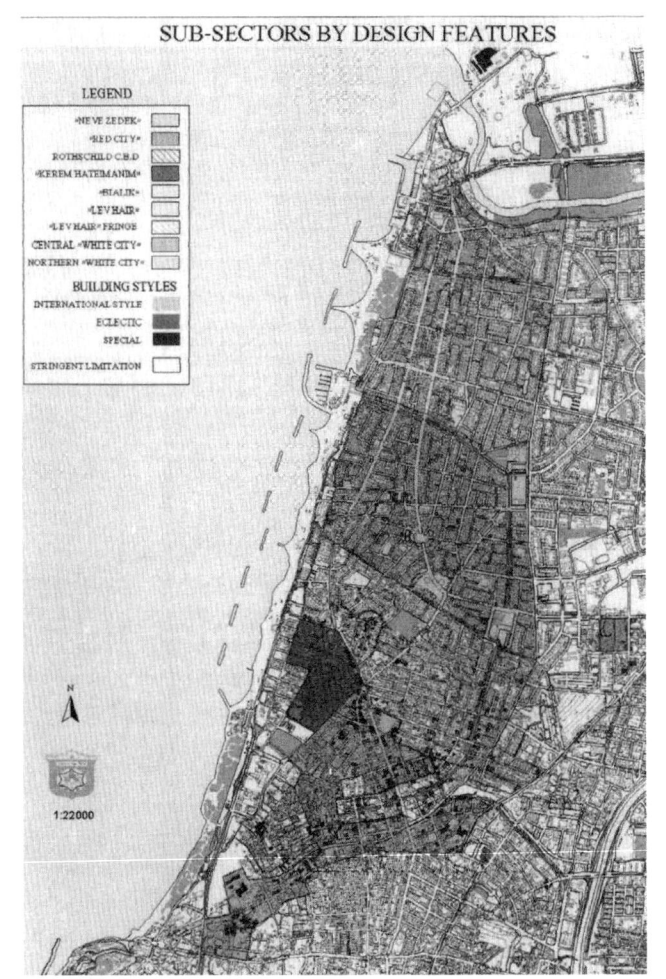

Historical districts and sub districts in the White City area, submitted to UNESCO, 2005.

MONUMENTALITY AND ITS BUFFER ZONE

Monumentality is accompanied by an "aura," a space characterized by a bidirectional relationship with the monument itself. The result is an extended zone of exclusivity, a buffer zone. The International Expert Meeting on World Heritage and Buffer Zones in Davos, Switzerland convened in 2008 on the initiative of the State of Israel in order to clarify key concepts concerning buffer zones surrounding World Heritage sites.[6] According to Francesco Bandarin, the director of the UNESCO World Heritage Center, these spaces are important tools for conservation and for the protection of an inscribed property.[7] They differ in various parameters such as their ability to unify or separate the monument from its surroundings, their spatial and formal characteristics vis-à-vis the monument, their use, etc. In Israel the manipulation of buffer zones serves as a political instrument.

RECREATED MONUMENTALITY

Israel renews the value of the monuments that strengthen its self-image. The post-modern process of monumentalization, a process of looking back to the past for the creation of contemporary monuments was the only method possible for the young state of Israel till recent years. It reached its apotheoses in the two decades that followed the Six Days War of 1967. Construction and destruction were used as complementary devices in this process.

During this period Israel created a portrait of a nation with strong roots in ancient history and biblical narratives. The freedom to recreate historic sites on recently occupied territories lead to an intense use of monumentality and its buffer zone as tools of sovereignty. The Old City of Jerusalem is a prominent example of a monument recreated in this period. It contains what I define as "nested monuments"; historical sites that are part of the old city but stand for themselves. For example, the Wailing Wall (known as the Kotel) in

Cover of *Living on The Sands: The White City of Tel Aviv, A World Heritage Site*, 2004.

City with Concept: Bauhaus in Tel Aviv, postcard, 1990's.

the Old City is a monument within a monument. As monuments they created a buffer zone around them. In Jerusalem the monumentality of the Old City and the Wailing Wall created a buffer zone in stone that sprawled through the whole metropolis, an echo of the ancient stone of the Holy Temple.

MODERN MONUMENTALITY: THE CASE OF TEL AVIV

The case of Tel Aviv demonstrates a contemporary approach towards using monumentality as a political tool. It illustrates the flexibility of this tool and its ability to adjust to contemporary needs and new political agendas.

According to Chezy Berkowitz, Tel Aviv's former city chief engineer, and Jeremie Hoffman, head of the preservation department of the Tel Aviv municipality, "the 'White City' of Tel Aviv is a district where European architects created an outstanding architectural ensemble showcasing aspects of the modern movement in a new cultural context".[8] In July 2003, UNESCO's World Heritage Committee recommended the inclusion of the 'White City' in the list of world heritage sites. In their own estimation

> [T]he White City of Tel Aviv is a synthesis of outstanding significance of the various trends of the Modern Movement in architecture and town planning in the early part of the 20th century. Such influences were adapted to the cultural and climatic conditions of the place, as well as being integrated with local traditions.[9]

Thus in 2003, Tel Aviv, Israel's most secular city, which does not possess any archeological or religious assets, and which was established in 1909 on the remains of Arab settlements, found its own way to become a Jewish monument, a modern Zionist monument.

In White City, Black City, Sharon Rotbard claims that UNESCO's recognition has implications beyond the history of the modern movement in architecture and that concern the Middle East and the state of Israel.[10] Rotbard notes how within a decade the narrative of the "Bauhaus style" and a "White City" has developed from a mere exhibition in a museum to a cultural and economic incentive that has transformed large parts of the city with minimal physical interventions.[11][12] Initially the change was mainly theoretical but soon enough it was recognizable in the real-estate market and in the uses and life in the city center.[13]

During the early 1990's, the municipality began to develop a series of preservation policies for the "White City." In 1994 Tel Aviv hosted several exhibitions and symposia all devoted to the "White City" and its cultural values. The next formal step was an application to the World Heritage committee, and UNESCO's 2003 declaration was soon followed by a variety of cultural events in 2004. This understanding of the potential of Tel Aviv's architecture was an important moment of cultural reflection. It was the first time that Israeli architecture was recognized for "making a history," "becoming history" and understanding itself as history.[14] The narrative of the White City enabled the relatively new city of Tel Aviv to have, like many important cites in the world, an "Old City," even though it was recreated as a cultural icon less then 50 years after its formation. Tel Aviv became that most unusual of places: historical and modern, as well as local and western.

The "Bauhaus Style" represented for the Israeli milieu a "rational attitude in planning" and "a social approach to architecture."[15] In fact, for the planners of Tel Aviv in the 1930's and 1940's, it was an opportunity to leave behind the eclectic mixture of both local-oriental and Eastern European styles and move forward to an enlightened, clean style. It was a style that allowed the settlers of Tel Aviv (most of whom immigrated from Eastern Europe) to disregard the history of their local environment and of their personal past.

But now that Tel Aviv found a way to enter the list of important cities of the world it needed both a "historic city" and a "corporate city."[16] According to Rotbard, there was a direct relationship between the iconization of the White City and the parallel development of the corporate city that evolved outside the city center, along the peripheral highway, to eventually become the largest business center of the metropolis during the 1990's.[17] This parallel development enabled to keep the White City intact while satisfying the corporate need for the development of high-rise buildings.

Defining the 'White City' as a preservation site addresses several contingencies. In most cases the boundaries of the World Heritage site and their buffer zones are clearly defined. Tel Aviv's 'White City' was built almost entirely during a period of 20 years, from the early 1930's until the 1950's. During this short period, there were no clear criteria or methods to identify and define the different historic developments in the city. The resulting district was based on an urban plan by Sir Patrick Geddes and reflected "modern organic" planning principles.[18] Buildings from the same period and with similar architectural characteristics can also be found in other areas of Tel Aviv and in adjacent cities such as Ramat Gan, Giv'ata'im and the controversial city of Jaffa (an ancient city with a majority of Arab population that lost its socio-economic superiority to the modern Jewish neighboring Tel Aviv). These cities were deprived of the monumental potential of their architecture. The area defined as a heritage site was only a limited part of the city center of Tel Aviv with a buffer zone around it. It was created as a monument of the prevailing "enlightened," affluent, secular hegemony.

Changes of function may contribute to the conservation of objects, just as easily as they might to their destruction.[19] Most of the time, using an object means wearing it out.[20] The basic idea of this new type of preservation enterprise is to use the buffer zone to create a living monument—a monument that function financially and socially, and that prevents the site from becoming a museum through curtailing daily activities and uses. In this unique case, the idea is to see the buffer zone as a supportive element for the world heritage site and as a connection to the rest of the city. According to Berkowitz and Hoffman, this progressive idea will be implemented, by using the buffer zone as a maintenance tissue for the heritage site, as a way of keeping it "a lively part of the city."[21] It will offer "communal facilities such as public parks, office spaces, parking and public buildings such as schools and hospitals" and "provide easy access to its inhabitants" even if such practices are hard to maintain in the center of a World Heritage site.[22]

In fact, the monumentalization of the White City as a cultural node was an incentive for the financial development of both the area that was declared as a preservation site and the buffer zone around it. Preservation and progression occur at once. So do conservation and renovation. And as reported in a New York Times article, Tel Aviv's real estate prices have risen steadily since 2003.[23] The dual movement of monumentality is not only a tool for political sovereignty: it is also a mechanism for increasing revenues.

In the end, the social and cultural elites of Tel Aviv have finally created a monument of their own and avoided the postmodern impulse to resuscitate ancient history and the search for biblical roots. The White City is a monument that legitimizes the Zionist enterprise by linking it to the white and clean, to Western Europe and to new beginnings.

NOTES

1. For more about the ideology of control through dispersion, see Peter Galison, "War Against the Center" *Grey Room*, Vol. 4 (Summer 2001), p. 29.
2. See also: Eyal Weizman, *Hollow Land: Israel's Architecture of Occupation* (London: Verso, 2007).
3. Weizman, *Hollow Land*, p. 39.
4. *Ibid.*
5. *Ibid.*
6. *International Expert Meeting on World Heritage and Buffer Zones*, Davos, Switzerland, 11 – 14 March 2008. accessed at http://whc.unesco.org/uploads/events/documents/event-473-1.pdf
7. *Ibid.*
8. UNESCO, *World Heritage and Buffer Zones*, p. 125.
9. *Ibid.*
10. Sharon Rotbard, *White City, Black City* (Tel Aviv: Babel Press, 2005), p. 13.
11. He refers to the exhibition: "White City: The architecture of the International Style in Israel; A portrait of an era" that took place in the Tel Aviv Museum of Art in 1984 and was curates by Michael Levin.
12. Rotbard, *White City, Black City*, p. 33.
13. *Ibid.*
14. *Ibid.*, 21.
15. Nitza Smock, *Houses From The Sand: The Architecture of the International Style in Tel Aviv* (Tel Aviv: The Tel Aviv Foundation for Development and The Ministry of Defense Press, Tel Aviv, 1994), p. 22.
16. Rotbard, *White City, Black City*, p. 31.
17. *Ibid.*
18. *Ibid.*, p. 125.
19. Gamboni, *The Destruction of Art*, p. 26.
20. *Ibid.*
21. UNESCO, *World Heritage and Buffer Zones*, p. 125.
22. *Ibid.*
23. New York Times real estate reporter Rina Castelnuovo wrote in July 2007 that "In 2003, the average price of an apartment was 896,100 shekels ($226,374); in 2008 it was 1,205,400 shekels ($304,509), according to the Central Bureau of Statistics, a government agency" (The New York Times, "great homes and destinations", 07.14. 2009). A slide show showing potential real estate properties attached to the article was described as: "Bauhaus in Tel Aviv".

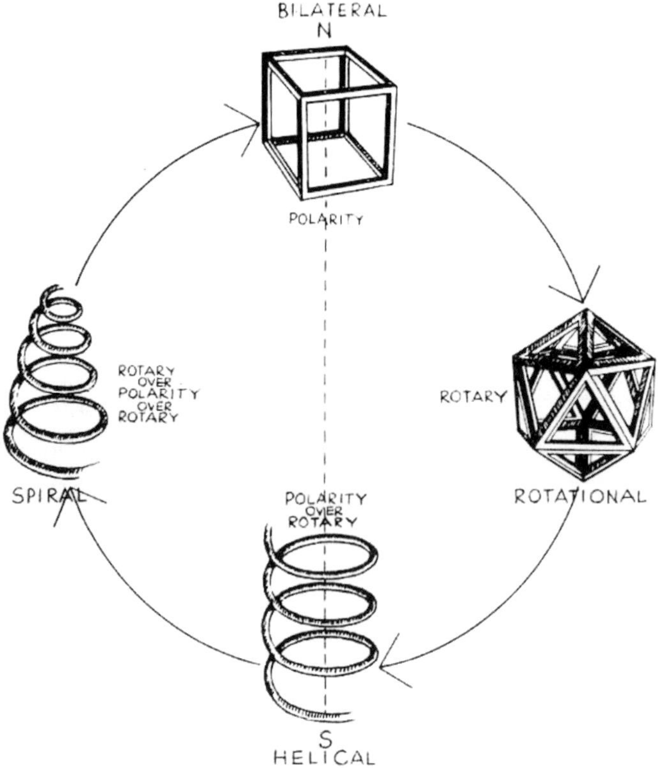
BILATERAL
N
POLARITY
ROTARY
ROTATIONAL
POLARITY
OVER
ROTARY
S
HELICAL
ROTARY
OVER
POLARITY
OVER
ROTARY
SPIRAL

*Anne Tyng, professor at the University of Pennsylvania for 27 years and a longtime collaborator with Louis Kahn, was instrumental in developing the mathematical and structural principles behind the *City Tower* project for Philadelphia. This interview, conducted by Sam Stewart-Halevy, explores the relationship between this project and Tyng's theory, proposed in a *Zodiac* article, of a cyclical history.

INTERVIEW*

ANNE TYNG
WITH SAMUEL STEWART-HALEVY

Sam Stewart-Halevy: I want to ask you about the structural ideas behind the City Tower. At the time, there was a lot of discussion about the spanning potential of the space frame. At the City Tower, you proposed to extend the frame vertically, turning it from a spanning device into a fully inhabitable high-rise construction. Did you see this vertical space frame as the logical next step? Were there any precedents of vertical space frames that you were looking at?

Anne Tyng: Well I had done my parents house on the Eastern Shore of Maryland. That was a wood space frame. It was totally triangulated with 3x4's on 7 foot centers that then crossed each other. The whole thing survived Hurricane Hazel while the other houses were blown to bits by 140 mile an hour winds. I thought that was a good test! I had also seen photographs of a thing called the "Swan" in National Geographic by Alexander Graham Bell-- it was a type of Kite structure-- and also a triangulated hut that he made so that he could watch the experiments with his father. So I was looking at that sort of thing.

> It seems like a major difference between these examples and the City Tower project is in the choice of material. In the Maryland House you were working with timber but then you switched to concrete for the Philadelphia project. Was the material choice intended from the beginning?

Well I think we had several versions. The concrete columns were thought of as hollow with tension cables inside so they could be post-tensioned. But that was a gradual development. The concept was based on a lower structure that I modeled with toothpicks. I think the idea of the concrete probably evolved. The steel always has the problem of fireproofing so the idea of having hollow tensioned concrete takes care of the fireproofing and the steel tensioning that you need. That's what we had in mind. These things evolve in the process of thinking about what you want to do in the actual building. The geometry came before the actual decisions about what materials might be used. In other words it was a continuous exploration.

> In adopting the tetrahedron form, you were working with an inherently strong geometry so was there an expectation the geometry would resolve itself in the structure?

Right, it resists compression beautifully. If one joint gives way, the load just goes to other joints. I remember asking an engineer what to do on my parents house and he just said not to worry about it. I did use connectors on some of it but mostly nails and glue at the joints. That survived a lot of stress for a wooden structure.

> In the City Tower, the joints are articulated in a really unusual way. The pyramid shaped capitals resemble fruit, hanging from the bottom of each plate. What was the intention behind these structural features? Were they meant to stiffen the connection between the columns?

There's nothing hanging out. It all gets connected into a joint. Kahn's big contribution to the design was to have these hollow capitals. He was the one who wanted to articulate the capital as some-

Studies for the *City Tower* project, Louis Kahn, 1952-1956, Philadelphia, PA.

thing that followed the geometry. The capitals would be a smaller scale than the major structure but would be big enough for a man to stand up in. It would have been easily accessible for maintenance.

DID YOU EVER THINK ABOUT DESIGNING THE ENTIRE PROJECT IN STEEL?

We definitely thought of steel. The surface treatment would have had a lot of steel. There's a mesh, a network, in order to reinforce the large panes of glass on the exterior. The mesh was almost like a three dimensional projection from the window. It was a similar geometry but a smaller scale than the bigger structure. That was the idea of the fine triangulation. It also would have made window washing much easier.

I'M CURIOUS ABOUT YOUR THEORY OF "STRUCTURAL CYCLES." AFTER READING THE ARTICLE THAT YOU WROTE FOR ZODIAC IN 1969 ON THE "GEOMETRIC EXTENSIONS OF CONSCIOUSNESS," I WONDERED WHETHER IT WAS POSSIBLE TO SYNTHESIZE A SPIRAL VIEW OF HISTORY WITH A HISTORY OF STRUCTURES AND ENGINEERING—WHICH SEEMS TO BE A LINEAR ONE OF PROGRESSION AND REFINEMENT. HOW DID THE CYCLICAL APPROACH PLAY OUT

> IN YOUR DESIGN OF THE CITY TOWER? WERE YOU CONSCIOUSLY RECALLING A PREVIOUS PHASE OF HELICAL STRUCTURES AS A WAY OF REIFYING YOUR THEORY?

I was simply showing how there could be smaller cycles within larger cycles-- forms within forms. I was using actual forms to show the cycles in architecture and in other fields. The spiral was a kind of a dematerialization since it was the most complex stage after the bilateral rotational and helical phases. Out of the complexity you get a new simplicity that includes the complexity.

> I THINK THIS NOTION OF CYCLES IS ESPECIALLY INTERESTING IN THE CONTEXT OF THE SPACE FRAME. IN READING ARTICLES FROM SOME OF YOUR CONTEMPORARIES LIKE WACHSMANN AND SAMUELY, IT SEEMS LIKE THERE WAS A SORT OF CULTURE AROUND THE SPACE FRAME. PEOPLE BELIEVED THAT IT BROKE THE CONTINUITY OF HISTORY BECAUSE THE TECHNOLOGY WAS SO NEW, ALMOST LIKE THE INVENTION OF THE VAULT IN GOTHIC ARCHITECTURE. WACHSMANN SAYS THAT ARCHITECTS NEED TO DISCARD THEIR OLD IDEAS AND START ANEW. THIS SEEMS DIRECTLY OPPOSED TO YOUR IDEA OF HISTORY AS A CYCLICAL REPETITION.

I think that's true. If you look back at the work of Alexander Graham Bell which preceded Bucky Fuller's stuff, that was an earlier cycle. I started architecture school at Harvard when the Bauhaus took over. It was a new world for everyone. Everyone was into low-cost housing. You had to know what every square inch of the house did in terms of detailing and that kind of thing. It felt like it was totally new and a break from the past, and in a way it was since it's relatively simple compared to Gothic architecture or previous Gothic cycles, or Gothic revival periods. I think people are more aware of a change when you get a simple thing after a very complex one so they feel as though they are starting a whole new world and everyone gets inflated. They're doing little boxes, they have to get inflated!

> ONE THING THAT IS INTRIGUING ABOUT BOTH YOUR WORK AND THE WORK OF KAHN IS THAT IT IS DIFFICULT TO PLACE IT WITHIN A SPECIFIC HISTORICAL PERIOD. IN MY PAPER, I AM ARGUING THAT THIS INITIAL DISPLACEMENT IS A

FORM OF INSTABILITY. IN THE CASE OF THE CITY TOWER, THIS INSTABILITY IS REVEALED IN THE STRUCTURE ITSELF SINCE THE TOWER APPEARS TO BE SWAYING BACK AND FORTH. IN READING KAHN'S RECOLLECTION OF TRAVELING TO PISA AS A YOUNG MAN AND SEEING THE LEANING TOWER, I WONDER WHETHER THE INSTABILITY OF THE CITY TOWER WAS A CONSCIOUS EFFECT OR WHETHER IT WAS ONLY REVEALED ONCE YOU WERE ABLE TO GRASP THE BUILDING IN THREE DIMENSIONS.

I think you may be mis-using the word instability because it's structurally very stable. It could be the innovative aspect to the building or some other word. Simplicity after complexity. You don't want to get stuck with a name that isn't open enough. It is universal and it does repeat itself but we just give it different names. Modernism or Post-modernism. It's really just the energy or the expression of the energy within it. Whether it's contained or very visible. Whether it has a dynamic effect or whether it's very serene and simple. That's part of it, I think. When you describe it try to use more adjectives. I think instability is the opposite of the beginning of a cycle. None of it is stable exactly--it's more complex. Sometimes I describe it as the dematerialization of matter with light before the beginning of a new cycle. And then you have new forms of life.

ALMOST LIKE A BREAKING DOWN OR DECONSTRUCTION?

Yes that kind of word, but it's so hard to pick the right one. Something that has a complex energy as well. It usually tends to be, in certain periods, very ornate as opposed to a very simple renaissance. I don't know! You have to look at a lot of cycles and then decide for yourself. It doesn't sound very positive to use the word instability when you use it that way. It could be excitement or multiplicity of form or highly energized form. That might say it. There's so many ways of saying it.

> I WONDER WHETHER YOU COULD APPLY THIS FRAGMENTATION IDEA TO THE EXISTING CITY HALL. AFTER I READ KAHN'S PASSAGE ON "HOLLOW STONES" I COULDN'T HELP BUT THINK OF THE GIANT MASONRY BUILDING THAT ALREADY STANDS ON THE SITE IN PHILADELPHIA. IS IT POSSIBLE TO VIEW THE CITY TOWER AS A DEMATERIALIZATION OF THE EXISTING CIVIC HEART OF THE CITY?

Goodness, that's a toughie. It probably does fit that case. The Philadelphia City Hall is one of those buildings that has different styles in it, more than one style. A number of the late 19th century buildings tended to be a mix of styles all in one building and I think the city hall has a bit of that quality. It's mixing styles. It's hard to know because it's a high building. William Penn up there makes it high I guess. I don't know, it's a mix. It doesn't have the spirit of the renaissance as a new expression of architecture. It's hard to say. What do you think?

> I RECALL THAT BUILDING FROM MY CHILDHOOD IN PHILADELPHIA AS AN IMPENETRABLE FORTRESS – THE OPPOSITE OF WHAT A CITY HALL SHOULD BE. I GUESS IT WAS SUPPOSED TO BE A SYMBOL OF STRENGTH AT THE HEART OF THE CITY. IT'S INTERESTING TO THINK ABOUT YOUR CITY TOWER AS A REPLACEMENT OF THAT BUILDING OR A NEW CIVIC FORM.

Well our building certainly wouldn't be very heavy. As Lou liked to say, most buildings were a woman wearing corsets and the City Tower was a woman without corsets. He didn't put it that way, something more expressive I guess--a woman braced against the wind. I think our concepts of what is rigid and what is not rigid have changed and the building itself has changed over time. The fact that it is centered in the middle of the city and that it's symmetrical tends to make it bilateral but because it's vertical it's probably both-- the end of the cycle and the beginning of one all in one building.

> DID YOU SEE THE CITY TOWER AS THE END OF A CYCLE?

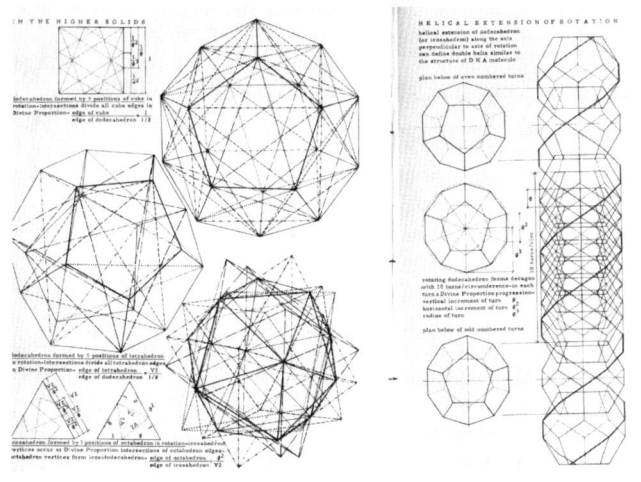

Anne Tyng, "The Geometric Extension of Consciousness," *Zodiac* (1969).

The tower has a consistent dimension all the way up. It doesn't taper, so it's not exactly a spiral marking the end of the cycle. The stuff that they're doing in Dubai is a good example. Those towers are definitely spirals. Dubai is a very good example as the end of the cycle although it's very hard to say where one thing begins and another ends. If you take the beginning of the 1920's Bauhaus thing and then you get more into bilateral forms after that, and then I think some of those new towers like the Gherkin in London are tending towards the spiral. There are a number of recent buildings that display spiral form. Right now because of all the things happening we may be at the end of a cycle and beginning of a new one.

THAT'S EXCITING!

FIGURE 1: *East Front of the New Theatre Royal*, Covent Garden (1809), Joseph Austin Benwell, hand colored engraving.

PERFORMING ON TWO STAGES
ARCHITECTURE OF THE COVENT GARDEN THEATRES

JOHN COOPER

On the night of September 19, 1808, during a performance of Richard Brinsley Sheridan's *Pizarro*, wadding from the firing of a stage gun shot into the ornate plasterwork of London's Covent Garden Theater, kindling a spark that set the stage alight. By the early hours of the following day, the theater and all its surrounding buildings had burnt to the ground. One day less than a year later, the theater's new stately Doric edifice was raised by the architect Robert Smirke.[FIG. 1] Adorned with *rilievo* and free-standing sculptural work by Flaxman, its austere grand entrance officially opened for a tragic rendition of *Macbeth*. Not a single line of the play was heard: tumultuous riots immediately arose in protest at the increased ticket prices of the new theatre, the players were driven off stage, and rowdy protestations spiraled into brawls, molestations, broken seats, and general civic disorder. Sixty days later the rioteers were appeased, old prices were restored, and the theater got back to the business of more restrained performance. But nearly forty years later, disaster would strike again on the night of March 4, 1856.

FIGURE 2: *Acting Magistrates commiting themselves being their first appearance on this stage as performed at the National Theatre Covent Garden. Sepr 1809*, (1809), George Cruikshank.

The inflammable drama of the theatre's ruin was preceded by an ominous prelude of magic, stunts, music and hocus-pocus, courtesy of the famous Professor Anderson, "Wizard of the North," who had already caused a minor fire at the Broadway theatre in New York and burned down Glasgow City theatre in 1845. During the debauchery of a *bal masque*—and in an ironic twist of fortune for a theatre with a Royal patent—to the tune of "God Save the Queen" Smirke's Doric temple to the dramatic arts went down in a blaze of theatrical glory.

Elaborate social performances marked the architectural entrance and exit of Smirke's opera house from the urban stage, and these became the stuff of ballad, legend, mockery, and criticism in the public imagination, which creatively remembered them in anecdotes, journalism, historiography, and most vibrantly, in images circulated in the printed press. While most critical-historical attention has been paid to the official repertoires of "high art" performances that happened onstage, here two unofficial performances will be put in the limelight. I will access these performances through their dense and highly constructed representation in printed imagery. The question, then, will be not What happened? but How did the visual strategies and technologies of depiction available at the time construct the historical event? And though I will not suggest that the fire of 1856 was basically a repetition of the 1809 riots, I am happy to acknowledge that both events were ruptures in the dispersed field of relations which I name "the public," both events caused the public to enter into economies of representation in extraordinary ways, and, moreover, both events were played out in the press through similar visual strategies—the most important of these being, to me, the theatricalization of a public ordinarily excluded from the franchise of performance.

***

Far from what ought to have been a scene of grand neo-classical civility, the opening night of Smirke's theatre was a shambles. Ticket prices in the cheap seats had been hiked without warning or apparent justification from three shillings sixpence to four shillings, and from six to seven shillings in the boxes. Dramatic protests ensued. In George Cruikshank's raucously vibrant cartoon of the event we see the main protagonists [FIG. 2]: the riotous audience, advertising their polyphonic complaint under the *baton* of a conductor confused at the sudden reversal of performance conventions. Cruikshank illustrates the diverse franchise of protest—from the cheap seats in the pit, up through the boxes to the so-called 'pigeon holes' in the roof. Only the bland dashes of color sitting in the most expensive seats presiding over the stage are untouched by the vituperative spirit. On stage are the three "acting" magistrates mentioned in the caption ("Acting Magistrates committing themselves: being their first appearance on this stage as performed at the National Theatre Covent Garden") and John Philip Kemble, the manager of the opera house.

The whole is rapidly but rigorously executed in quick lines and succinct color washes to ensure maximum expediency through the press and profitable exposure via the multiple channels of London print shops and subscriptions, making the event quickly available to the middle and upper circles of society—especially after its probable production of an extensive traffic of cheap spin-offs, piracies, and ephemeral versions.

Within the illustration, a panoply of amateur print matter communicates the specific grievances of the public. Amid signs publicizing the demand for "Old Prices" to be reinstated, other complaints surface. "John Bull against John Kemble" pits the archetypal English Everyman against the theatre's wealthy entrepreneur; "No Italian Private Boxes" protests against the division of space into a profitable and elitist economy associated with continental practice; and nationalistic overtones are amplified by calls for "No Catalani"— meaning Angelica Catalani, the famed Italian soprano, rued for her displacement of "native" singers. The riots' commandeering of the attitudes and effects of stage performance, coupled with the production of printed matter, asserted the agency of the audience in the production and circulation of signs.

Such noisy perversions of the conventional protocols of the English theatre brought Read and Nanes, two of the Bow Street "Acting" magistrates portrayed by Cruikshank, on stage to perform advocacy of the law. The Riot Act which they performed—the central pun of Cruikshank's image—was a 1713 Act of Parliament which empowered local authorities to declare any group of more than twelve people to be unlawfully assembled, and to have them dispersed or face punitive action. Here, Cruikshank's transformation of the theatre into a law court does not entail a radical restructuring of the proscenium, stage, and pit; rather, the architectural grammar of the law is depicted as being already implicit in that of the stage. As Cruikshank astutely disclosed, this architectural transformation entails both a mockery of the law and the transfer of power from magistrate to mob—a transformation that was to be repeated and exacerbated during riots that took place during the following sixty nights.

Sixty days after the Old Price Riots began, Kemble finally relented. Prices were returned to pre-1809 rates, the audience was satisfied, and the focal spirit of performance withdrew back behind the proscenium to its conventional architectural location: the stage. But what becomes clear from the annals of the Old Price Riots is that performance, as something like a *right* or *entitlement*, came into conflict with the architectural economy of the stage. The right to performance was claimed by the public, and the assertion of that right itself took the form of a performance which inverted the internal architectural divisions of the theatre. The building was turned upside down and inside out so that the confrontation between players and audience, pit and stage, became a confrontation between the public spaces of the street and the private spaces of a business. Reflecting on the Autumn disturbances of 1809, some months later, the anonymous author of *Considerations on the Past and Present State of the Stage* summarized this point of view. Arguing that though the management and landlords "may possibly have an indisputable title to the ground on which the boxes are built," the author remarked that "the boxes themselves, *as places of theatrical exhibition*... hold, as it were, in trust, and under various limitations, for the behoof of the public."[1]

***

By March 5, 1856 the theatre and its whole contents were utterly burned to the ground. The dramatic ceremony which memorialized the completion and public opening of Smirke's theatre was matched by the dramatic public performance that attended its sudden destruction. During the climax of Professor Anderson's six week season of "wizardry," as the orchestra belted out the obligatory national anthem, "the sudden descent of a flaming beam," according to the *Illustrated Times*, "gave the first intimation of the catastrophe; the exciting pleasure of the dance was immediately turned to horror and tumult; there was something hideous in this sudden change from mad revelry to ghastly fear; the terror-stricken maskers rushed to every outlet, and many women were trampled on and carried out fainting."[2]

Along with, and often next to, such literary narratives, a rich imagery of peripety and artful disaster was quickly disseminated via the highly efficient channels of print circulation available to London illustrators and journalists. Carefully colored, batch-produced images would have been available for display and purchase for a moderate price in the commercial print galleries collected around Covent Garden piazza behind the opera house itself. But—whether legitimately or by piracy—such imagery could also serve as the basis for reduced, plagiarizing versions published in the popular press. Thus, via a rapidly functioning system for the batch production of images, the enclosed interior performances of the theatre were published in public spaces.

In a single plate colored lithograph, printed in the immediate aftermath of the fire, the energetic momentum of the press doubles the choreographic movement of the fleeing bodies.[FIG. 3] With the fire raging and the flaming beams of the proscenium falling, the place designated for performance becomes inaccessible. In the crumbling of this architectural fabric, performance is forced to take place elsewhere: in the wings, the pit, behind or outside of "the scene." The actors, dancers, and administrators of this performance spontaneously assume balletic poses or strike thespian gestures. It

FIGURE 3: *Interior of Coven Garden Theatre, First Alarm of Fire at the Conclusion of the Bal Masque*, (1856), George Cruikshank, hand colored lithograph.

is as if these figures are drawing on a public store of choreographic memory. The hallmarks of dramatic disposition are everywhere in evidence: poised, sprung bodies, expressively outstretched arms, earnest claspings of fellow protagonists, and animated faces. Consider, on the one hand, a couple dancing, with some urgency, a sort of fleeing *pas de deux* [FIG. 4], or three Iberian or Troubadour-looking masqueraders, two of them striking the poses of the Spanish Bolero. [FIG. 5,6] By a lucky twist of fortune, this spontaneously-produced company of actors is already dressed for the part. It is as if, in crisis mode, the amateur public remembers the aesthetic protocols of the professional stage.

During the Old Price Riots, the public had a clear agenda, but that is not the case where the fire of 1856 is concerned. The public did not "burn the house down" with the intent to express a collective consciousness; it was not a carefully planned revolutionary coup. Rather, as communicated by the illustrated accounts of the fire, *the public spontaneously adopted aesthetic protocols in a time of crisis*. It must be said, to be more accurate, that it was the curators of this history—the illustrators and journalists who documented the event—who constructed crisis by means of the visual and verbal techniques of the stage.

The Covent Garden site, even in the absence of an ordinarily functioning architecture of performance, was saturated with the attitudes, responses, movement, spectacle, and perspectives of theatre.[3] Why does such a transformation of public space matter? It could be merely an entertaining trope, a decoration of public life with the filigrees of the stage. Yet it is more than a decoration, I propose, because such a transformation authenticates the artfulness of everyday life. By this I mean that the fire demolished the architectural equipment which regulated distinctions between "art" and "non-art." Events during the fire enfranchised non-professional artists into a realm of experience and expression normally reserved for "official" or "professional" artists. The means was an infernal crisis, as the Old Price riots were a discordant one, but what these crises exposed was the underlying public presence of *aesthetic ambition*.

FIGURE 4 & FIGURE 5: Details of figure 3.

FIGURE 6: *La Castilliana Bolero Danced by Madelle Fanny Elssler, & Monsr Perrot. in the ballet divertissement Le Delire d'un peintre*, (1843), Jules Bouvier, hand colored lithograph.

NOTES

1. Anon, *Considerations on the Past and Present State of the Stage*, with reference to the late contests at Covent Garden (London: C. Chapple, 1809).
2. *llustrated London News*, 15 March 1856.
3. This hiatus lasted for two years—until May 15, 1858, when E. M. Barry's Italianate opera house was completed. Barry's building remains, with modernizing alterations, to this day.

trial 0 initial settings

trial 1 cellular office and hoteled space

presentation (grey)

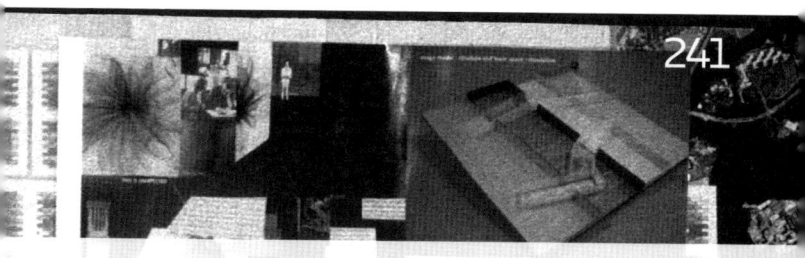

GHOSTS OF THESES PAST

NICHOLAS DE MONCHAUX
INTERVIEWED BY PIDGIN

Nicholas de Monchaux, Thesis, 2001

PIDGIN: COULD YOU BRIEFLY TALK ABOUT YOUR THESIS PROJECT?

Nicholas de Monchaux: Gosh, it's been a while. It was basically a project about emergence and organization in man-made and natural systems, in the form of a new kind of 'office park' (sited near Princeton) that would dispense with organizational hierarchy for a form that would emerge out of interactions amongst its workers, as well as the cycles and flows of the surrounding ecology. It was a play in part on the fact that the main force in midcentury office design (comming from Germany) was something called "burolandschaft" or office landscaping - so both taking that to its natural conclusion and bringing in ideas about complexity and self organization, which were at the time completely unknown, and not quite yet fashionable in architectural discourse.

WHERE DID THESE INTERESTS COME FROM? WERE THESE THEMES THAT YOU HAD BEEN THINKING ABOUT FOR SOME TIME, OR WAS IT SOMETHING NEW THAT YEAR?

I had been exposed to these ideas in a class at the Woodrow Wilson School, not the School of Architecture. In hindsight of course, it seems perfectly natural to see the formal and ecological ideas inherent in ideas of emergence, but at the time it wasn't and the thesis was my attempt to start figuring this out. And because the course at Woodrow Wilson had been one on organizational theory for organizations (NGOs etc), I started with the notion of designing for a non-hierarchical organization, and how that would change the (kind of amazing in its own way) architecture that surrounded Princeton. I had taken that course the preceding spring, and was busy working up a thesis about ideas that were then much more under discussion - about nationality, identity and displacement on the railway border between France and Spain. I even went and did site documentation that summer. But then there was sort of a 'slow burn' with these issues of self-organization, and I found myself fascinated enough to discard the border thesis in favor of experimenting with something that I had very little expertise about at the time!

> IT SEEMS THAT ARCHITECTURE IS SO OFTEN ABOUT THESE HAPPY ACCIDENTS, OR REDIRECTIONS. WERE THE PROFESSORS AT THE SCHOOL SUPPORTIVE OF THIS? WHAT ROLE DID THEY PLAY IN SHAPING YOUR IDEAS?

Well, yes and no. I think there was some sincere confusion about why I was interested in two things - landscape and ecology on the one hand, and organizational theory on the other - that were at the time not well-represented intellectually in the faculty. Which is not to say that I didn't find support in principle, just that the thesis was way outside the mainstream of topics that year. Which you can really hardly blame the faculty for! Both of those interests on my behalf had come from courses at Princeton, but courses outside the architecture school. Which is part of how an institution like Princeton should work, and probably the thesis in particular.

> IF THESE INFLUENCES THAT WERE NOT NECESSARY "MAINSTREAM" IN THE SCHOOL SHAPED YOUR THESIS, HOW DID THE THESIS BEGIN TO INFLUENCE YOUR WORK OUTSIDE OF SCHOOL? BOTH IN THE IMMEDIATE SENSE, AND UP TO THIS POINT?

Well, enormously influential would be an understatement! I am not sure if it is still like this, but there is an enormous amount of pressure on the thesis to represent the school well. Looking back at the choice I made to do a thesis slightly outside of the mainstream, it seemed an awfully nerve-wracking one at the time. But then looking at what I have done since, it was enormously helpful. As far as my own intellectual development, I first went to work for Liz [Diller] for a while, which was fantastic, and then starting a few years later, I did two things very related to my thesis, and instrumental in my own creative development. First, I started teaching on a combined faculty of Architecture and Landscape Architecture (at the University of Virginia), where in many ways I learned how much I hadn't known during my thesis about both the practicalities and theoretical underpinnings of landscapes. And then starting in 2002 I became a visiting researcher at the Santa Fe Institute, whose work I had discovered in researching my thesis. And they have been both enormously supportive and instrumental in giving me a strong theoretical grounding in the issues - of emergence, complexity and change in natural and manmade systems - that I only skirted the surface of in my thesis. So in many ways I made a calculated, if uncertain decision to do a thesis that was less about displaying competency, than a calculated incompetence, in these subjects that I was really interested in but knew (especially in retrospect!) very little about.

> I AM REALLY INTERESTED IN THE IDEA OF A THESIS OR DISSERTATION AS AN EXTENDED PROJECT THAT IN SOME WAYS IS A "MISTAKE," TO USE A HYPERPOLE, OR, A REHEARSAL. COULD YOU TALK MORE ABOUT YOUR EXPERIENCE AT UVA - ABOUT LEARNING MORE ABOUT YOUR SUBJECT, AND THEN, ABOUT TEACHING?

Well, I went to UVA as a visitor, and stayed for several years largely because of the opportunity to work with what was at the time one of the strongest faculties in landscape architecture in the country. In particular, I relished several joint studios taught with landscape faculty like Beth Meyer and Julie Bargmann, and a conference that Beth, Julie and I organized for the Lanscape Architecture Foundation on Landscape, Culture, and Technology. It's an old saw that there's no better way to learn something than to teach it, but probably true. That said, I think the opportunity I had to "start" teaching at Princeton, as a TA for courses in theory, design, and computing gave me an essential confidence about teaching, which, while sorely tested once or twice in my first years at UVA, stood me in very good

Nicholas de Monchaux, *Thesis*, 2001

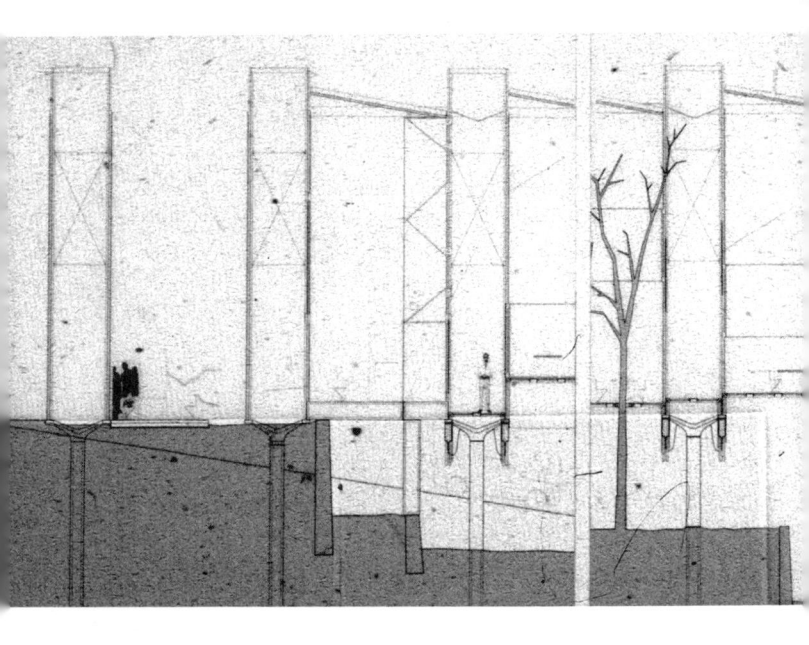

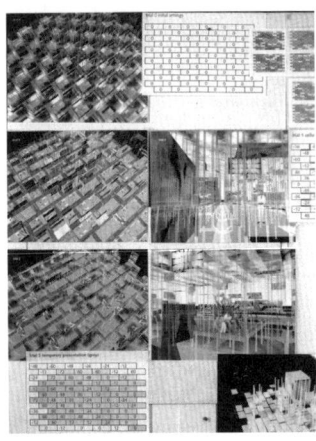

(Above) Nicholas de Monchaux, Thesis, 2001, Fig 4. (Bottom Left), Fig. 5. (Bottom Right)

246/247

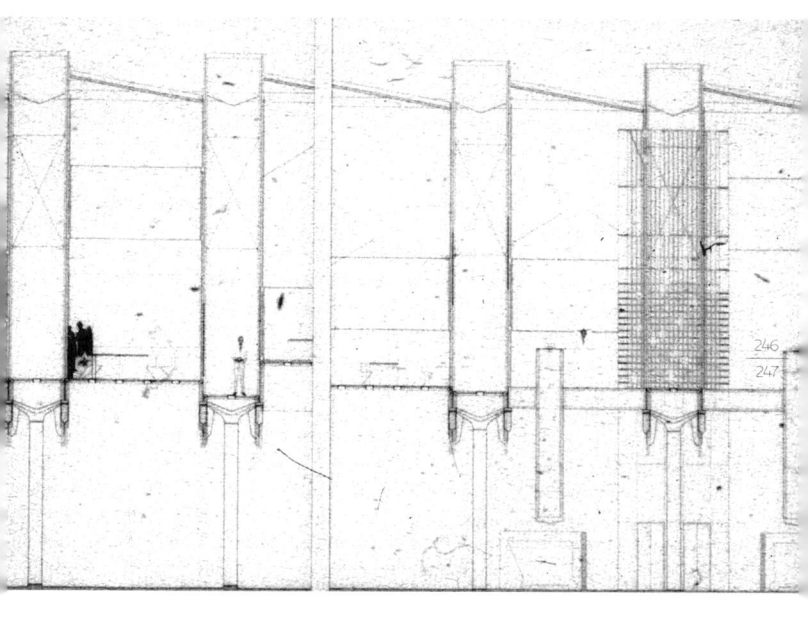

stead as a young design instructor in particular. That experience also gave me a useful saying - I think from Liz - that the most interesting things to teach are beginnings and endings, which brings us back to Thesis. At least related to design, I think they are actually two kinds of beginnings, the first the real introduction, where you have to find everything in a student's experience that might lead them to be a good designer, and filter out everything that will do the reverse and then the thesis, which is its own kind of introduction, certainly in my own experience, to the issues and ideas you'll knaw away at for the rest of your career.

> I THINK YOUR EXPERIENCE WITH THE THESIS SEEMS TO BE REALLY PRODUCTIVE, BUT THERE ARE OPINIONS OUT THERE THAT QUESTION HOW MUCH THE THESIS CAN BE A "BEGINNING." WHAT IS YOUR OPINION OF THE THESIS TODAY, IN ALL ITS FORMS?

Well, a good thesis needs several ingredients; highly motivated students, who have developed a certain intellectual confidence; a strong skill-set in place as far as moving a design forward stage by stage (without drama or all-nighters!); and then, to top it off, a faculty willing to engage with each student robustly. The fact is that in today's climate of architectural education, it is not necessarily easy to get all three of those ingredients present, at the same time and, in the same place.

I think schools that are everyone's top choice start out with confident students, but they don't always do the best job of maintaining the right balance of confidence and humility as students go along. This is a general observation not specific to Princeton, or Berkeley for that matter! For the second part, I think managing the mechanics of a design process is something that is often taught by example, but sometimes can be the ghost in the room in a thesis discussion. You need some really good experiences managed by someone else (a critic) before you can really take off and bring a project to a good conclusion "on your own." And for the third part, you need a faculty/student ratio, and commitment on the part of the faculty, that treats each thesis as worthy of robust, and sustained criticism. I don't know if it's still done, but one nervous-making but really important part of my Princeton Thesis experience was the presentation by each student of their thesis statement to a conference room of the whole faculty. Which while it shared a certain architecture of inquisition, in retrospect also gave an important signal that each thesis was worth the time and attention of some fairly busy and distinguished architects and practitioners, which was sustained over the course of the semester. When I think how difficult it is to fit something like that into my own schedule now, I realize that it was an especially important commitment on the part of a faculty much busier than even myself.

IF ALL THE "INGREDIENTS" AREN'T THERE, OR CAN'T BE THERE FOR SOME REASON, WHAT ARE SOME ALTERNATIVE DENOUEMENTS TO THE ARCHITECTURAL EDUCATION?

I hold two (possibly contradictory) ideas about this. First, I would fight to the death (or at least the equivalent in academic bureaucracy!) for the ability of any strong student at any school I teach at to do a thesis, and to have that thesis robustly engaged by the faculty. That said, I think there are some great alternative models that can accomplish many of the same goals for many students. Especially when they focus on collaborative models of working that reinforce the fact that the 'sole investigator' model of the traditional thesis is in its own way enormously obsolete. Just as a traditional thesis (in my view) is only succesful if it positions itself in a larger collaborative intellectual web, so are some alternative models really succesful in creating such a web internal to a 'research studio' or 'superstudio.' In the past year at Berkeley I guided three group projects that were done as an alternative to the thesis process, and I can say sincerely that each project moved much further than a single thesis could have, but with enormous individual benefit to each student. The three projects were also inter-related, and related to my own work and research, which made the expenditure of an enormous amount of effort by everyone worthwile. (That said, you should probably ask the students for their own thoughts!) Collaborative models seems to be incredibly important for education and for practice, how do we better connect these two spheres, i.e. how does working together in school help students work together in the field? I think I was enormously fortunate in a very dumb way in that my first architectural jobs before I got to Princeton, and before I did my thesis, were in London - with practices like Micheal & Patty Hopkins', and then with Diller and Scofidio when we were just 5-6 people. And in each case the process of moving a design forward was, either through the culture of offices like Foster & Hopkins, or the particular nature of D+S, enormously collaborative with engineers, specialists etc. Not just brought in for a meeting, but sitting next to you all the time, especially in London. So the notion of architecture as a collaborative practice was the first idea I had, before I got to school. (So even with my 'individual' thesis, for example, I spoke with HVAC people, acousticians, GIS specialists, etc., just because it was what I was used to.) So, even though the role of architectural education, especially towards the end of the 20th century, has been seen to give us everything we won't get in practice, ie, the opportunity for self expression, I think it's possible not to lose the best parts of that model but develop a much more relaxed attitude towards individual authorship. But one in which everyone gets credit!

I HAVE TO ASK YOU ABOUT YOUR BOOK. AND WHAT ELSE IS KEEPING YOU BUSY THESE DAYS?

Well, the book is about landscape, cities, and spacesuits, and started as an essay for Georges Teyssot at Princeton, one that was actually 21 one-page essays, recapitulating the 21-layered form of the Apollo A7L spacesuit, which was hand-stiched by the Playtex bra company. It became a larger project when I was invited to give a public lecture at the Santa Fe Institute in 2003, and gave 21 short lectures on the same theme, but connecting it more explicitly to organizational and natural ideas. Then I had a fellowship in 2005-2006 at the National Air and Space Musuem that gave me access to all the source material I needed to make it into a 100,000 word opus! And then I am doing related design work on how we as designers should address recent changes in the technology of place. I recently completed an installation around this project at the Biennial of the Americas, in Denver Colorado this summer.

So yes, technology, landscapes and emergence, just like my thesis!

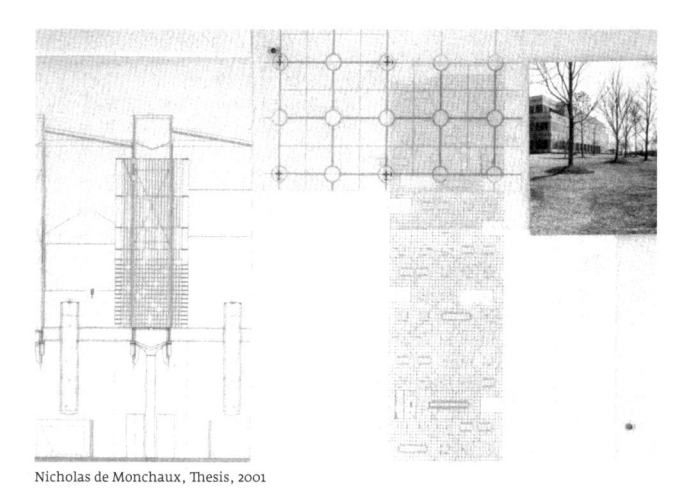

Nicholas de Monchaux, Thesis, 2001

PIDGIN
NUMBER
NINE
Fall 2010

ISBN:
978-0-9815016-5-9

COPYRIGHT:
© copyright 2010 Pidgin Magazine, all rights reserved.
All material is compiled from sources believed to be reliable, but published without responsibility for errors or ommissions. We have attempted to contact all copyright holders, but this has not been possible in all circumstances. We apologize for any omissions and, if noted, will amend in any future editions.

CONTACT:
pidgin@princeton.edu
www.pidgin-magazine.net

Pidgin Magazine
School of Architecture
Princeton University
S-110 Architecture Building
Princeton NJ 08544-5264

EDITORS:
Matthew Clarke
Brandon Clifford
Ang Li
Enrique Ramirez
Irene Sunwoo
Philip Tidwell

COVER:
Philip Tidwell

TYPOGRAPHY:
Fedra and Irma type families by Peter Biľak

PRINTING:
Printed in Iceland by Oddi Printing
www.oddi.com

COLOPHON

Pidgin is a publication edited and designed by graduate students at the Princeton University School of Architecture. The views and opinions expressed herein are those of the authors and do not necessarily reflect the attitudes and opinions of the editors or of the school. We are indebted to Dean Stan Allen for his sustained enthusiasm and support. Many thanks, as well, to the faculty and staff of the School of Architecture for all of their efforts and encouragement. Pidgin is made possible by the generous support of the Princeton University School of Architecture, as well as Elise Jaffe + Jeffrey Brown.

IMAGE CREDITS

page

4-5	British Airways, British Aerospace Systems (BAE), and Royal Air Force Museum
7	Robert J. Serling, Richard K. Smith, and R.E.G. Davies, *The Jet Age* (The Epic of Flight) (Alexandria, Virginia: Time-Life Books, 1982).
8	W.J. Duncan and A.H. Wheeler. *Report of the Court of Inquiry into the Accidents to Comet G-ALYP on 10 January, 1954 and Comet G-ALYY on 8 April, 1954*, HMSO, London (1955)
11	W.J. Duncan and A.H. Wheeler. *Report of the Court of Inquiry into the Accidents to Comet G-ALYP on 10 January, 1954 and Comet G-ALYY on 8 April, 1954*, HMSO, London (1955)
12	Robert J. Serling, Richard K. Smith, and R.E.G. Davies, *The Jet Age* (The Epic of Flight) (Alexandria, Virginia: Time-Life Books, 1982).
14-15	Robert J. Serling, Richard K. Smith, and R.E.G. Davies, *The Jet Age* (The Epic of Flight) (Alexandria, Virginia: Time-Life Books, 1982).
38	Image accessed via Photobucket, http://www.photobucket.com
43	Monument detail courtesy of Panoramio user Francisco Edson Mendoso
	Photographer images courtesy of *Arquivo/Agência o Globo*, Neg. 55651 & 54707
46-7	Digital Image © The Museum of Modern Art / Licensed by SCALA / Art Resource, NY
48	Image courtesy of the *Arquivo Geral da Cidade do Rio de Janeiro*
50-1	Photo by Benício Whatley Dias, courtesy of *Acervo Fundação Joaquim Nabuco*
52	Image courtesy of *Rio: Guanabara em Nova Dimensão*
55	Image of Ghandi statue accessed via Flickr, http://www.flickr.com/people/gijlmar
81,84	Jean-Claude Lemagny, *Visionary Architects: Boullée, Ledoux, Lequeu* (Houston: University of St. Thomas, 1968) 27, 21, 34, 33.
88-91	Andrew Robison, *Piranesi: Early Architectural Fantasies* (Meriden CT: Meriden-Stinehour Press, 1986) 163, 196, 179, 209.
114	Digital image @ Flickr, http://www.flickr.com/photos/simon-crubellier/188624668
138-147	Images courtesy Galerie Daniel Buchholz, Cologne/Berlin.
156-7	Image courtesy of the *FABLab : University of Michigan Taubman College of Architecture and Urban Planning*.
158	Image accessed via ChestofBooks, http://chestofbooks.com/
160-64	*Arte Programmata*, Exhibition Catalog, 1962.
166-74	*Almanacco Letterario Bompiani*, 1962
176	"Premio In/Arch Domosic 1963," L'architettura: Cronache e Storia, no.106 (August, 1964).
189	Image of Lascaux Cave Paintings courtesy of Prof. Saxx - http://commons.wikimedia.org/wiki/File:Lascaux_painting.jpg
210	(top) Image of Western Wall in, Eyal Weizman, *Hollow Land: Israel's Architecture of Occupation* (London: Verso, 2007), 39.
210	(middle left) Shmuel Yavin (ed), *The renewal of The Bauhaus in Tel Aviv: The Preservation of The International Style in the White City*, (Tel Aviv: The Bauhaus Center, 2003).
210	(middle right) Ha'ir (The City, Tel Aviv's local newspaper), "The White City," 3 June 2004 in Sharon Rotbard, *White City, Black City* (Tel Aviv: Babel Press, 2005), 13.
210	(bottom) Image of "sprawling monumentality" in, Eyal Weizman, *Hollow Land: Israel's Architecture of Occupation* (London: Verso, 2007), 35.
212	Monk, Bertrand, *An Aesthetic Occupation: The Immediacy of Architecture and the Palestine Conflict*, (Durham, NC: Duke University Press, 2002).
214	Sharon Rotbard, *White City, Black City* (Tel Aviv: Babel Press, 2005), 39.
216	(top) Cover of the exhibition: Living on The Sands, curator: Nitza Smock, Helena Rubinstein Pavilion, Tel Aviv Museum of Art, 2004.
216	Sharon Rotbard, *White City, Black City* (Tel Aviv: Babel Press, 2005), 28.
230	Image of east front of New Theatre Royal courtesy of Victoria and Albert Museum
232	Image by George Cruikshank (1809) courtesy of The Trustees of the British Museum
237-8	Image by George Cruikshank (1856) courtesy of Victorian and Albert Museum
239	Image by Joules Bouvier courtesy of Victoria and Albert Museum

AUTHORS

Marcus Carter
Marcus Carter is an architect at Steven Holl Architects. He collaborates on design research with Christopher Lee as CLAD. While completing his M.Arch at Yale, he was editor of Perspecta 38: Architecture After All.

Patrick Ciccone
Patrick Ciccone is the managing editor of Future Anterior, a journal of historic preservation, and maintains the blog An Uncommonplace Book. He lives in New York City.
http://uncommonplacebook.blogspot.com

Joseph Claghorn
Joseph Claghorn is a practicing landscape architect based in Hong Kong, with training in both architecture (MArch Georgia Tech) and landscape architecture (MLA Harvard).

Brandon Clifford + Wes McGee
Brandon Clifford and Wes McGee are co-founders of Matter Design. Brandon is a M.Arch candidate at the Princeton University School of Architecture. Wes is a Lecturer in Architecture and the Director of the FABLab at the University of Michigan Taubman College.
http://www.matterdesignstudio.com

John Cooper
John Cooper read English at Clare College, Cambridge before taking an MA at the Courtauld Institute of Art, London. He is currently a Mellon Fellow in Art History at Yale University where he is writing a dissertation on the history and aesthetics of dance.

Five Fellows
Five Fellows LLC. is comprised of Ellie Abrams, Meredith Miller, Thomas Moran, Catie Newell, and Rosalyne Shieh. All are 2009-2010 post-graduate design fellows at the University of Michigan's Taubman College of Architecture and Urban Planning. Both Miller and Shieh received their M.Arch degrees from the Princeton University School of Architecture.
http://www.taubmancollege.umich.edu/architecture/faculty/fellowships/5fellows/

Jorge Orozco Gonzalez
Jorge Gonzalez is a M.Arch candidate at the Princeton University School of Architecture.
http://jorgeorozcogonzalez.com

Jimenez Lai
Jimenez Lai is currently clinical assistant professor at University of Illinois at Chicago. Previously, Lai has lived and worked in a desert shelter at Taliesin, AZ, and resided in a shipping container at Atelier Van Lieshout on the piers of Rotterdam. Since founding Bureau Spectacular, Lai has been making new drawings and installations.
http://bureau-spectacular.net

Jesse LeCavalier
Jesse LeCavalier is trained as an architect, with degrees from Brown University and the University of California, Berkeley. He is currently a doctoral candidate at the ETH Zurich and will be a Sanders Fellow at the University of Michigan TCAUP for the 2010-2011 academic year.

Lisa Lee
Lisa Lee is the 2009-2010 Chester Dale Fellow at the Center for Advanced Study in the Visual Arts and a PhD candidate in Art and Archaeology at Princeton University. She is at work on her dissertation, Sculpture's Condition / Conditions of Publicness: Isa Genzken and Thomas Hirschhorn.

Joshua Longo
Joshua Longo is a Brooklyn Based artist, designer, teacher, and motivational speaker. He is the CEO and Creative Director of Longoland and is a Visiting Instructor at Pratt Institute.
http://www.longoland.com

Nicholas De Monchaux
Nicholas de Monchaux is an architect, urbanist, and critic, as well as an Assistant Professor of Architecture and Urban Design at the University of California, Berkeley.

Enrique Ramirez
When he's not breaking storm windows or playing air guitar, Enrique Ramirez is a Ph.D candidate at the Princeton University School of Architecture. He's also from Texas.
http://www.aggregat456.com

Garrett Ricciardi + Julian Rose
Garrett Ricciardi and Julian Rose received their M.Arch degrees from the Princeton University School of Architecture in 2010.

Bryony Roberts
Bryony Roberts is a M.Arch candidate at the Princeton University School of Architecture.

Catherine Seavitt Nordenson
Catherine Seavitt Nordenson is principal of Catherine Seavitt Studio, an interdisciplinary practice for architecture, landscape, and public infrastructure. Seavitt currently teaches architectural design at Princeton University. She was a 2001-2002 Fulbright Fellow in Brazil.

Samuel Stewart-Halevy
Samuel Stewart-Halevy is a M.Arch candidate at the Princeton University School of Architecture.

Osnat Tadmor
Osnat Tadmor is a M.Arch candidate at the Princeton University School of Architecture.

AVAILABLE ONLINE AT
WWW.PIDGIN-MAGAZINE.NET
AND IN SELECT BOOKSTORES.